Abandoned in the Heartland

THE GEORGE GUND FOUNDATION
IMPRINT IN AFRICAN AMERICAN STUDIES

The George Gund Foundation has endowed
this imprint to advance understanding of
the history, culture, and current issues
of African Americans.

Abandoned in the Heartland

Work, Family, and Living
in East St. Louis

Jennifer F. Hamer

UNIVERSITY OF CALIFORNIA PRESS
Berkeley   Los Angeles   London

University of California Press, one of the most distinguished university presses in the United States, enriches
lives around the world by advancing scholarship in the
humanities, social sciences, and natural sciences. Its
activities are supported by the UC Press Foundation and
by philanthropic contributions from individuals and institutions. For more information, visit www.ucpress.edu.

University of California Press
Berkeley and Los Angeles, California

University of California Press, Ltd.
London, England

Library of Congress Cataloging-in-Publication Data

Hamer, Jennifer.
    Abandoned in the heartland : work, family, and living
in East St. Louis / Jennifer F. Hamer.
        p.   cm.
    Includes bibliographical references and index.
    ISBN 978-0-520-26931-6 (cloth : alk. paper)
    ISBN 978-0-520-26932-3 (pbk. : alk. paper)
        1. East Saint Louis (Ill.)—Social conditions—21st cen-
tury.   2. East Saint Louis (Ill.)—Economic conditions—
21st century.   3. Working class—Illinois—East Saint
Louis.   4. African Americans—Illinois—East Saint
Louis.   I. Title.
    HN80.E27H37   2011
    305.5'620977389—dc22   2010052399

Manufactured in the United States of America

20   19   18   17   16   15   14   13   12   11
10   9   8   7   6   5   4   3   2   1

In keeping with a commitment to support environmen-
tally responsible and sustainable printing practices, UC
Press has printed this book on Rolland Enviro100, a 100%
post-consumer fiber paper that is FSC certified, deinked,
processed chlorine-free, and manufactured with renew-
able biogas energy. It is acid-free and EcoLogo certified.

For my family: Especially to my son, Nile; daughter, Zoe; and spouse, Clarence E. Lang; grandmother Frieda Lewis; mom and dad, Elsie and Johnnie Hamer; mother-in-law, Delores Lang-Patton; sisters, Frieda, Stephanie, Sonnie, Khadija, and Sheri; brothers, Lawrence, Mark, and Tom; nieces and nephews, Rabha, Regge, Mark, Lily, Olivia, Sam, Ben, Johnnie Dennison (J.D.), and Macy; and the many families and children in East St. Louis, Illinois

CONTENTS

ILLUSTRATIONS

Following page 57.

ACKNOWLEDGMENTS

I dedicate *Abandoned in the Heartland,* a book about families, to my own family of children, a spouse, parents and grandmother, sisters, brothers, nieces, and nephews. Yet, my definition of family, as many know, extends well beyond the traditional categorization and includes a larger community of others. I list these others below and hope they understand that the appearance of their names, in no way, adequately reflects the sincere appreciation that I have for the tremendous and varied support that each has contributed to the development and completion of this work. To begin, Clarence E. Lang, my spouse and colleague, more than anyone, supported the realization of this manuscript. His own work on class politics and the black struggle for rights in St. Louis, Missouri, informed my theoretical understanding of the heartland and its meaning for African Americans and working families. His expertise informed the project. Yet, while this was certainly critical, it was the strength of his coparenting, love, and partnership that made the book's completion possible. East St. Louis resident Sharon Ward, a long-time friend and colleague, has worked tirelessly and admirably for her city. She was instrumental in my ability to access residents, to observe the space, and to better appreciate the rich potential of this declining but hopeful place. I must thank Christopher D. Benson, award-winning journalist and author of *The Death of Innocence: The Story of the Hate Crime That Changed America*. His passion for equity and justice inspired my analysis and affirmed the meaning of this book project for families and communities. Equally important, his presence was essential to my ability to balance the demands of the project with other professional obligations and family. He, Adlai Murdoch, Robin Jarrett, and William E. Berry, provided the gentle steering and the push that only the dearest friends and colleagues know how and when to deliver. I thank Joseph Pleck, Geraldine Peeples, and historian Vernon Burton, who invited me onto projects that further grounded me in the city of East St. Louis. William T. Summerville, Abdul Alkalimat, Regina Stevenson, Kevin Franklin, Brendesha Tynes, Lou Turner, Ruby Mendenhall, Jorge Chapa, William Patterson, Sundiata Cha-Jua, Helen Neville, Ray Muhammad, Erik McDuffie, and Tom Weissinger, all part of the University of Illinois at Urbana-Champaign, were supportive colleagues. I'm grateful especially to David Ivy and Shirley Olson, of the Department of African American Studies at the University of Illinois at Urbana-Champaign; Shirley was especially invaluable as she helped me to manage my time while I served as the head of a department, university administrator, and member of the faculty. Many current and former graduate students assisted me as well. From Southern Illinois University at Edwardsville: Kathleen Marchioro, Aishia Jefferson, Faith Barnes, and Darla Hernandez; Wayne State University: Waverly Duck; and the University of Illinois at Urbana-Champaign: Mario Perez, Shywon Berry, Kisha (Ishywanza) Rivers, and Tony Laing supported the research by collecting data, reviewing past literature and drafts of the manuscript, challenging my analysis of findings, or buttressing my other obligations as I attended to interviews, analysis, travel, and writing. Jabari Asim, award-winning author and editor of *The Crisis* magazine, reviewed the manuscript and sharpened its thesis. Together, he and Clarence E. Lang inspired and guided the conclusion of the text. Renowned family scholar Robert Hill generously gave his time to review the earliest drafts of this manuscript. I was overwhelmed by his encouragement and his affirmation of my skills as a family scholar. I will forever appreciate all that he continues to offer to the field of family studies and policy. I was fortunate as well to develop long-lasting friendships with Venessa A. Brown and Stephen Hansen, who are both faculty and administrators at Southern Illinois University at Edwardsville and who offered both personal and professional guidance early in the book project. The Institute for Urban Research at Southern Illinois University at Edwardsville offered seed funding to support the early stages of research. Artist Melodye Rosales generously provided creative guidance to the search for images to build into the text. The insert of archived and newly produced photographs, I hope, brings the narrative to life for those unfamiliar with the city and its residents. Odell Mitchell, whose brief biography appears elsewhere in this book, was sensitive yet meticulous in his production of photographs that captured life in East St. Louis today. I must also thank Alford Young, who provided critical theoretical direction to the book content at varying stages, as well as Leon Wilson, James Loewen, Eduardo Bonilla-Silva, Anthony Lemelle, Robert Chrisman, and Robert L. Allen for steadfast support at varying times in the project's development. My intellectual engagement especially with the last two (both of whom are co-editors of the *Black Scholar*) led me to reconsider my original approach to understanding and interpreting my observations of East St. Louis and the circumstances of Black America. I am indebted to them for sharing with me their experiences and knowledge and for encouraging me to join them in efforts to address continued inequities. I'd like to acknowledge Kevin Roy, Robert Marsiglio, and Greer Litton Fox for comments on the chapter on men and the protection of children in the city, a version of which was published in their edited volume, *Situated Fathering* (Rowman and Littlefield, Inc., 2005). Archivists Stephen Kerber, Southern Illinois University, and Charles Brown, Mercantile Library at the University of Missouri-St. Louis, spent hours helping me to locate and identify historical images; the insight and previous works offered by Andrew Theising, Bill Nunes, Edna and Reginald Petty, and Eugene Redmond were a scaffolding for the project. Former East St. Louis mayor Carl E. Officer, current mayor Alvin Parks, former city manager Robert Betts, Doreen Hoosman, East St. Louis city clerk, and Norman E. Ross, director of the Greater East St. Louis Chamber of Commerce, were generous with the time they gave to me and Sharon Ward. Each shared essential information about the workings of the city, its difficulties, and its promise. In addition to the network of family, friends, associates, and colleagues, above, I am forever grateful to Karen Hewitt, Rita Davis, James Stewart, Alison Weingartner, Nancy Yeagle, Kassie Patton, Samuel Smith, and Colleen and Glen Berman, friends who steadfastly admired my work and went out of their way to support me both personally and professionally. They did this even when I was too busy researching, writing, parenting, and otherwise working to be the good friend that they deserve. I must also thank my editors and copyeditor. Naomi Schneider, executive editor, Jessica Moll, and Kalicia Pivirotto, assistant editor of Acquisitions at the University of California Press, guided me through manuscript preparation for production with the press. Naomi offered extreme patience and a gentle but firm editorial hand. Indexing services were provided by J. Naomi Linzer. Irv Murchnick provided exceptional services as a copyeditor. Remarkably and fortunately, he brought his own personal knowledge and interest in East St. Louis to the manuscript. He was committed to the subject matter itself, and not just the technical production of the narrative. This, I believe, made possible a story accessible to multiple audiences and one that fully captures the depth, difficulties, and emotion of working-class family life in America's heartland. Clearly, a book project is a social endeavor. A meaningful product requires the exchange of ideas and a selfless network community of theorists, methodologists, editors, family, friends, and colleagues who are willing to share their time, lives, and expertise. I deeply thank all of those who have so graciously defined my community.

Prologue

East St. Louis, Illinois, embodies at least three core elements of American national life: it is a suburb in the heartland, it is predominantly African American, and it is poor. Taken together, these three elements overlap one another and overwhelm the popular imagination, for they also, counterintuitively, contradict one another. The goal of this book is to capture these complexities in the glorious resilience of East St. Louisans, as well as in the more commonly observed desperation and helplessness of the city itself.

What does this messy picture mean for the United States as a whole? I contend that embedded in a historically fascinating, if seemingly snakebit and definitely abandoned, place is nothing less than the face of American poverty in the twenty-first century. Over the last decades, the locus of poverty shifted from the rural South to the industrial cities of the North. Today, its most poignant manifestations lie buried in our inner-ring and formerly industrial suburbs, such as East St. Louis; Paterson, New Jersey; and Gary, Indiana. These and similar places are part of the "new suburbia" that is not white, upwardly mobile, or middle-class. Instead, they are among a growing number of working-class cities that were historically built on heavy industry, such as meatpacking, assembly lines, steel mills, paint factories, and other manufacturing. These older working-class suburbs are mostly located in the Northeast and the Midwest.[1] The departure of industry from these and similar places left cities and residents abandoned and living in increasing poverty. Today, people here live with suburban blight and troubling rates of crime. They live amid waning social services and infrastructures, move in and out of unemployment, from one less-than-living-wage job to the next, raise their children, and age without stability or economic security. This is a fair description of East St. Louis. It is a suburb where residents are overwhelming working-class but poor,[2] and the municipality is in persistent decline. And, should current economic and employment trends continue, this city will perhaps serve as a foretaste for America's working-class places and people in general. Located directly across the Mississippi River from St. Louis, Missouri, East St. Louis has a reputation—for bawdiness and for civic dysfunction—bordering on mythology. Both aspects of that myth more readily suggest an inner-city neighborhood than a midwestern suburb. Yet a midwestern suburb it is.

Once we make that leap in understanding that East St. Louis is actually a suburb, not an inner city, the conventional insights pile up in unconventional ways. East St. Louisans depend on automobiles to make their personal and work lives function, just like other suburbanites—except that here, uniquely, car convenience confronts numerous economic and social barriers. With the decline of hard industry, East St. Louisans seek jobs in the new service economy, just like other suburbanites—except that few jobs within reach of their education levels, much less their limited transportation access, have viable futures. In such an environment, an underground economy inevitably flourishes, serving internal community needs. This is a rational response to conditions, even if the larger community perceives the consequences as unseemly or illegal.

The final contribution of East St. Louisans to our appreciation of the new suburbia—a powerful if, perhaps, even more counterintuitive contribution—centers on the meaning of family. The experiences of women, long into their own senior citizenship, who care for extended family members and of disenfranchised men who struggle more than anyone knows for the physical and spiritual safety of their children combine to challenge our assumptions about green lawns with picket fences, well-maintained parks, nurturing schools, and other icons of American geography. The moving stories of these suburban soldiers need to be chronicled, not just for the intrinsic human value of their examples of courage and fortitude, but also for what they reveal about the transformed circumstances of family life for all of us as the population ages and public services become increasingly stretched and malnourished.

.   .   .

Where we live matters. It affects our quality of life. It impacts our children's access to a good education; our ability to seek, attain, and maintain decent jobs; our health and safety. This is not news for African Americans especially. With the demise of Reconstruction after 1877, a new system of racial segregation, colloquially known as "Jim Crow," emerged in the South to reassert black subordination in the absence of legal slavery. Many African Americans responded to this "nadir" in U.S. race relations by launching internal migratory movements within the region and outside it. In 1879, thousands of ex-slaves began a mass exodus to Kansas in search of homesteads, launching the first major black migration following the Civil War. The riverfront city of St. Louis, Missouri, became a way station when the "Exodusters," with little more than the clothes on their backs and the belongings they could carry, arrived with few means to complete the journey. Members of the city's established black community drew upon their own resources to feed, house, and clothe them, as well as to fund their settlement in the West. Directly across the Mississippi River, East St. Louis drew its own black migrants, attracted by a burgeoning industrial economy in the 1890s. Like a number of other small and midsize communities in the urban Midwest during this period, the city became home to an African American population that leveraged the power of its wages and numbers to amass political influence. Migrant families were in search of employment, education for their children, and an escape from the bitter violence and Jim Crow practices pervasive in the southern states. For this, many moved to St. Louis, Detroit, Chicago, and other midwestern and northeastern cities.[3]

On the upside, migrants as a whole experienced considerable gains in education and work opportunities. The flip side? Neither space nor place eliminated the meaning of the color line. Black families during this period moved into crowded, segregated, and inadequate housing that was often all that was available to them—living quarters that were cast off by the white immigrants who had preceded them and then moved into better spaces.

The early period of migration was a relative trickle, however, in comparison to the flood of black migration set in motion by U.S. involvement in World War I. Boll weevil infestations of cotton crops, floods, falling agricultural prices, and the consolidation of Jim Crow, backed by racial terrorism and indignities, pushed them out of the South. Meanwhile, the cessation of European immigration, accompanied by a growing demand for labor, pulled millions of African Americans to teeming midwestern urban centers such as Chicago and St. Louis and regional industrial satellites such as East St. Louis, in search of both economic opportunity and expanded social freedoms and rights. As had been the case during earlier migratory waves, the new black settlers were not passive subjects of impersonal forces or white initiatives. Responding to kinship and information networks and the prodding of the black northern press, they acted consciously and meaningfully on their own behalf. This developing "Great Migration" contributed to the mass urbanization and spatial concentration of the nation's black populace—the concentration being the outcome of racial discrimination in housing markets. Yet, the expansion of the black urban-industrial working classes, as well as the middle-class entrepreneurs and professionals who attended to the needs of the working classes, lent greater diversity, complexity, and institutional resources to African American communities. Even still, the urban North fell short of the "Promised Land" that many had envisioned. Racist practices in employment, education, and city government proved resilient, while anti-black pogroms drove black residents out of small northern towns altogether. The resurgence of the Ku Klux Klan, headquartered in Indiana, demonstrated the anti-black sentiments pervasive above the Mason-Dixon Line, as did the widespread popularity of the film *Birth of a Nation,* which romanticized the Klan's post-Reconstruction origins in the South. Horrific race riots also characterized the black northern experience during this period. Whether occurring in Chicago, Tulsa, Oklahoma, or, most notoriously, East St. Louis in the summer of 1917, white mob violence was aimed at checking the ambitions of African Americans who competed with white workers for jobs, public space, housing, and political clout. Although sustained by the strength of their institutions, black East St. Louisans were essentially stripped of power following the bloodshed of 1917, when white reformers adopted a commission form of governance and citywide elections to dilute their numbers.[4]

Some of the best early documentation of racial problems in the American landscape can be found in W. E. B. Dubois's *Philadelphia Negro* (1899) and *Negro American Family* (1908), E. Franklin Frazier's *The Negro Family in the United States* (1939), St. Clair Drake and Horace Cayton's *Black Metropolis* (1945), and Charles S. Johnson's *The Negro in Chicago* (1922). These authors established the pervasiveness of the economic and social discrimination, housing, and school segregation that collectively took their toll on black men, women, and children in the inner-city neighborhoods.

Significantly, these researchers also noted the complexity of black urban communal life. It was not a monolithic life but one richly textured by class and status. As early as 1908 in *Negro American Family,* Dubois described four distinct grades or classes within black society that were born of historical and contemporary U.S. inequities. Out of these social conditions a relatively small middle-elite class and a larger working class developed. Each of these strata was defined by a stable home life, employment, and relative socioeconomic comfort. Beneath the working classes he observed a poor sector that struggled daily against marginal employment, marital disruption, and inadequate housing. At the very bottom of the hierarchy he discovered a vicious and criminal population that he argued had little regard for the values and practices that provided for mobility. Research on the South, such as Hortense Powdermaker's *After Freedom: A Cultural Study in the Deep South* (1939) and John Dollard's *Caste and Class in a Southern Town* (1937), along with studies of urban places, reported variations of Dubois's class gradations. In 1939, E. Franklin Frazier found similar distinctions between low-income blacks and those with greater means. St. Clair Drake and Horace Cayton, as well as Charles S. Johnson, reported challenges especially for those southern-born blacks who were new to the metropolises. In these early decades the newest arrivals were often perceived as caustic and ill-prepared for urban living—so much so that black newspapers would print instructions for how recent migrants should behave, according to historian Clarence Lang in *Grassroots at the Gateway: Class Politics and Black Freedom Struggle in St. Louis, 1936–75* (2009), which focused on working-class politics.

Urban inner-city, black, poor, crime-ridden, "ghetto" neighborhoods emerged as the leading descriptor of the black urban experience, and the public was anxious to understand why these families appeared to be so different from the white mainstream. This shorthand description of the black experience found full expression in the 1965 report, *The Negro Family: The Case for National Action*, led by Daniel P. Moynihan. His review of the historical literature and an analysis of then current trends highlighted growing rates of out-of-wedlock births, matriarchal family systems, and unemployment, particularly relevant among inner-city black males. The report acknowledged historical and structural conditions of discrimination and segregation. It simultaneously argued that such conditions created the basis for the development of a culturally distinct matriarchal black family structure in which men remained mostly unemployed, disconnected from the marital institution, and unable to provide for the household. The values and practices of low-income ghetto families were out of sync with mainstream norms. Worse yet, these characteristics were transmitted from one generation to the next, creating a pathological culture that was contrary to social and economic mobility. In other words, poor black people and their cultural deficiencies were to blame for the group's inability to move beyond their own failures.

Still, increased social and economic opportunities witnessed after World War II brought greater mobility for many African Americans and allowed for growing strata of working- and middle-class families—many of whom pursued improved housing, education, and work prospects in the suburbs, spaces beyond the borders of the blighted inner-city cores.

Simultaneously, inner-city poverty became more concentrated in the following decades, as industry leaders closed or moved plants to U.S. suburban, southwestern, and southern sites that offered lower taxes and nonunion labor. (In the latter part of the twentieth century, industries began leaving the United States entirely.) The economy was shifting as well, with manufacturing occupations increasingly replaced by technical and service-related occupations. Poor black inner-city families, for many reasons trapped within core boundaries, became the face of America's poverty, effectively racializing, in the public mind, the notion of poverty and its solutions altogether.

In a critique of Moynihan's intergenerational poverty thesis, scientists presented an alternative explanation of inner-city black community life. Carol Stack's *All Our Kin: Strategies for Survival in a Black Community* (1974), Andrew Billingsley's *Black Families in White America* (1968), Elliot Liebow's *Tally's Corner: A Study of Negro Streetcorner Men* (1976), Ulf Hannerz's *Soulside: Inquiries into Ghetto Culture and Community* (1969), Robert Hill's *The Strengths of Black Families* (1972), Lee Rainwater's *Behind Ghetto Walls: Black Families in a Federal Slum* (1970), Betty Lou Valentine's *Hustling and Other Hard Work: Lifestyles in the Ghetto* (1980), and Joyce Ladner's *Tomorrow's Tomorrow* (1995) all interpreted the everyday cultural practices of low-income black urbanites as resilient and dynamic adaptations to historical and persistent conditions. The problem was not black pathological culture but the poverty and racism that were imprinted on the structures of society.

Race and place mattered throughout the twentieth century. Gunner Mrydal's *American Dilemma* (1944), Karl Tauber and Alma Tauber's *Negroes in Cities: Residential Segregation and Neighborhood Change* (1965), and the findings of the *Report of the National Advisory Committee on Civil Disorders* (1968) drew attention to the physical isolation of low-income African Americans in blighted neighborhoods. These works asserted that these conditions had a negative impact on the social and economic mobility of residents.

In 1987 William J. Wilson's *The Truly Disadvantaged* explained to the world that whatever was happening in America's inner-city ghettos, it had little or nothing to do with racism and much to do with class. His argument was threefold: (1) the movement of industry and the shifting emphasis on service occupations left unskilled workers, including but not exclusively blacks, without jobs; (2) ghetto-specific culture (for example, poor attitudes and behaviors in regard to work, family, and education) inhibited the ability of poor black men especially to access the formal job market; and (3) affirmative action programs and acquired skills had enabled working-class and middle-class African Americans to move into suburbs and maintain economic movement and stability. In *When Work Disappears,* Wilson continues his assessment and argues that when working- and middle-class blacks departed from the ghettos, the poorest were left behind without role models to guide their development into decent families and workers. Wilson's argument inaccurately presumed that suburban space was an idyllic one for working- and middle-class blacks. This was hardly the case, and his assertions were widely criticized despite their popularity. Doug Massey and Nancy Denton's *American Apartheid: Segregation and the Making of the Underclass* (1993), Paul Jargowsky's *Poverty and Place: Ghettos, Barrios and the American City* (1996), Harry Holtzer *What Employers Want: Job Prospects for Less Experienced Workers* (1999), and others demonstrate that African American movement into the suburbs occurs under conditions of segregation and discrimination via discriminatory highway development, mortgage and small business lending, realty practices, and labor market practices.[5] These persist into the twenty-first century.

In the past, as in the present, when working-class and middle-income African Americans move into the suburbs they are qualitatively better off than those who remain in inner-city neighborhoods. But as Melvin Oliver and Thomas Shapiro make clear in *Black Wealth White Wealth* (2nd ed., 2006), and as Mary Patillo-McCoy points out in *Black Picket Fences: Privilege and Peril among the Black Middle Class* (2000), and as sociologist Robert Bullard sums up in *The Black Metropolis in the Twenty-first Century* (2007), African Americans hold relatively less accumulated wealth and lower incomes, live in neighborhoods with poorer infrastructures, experience higher rates of crime, and are more likely to reside in mixed-income areas than whites in suburban spaces. Furthermore, recent studies indicate state retrenchment. When Sharon Hays, in *Flat Broke*, interviewed welfare mothers about their experiences after the passage of the Personal Responsibility and Work Opportunity Reconciliation Act of 1996 and Barbara Ehrenreich described the world of low-wage workers in *Nickel and Dimed,* they each demonstrated that class matters as well. They found that the state is increasingly impersonal and disconnected from those at the bottom, those most in need. Black people are disproportionately located in this stratum. The declining role of the state, especially in predominantly black places, is further made clear in Beverly H. Wright and Robert D. Bullard's analysis "Black New Orleans: Before and After Hurricane Katrina" (2007). Here institutions, homes, schools, businesses, and lives were devastated from the 2005 hurricane—but it was those in black spaces and places in and around the city who were traumatized the most severely from discriminatory state inaction and from neglect and inadequate recovery efforts.[6]

The status of East St. Louis as a transportation hub defined the city's prominence in the early half of the twentieth century, but its marked decline distinguished it thereafter. By the 1950s, it was the fourth largest city in Illinois and the second of its size in the St. Louis, Missouri, metropolitan region. In the 1960s East St. Louis arose as a city of interest for researchers. Although several older cities were beginning to experience decline, according to a 1967 advisory study by Southern Illinois University at Edwardsville, ". . . Why East St. Louis Needs to Be a Demonstration City," few had the degree of social and economic problems that were plaguing East St. Louis. The city, authors of the document assessed, was one of the most deprived areas in the state of Illinois, a circumstance that impacted both white and black families:

In 1964, in comparison with sister Illinois cities of 50,000 or over, East St. Louis ranked first in percentage of families with income less than $3,000 (30%); first in percentage of the civilian labor force unemployed (10.5%); first in percentage of adults with less than

eight years of formal education (33.4%); first in percentage of tuberculosis incidence (.07); first in rate of infant mortality (3.4%); first in
percentage of unsound housing units (43.3); and second in rate of
criminal offenses (.02%).[7]

At the time, well over one-half of the population was African
American. The circumstances of decline were far more harmful to them than to their white neighbors. According to a U.S.
Bureau of the Census report for 1960, 66 percent of the nonwhite
population were employed as operatives and laborers and in service occupations compared with 48 percent of the total population. Over one-half of black households earned less than three
thousand dollars per year, and among those unemployed, about
80 percent earned less than two thousand dollars the year prior
to the report. For white families in the city, the rates were 32 percent and 44 percent, respectively. Black family members who
remained in the workforce were more likely to be employed
in St. Louis than on the east side of the Mississippi.[8] And, in
terms of housing, in general about 60 percent of the stock with
full plumbing facilities was in good condition. Yet, this was the
case for only 32 percent of housing in which the black population resided.[9] In sum, place matters, but no space—rural, urban,
or suburban—is an escape from the negative effects of race for
African Americans—a truth that the circumstances of East St.
Louis unfortunately demonstrate.

SUBURBIA IN BLACK AND WHITE

American suburbs historically and to this day have been popularly perceived as homogenous—predominantly white, middle-
class, and socioeconomically mobile and affluent—residential

retreats that exist beyond the edges of metropolitan centers.[10] These spaces were understood to offer these families respite from the harshness of city life—its dangerous streets and criminal kind, its loud noises and dense populations, its unpredictability, lack of personal space, pollution, and, yes, its dark racial element. In *Crabgrass Frontier,* Kenneth T. Jackson adds that relative to suburban life in other nations of the Western world, American suburbs are distinct in the following ways: "Affluent and middle-class Americans live in suburban areas that are far from their work places, in homes that they own, and in the center of yards that by urban standards elsewhere are enormous. The uniqueness thus involves population density, home-ownership, residential status, and journey-to-work." [11] Sylvia Fave declares that suburbia was much more than just space and place. Rather, it represented a lifestyle with distinct cultural meaning. In other words, the differences between urban and suburban life were viewed as marked and distinct.[12]

When sociologist Herbert Gans lived in Willingboro, New Jersey, for two years to conduct his famous 1967 Levittown study, he provided some texture to these popular notions of suburban space. He concludes that this suburban community was quite homogenous but permitted greater opportunity than central city life for leisure and family-bonding activities as well as for socialization with neighbors. Suburban neighborhood "blocks" became the social units whereby stay-at-home mothers established friendship networks and supported one another in the absence of extended family. In the meantime, working- and middle-class husbands commuted to the city and worked in family wage jobs. The regular weekday travel, Gans asserts, was welcomed by men and offered them some solitude and privacy in between work and family life. But he also reasons that it was the people, not the space, that defined a dynamic suburban life.[13]

Suburbia was further complicated when evidence showed that both middle-class and working-class suburbanites seemed to share a strong work ethic and commitment to family. Further, many had *reluctantly* followed industry and jobs to the suburbs, leaving behind cherished inner-city neighborhoods, neighbors, and extended kin. According to Bennett M. Berger in *Working-Class Suburb,* a 1969 study, autoworkers who moved into the suburbs brought with them a lifestyle that contrasted with the suburban myth. Indeed, Bennett argues that the experience of suburbia is based on the backgrounds of residents rather than on space. Workers did not necessarily move to escape city life as much as for work opportunities, and their aspirations moved with them. Living in suburbia did not increase mobility, as all autoworkers saw their quality of life improve. Bennett further suggests that middle-class suburbanites held higher definitions of success than their working-class counterparts, and these are then passed on from one generation to the next.

Despite the nuanced descriptions and analyses offered decades ago by both Gans and Berger, as well as others, the image of suburbia, as an idyllic cookie-cutter space and existence, seems firm in its persistence. This image endures despite the analyses of recent revisionists whose work draws a complex, multifaceted, and diverse picture of suburbia. They note that even in the early part of the twentieth century, suburbia's beginnings encompassed not just the white affluent middle class and the white working class but also persons of color—all striving for the American dream to own a home and surround themselves with green grass, trees, quiet, and so on, often under difficult circumstances.[14]

SUBURBIA IN COLOR

For sure, the United States is nothing if not racially diverse. Even Gans, in *Levittown,* notes the existence of a few families of color, Chinese and Japanese, in particular. Though he does not spend much time examining them as a distinct population, he does note that they were more socially isolated than their white suburban neighbors. Yet, despite research reports and media presentations that place black Americans primarily in the poor urban core, this population, too, was also among those who chose to live outside central cities. According to Andrew Weise, in *Places of Their Own: African American Suburbanization in the Twentieth Century,* "During the Great Migration of the 1910s and 1920s, one in six African American migrants to the urban North moved to a suburb. In the South, black residence on the urban fringe was even more widespread; in fact, it was characteristic of the region before World War II. By 1940 more than a million African Americans lived in suburban areas, and suburbanites represented one-fifth of the black population in the metropolitan United States."[15]

Movement to the suburbs for African Americans and blue-collar workers, especially, was a bittersweet challenge. In *Working-Class Heroes: Protecting Home, Community, and Nation in a Chicago Neighborhood,* Maria Kefalas observes that in the early twentieth century, many moved onto empty lots and set up tents and temporary shelters as they built, with their own hands, some semblance of their dream home; they often lacked running water and traveled dirt roads to and from their work in the city and their place in the suburbs. Materials for housing construction were accumulated over time, paycheck by paycheck. Neighbors, friends, and children were the hands and labor that built the walls, roofs, and other parts of the permanent structures. Families used skills developed through trades and in childhood to assemble these houses.

As time passed and social and economic opportunities increased, so, too, did the quality of suburban life. In the 1950s, when many African American central-city residents witnessed marked decline in employment opportunities, amenities, and housing quality, suburban life seemed to hold great promise for those who managed to make their way into these locales. In the Midwest, Gary, Indiana, Highland Park and Benton Harbor, Michigan, East St. Louis, Illinois, and other industrial and first-ring suburbs offered manufacturing jobs and opportunities to move solidly into America's working class. Many blacks of these cities purchased homes, automobiles, elected African American city officials, and, like white Americans, carved out their own suburban space.

Black working-class migrants, men and women alike, often encountered white hostility in suburbs. They were excluded from jobs, restricted to menial, often-dangerous occupations, and racially segregated into crowded, high-rent slum housing or certain sections of town. Their children were educated with dated books and materials; they themselves often had to return to the "black side of town" before sunset to avoid physical attacks by white civilians and harassment and arrests by police.[16] Both Kenneth Kusmer and Weise abundantly illustrate this deprivation and oppression.

As the civil rights movement gained momentum, African American employment opportunities expanded and standards of living increased. Mark J. Stern cites other factors: a booming economy's demand for new workers, a federal welfare state forged during the 1930s, and union desegregation. With these new civil and purchasing powers, African Americans increased their financial and intellectual contributions to local, regional, and national policies and politics, furthering a climate of racial and economic reform. Their hard-earned dollars contributed to the building of county buildings, the beautification of parks, and the development of public schools. Their taxes and patronage also sustained shopping malls, grocery stores, and cultural centers.[17]

But economic booms do not proceed indefinitely. Nor do they include everyone. Relative to black men and women arriving in midwestern cities and suburbs in later years of the twentieth century, those who arrived in the earlier decades were more likely to have hired into at least an entry-level position and slowly moved their families into the stable working class. Such families and their offspring were eventually able to move to more upscale housing and schools within the central city or in metropolitan-area suburbs and small cities. Regardless of place, most African Americans lagged far behind working-class whites. In 1964, fewer than 10 percent held professional or managerial positions, compared with almost 25 percent of whites. In his summary and analysis of data from the 1960s, Dalton Conley reports that approximately 40 percent of black children lived below poverty, compared with 10 percent of white children. Being denied access to low-interest loans, possessing low levels of accumulated wealth, and experiencing continued residential segregation meant that many blacks remained within or on the borders of predominantly black, low-income areas. Unlike white men, black men were less able to pass their occupational successes on to their sons or daughters. Black men were more likely to end up in manual occupations regardless of education level and the benefits of parental contacts. Unlike those in central cities, many families in East St. Louis continued to live in poor-quality, makeshift houses and without running water well into the 1970s.[18]

The statistics reveal both the progress and the magnitude of the continuing gaps. By 2007, according to the U.S. Census Bureau, one-half of African American householders were homeowners, compared with three-quarters of whites. Between 1970 and 2004, life expectancy for blacks did rise from sixty-four to seventy-three. Today, African Americans are more likely than before to attend school regularly and graduate from high school. Black men and women are also more likely now than in the past to complete a bachelor's degree, though recent trends indicate that women are more likely to do so than men. Policy makers of both conservative and liberal stripes are quick to point out these trends as an indication of growing U.S. racial equality.[19] Too quickly, in my view.

The countervailing truth was that in midcentury central cities and industrial suburbs, many black residents witnessed their labor becoming increasingly dispensable. Heavy industry began to leave industrial suburbs as well as central-city cores, and the number of low-skill entry-level jobs decreased where most African Americans were concentrated. As access to higher education increased for the U.S. population, employers were able to hire those with technical training and college degrees for the same jobs that were once open to those with less than a high school education. This quelled the need and desire for low-skilled, poorly educated workers, of which African Americans, especially males, were and remain a disproportionate number.[20] In short, just as African Americans were poised to make their biggest economic and political gains, corporate board members and policy makers made decisions that dramatically shifted the economy in directions that effectively undermined the quality of life for many urban workers and families, leaving in the wake of these decisions a trail of distressed, and essentially abandoned, places and people, such as the city and residents of East St. Louis.

DISTRESSED AND ABANDONED
WORKING-CLASS SUBURBAN PLACES

What, exactly, is a distressed and abandoned place? What are its characteristics? Foremost, the "widespread, systematic disinvestment in the nation's basic productive capacity" is a central feature.[21] Essentially, corporate leaders no longer invest in basic industries, choosing instead to build and maintain profits through mergers, acquisitions, and foreign investments. They may choose to shut down plants or redirect profits away from a particular industry or activity. They may shift equipment from one plant to another, reducing production at the initial site. Regardless of the form of disinvestment, the effect is the same: payrolls are reduced and people are laid off. Relative to other groups, African Americans are least likely to find subsequent employment or a job that is comparable to their former position.

In the 1970s, between 450,000 and 650,000 jobs in the private sector, in both manufacturing and nonmanufacturing, were wiped out somewhere in the United States.[22] In this past decade, massive layoffs have eliminated many more.[23] Over the past ten years, millions of men and women have lost their jobs to corporate shutdowns. In the first ten months of 2003, there were 15,596 mass layoffs in the United States, displacing almost 1.6 million workers.[24] From December 2007 to February 2010, the total number of mass layoffs was 55,309 and the associated number of first-time unemployment claims was well over five million (5,580,819). In February 2010 alone, 155,718 workers filed jobless claims, about one-quarter of whom were in manufacturing industries.[25] Among states in the Midwest, Illinois leads as the one with the highest number of mass layoffs and new unemployment filings. It is fifth in seasonally adjusted unemployment in general.[26]

High rates of unemployment and limited investment in the city by major industries and smaller employers contribute directly to the lack of development and maintenance of a place. Yet, distress and abandonment do not mean that a city is without value; they do not preclude a continued siphoning of resources from poor communities. To the contrary, the location of these communities, their property, and their cheap labor are attractive to investors, grant seekers, and those who own or manage the low-paying service industries that dominate the local and surrounding area. In other words, the "abandonment" of a place is actually the rejection and neglect of its population. In an abandoned place, relatively little investment is made in the academic training and success of children and youth, including their college preparation; younger generations, after all, are no longer a necessary potential part of the work force. An abandoned place has minimal investment in residential policing; limited transportation in and out of the city; little investment in city infrastructure and amenities (stop lights, paved roads, road signs, trash pickups, parks, and libraries); dilapidated structures that cause health risks for local residents; and political corruption that occurs with the complicity of higher government structures.

PEOPLE IN DISTRESSED
AND ABANDONED SUBURBAN PLACES

Paychecks are only part of what is lost when working-class men and women do not have family-wage jobs or career opportunities. Communities and families suffer as well. Cities experience a loss of revenue that leaves them unable to support basic infrastructures adequately. Municipal buildings crumble. Public facilities such as libraries, zoos, and parks receive reduced attention in city and county budgets, threatening the city's cultural and recreational environment. Pothole repairs are neglected or abridged for other community needs. Police and fire departments must reduce their personnel, equipment maintenance, and purchases, threatening the safety and protection of citizens. Schools must reduce the costs of faculty and other staff. They necessarily cut academic and extracurricular programs and charge families more for book rentals and other supplies. This occurs at a time when families in the city have less to spend. Bluestone and Harrison summarize the phenomenon:

> The costs of disinvestment go well beyond lost wages and foregone productivity. Workers and their families suffer serious physical and emotional health problems when their employers shut down operations, and the community as a whole experiences a loss of revenue needed for supporting police and fire protection, schools, and parks. Entire cities and towns can be brought to the brink of bankruptcy, as has happened in Detroit, Cleveland, and a host of smaller municipalities throughout the industrial Midwest.[27]

By the 1970s, the composition and governance of former manufacturing suburbs such as Gary, Indiana; East St. Louis; and Newark, New Jersey, and central cities such as Detroit, Michigan, had reached or nearly reached a black majority. In spite of this accomplishment, they had also begun to show the signs of beleaguerment by disproportionate poverty, the loss of tax dollars, and diminishing living-wage jobs. Meanwhile, groups of white ethnics who were not subject to the same degree of job discrimination and low pay, residential or other forms of systematic segregation, and other inequities continued their ascent from the working class into a more comfortable middle stratum of society.

. . .

My interest in the city of East St. Louis and its population began in 1996, when I began my career as an assistant professor of sociology at Southern Illinois University at Edwardsville (SIUE). The university is located just fifteen minutes from the city of observation, East St. Louis, where it had established the Southern Illinois University at Edwardsville East St. Louis Center to offer programs and services to the area. University and center leadership encouraged faculty to consider the city of East St. Louis, its geography, and its people as a lab or program site, especially if such activities could generate grant dollars for both entities.

New faculty members were given a tour of the center and an orientation that included a packet of statistics. These numbers summarized the city's misery—among them, high rates of poverty, low median income, joblessness, and low academic achievement. I would later learn that these statistics and trends often served as the basis for public and private grants written by center staff and university faculty members to attract and win grant dollars for research and programs. Millions of dollars poured through both the university and center sites annually, seemingly with a goal to improve the city and the lives of its residents.[28]

These same statistics, however, had a latent function: they fed and perpetuated popular fears and notions that the general public had about black people broadly and in East St. Louis in particular.

The city certainly had a reputation. It was infamous for its political corruption, homicide rate, and welfare caseload. It was also predominantly black—a fact that was filtered through almost every East St. Louis news item that made its way across the wire. Black faces were jobless, homeless, lazy, welfare abusers, homicide victims and perpetrators, shady public officials, and crooked ministers. A new faculty member, if he or she was so inclined, might wonder: were there any "regular" people in this town? If there were, they were well hidden from the public view.

Despite the monetary appeal of grant dollars (especially since I had a huge student-loan debt), my initial forays into the city were not related to research. I was trained as a family scholar. However, I am also an activist at heart; I was interested in black and working families and what my area of expertise could do for these populations. In my first year at SIUE, I developed a friendship with Sharon Ward, who was at the time a research associate with the university, a lifetime resident of East St. Louis, and a member of numerous boards and committees both within the city and connected to projects at the East St. Louis Center. She was, in many ways, an activist who had spent her adulthood voicing the concerns of residents and working within the system to bring programs and services to the area. She was committed to the city and held a deep appreciation for the residents, especially those who tried to organize around issues and challenge local and regional politics. Through her connections, I was invited to conduct varying workshops and write grants that focused on leadership, faith-based organizing, and after-school and adult-education programs. This network introduced me to city leaders and agency directors but also to the city itself, its political history and current issues, its faith-based organizations and educational system, and diverse residents.

Outside the official university orientation, I quickly observed a city more complex than what was formally presented. Workers waited at bus stops on any given weekday morning. Mothers dropped off and picked up their children from the Head Start program housed at the East St. Louis Center. Men and women opened and closed the McDonald's and KFC restaurants. Maintenance workers mopped the floors inside St. Mary's Hospital. Children skipped home from school, their backpacks stuffed with school projects. These observations, the research that I had to conduct to write grants for organizations and agencies, and my interaction with residents through workshops and other activities made it clear to me that despite all of the research conducted within these city's boundaries, we actually knew very little about these people or the political economy that defined their physical space.

In my first book, I described how black fathers who lived away from their children managed their parenting as black, low-income, never-married men. My findings suggested that this demographic group may have been redefining fatherhood in a way that better reflected what they were able to do as poor men who lived away from their children. That is, they seemed to be placing an emphasis on emotional, expressive care-giving rather than on monetary or instrumental functions. Given the steady decline in wages for those with only a high school education and the falling number of manufacturing jobs, I was interested in further exploring how these men understood their work prospects and what this meant for their parenting and contributions to families and communities. I felt that East St. Louis provided an excellent opportunity for this research, given its high rate of joblessness and my proximity to the population.

Not long after I began work in East St. Louis, the U.S. Con-

gress passed and President Bill Clinton signed the Personal
Responsibility and Work Opportunity Reconciliation Act of
1996. The news gripped the attention of social scientists, social
service agencies, residents, and local officials and started a panic
among many, as we all wondered about and thought through its
implications for all levels. In response to the new legislation, the
State of Illinois sponsored several public meetings in East St.
Louis and elsewhere in the state in an attempt to educate welfare recipients, agencies, and workers about the changes in policy and related organizational changes to public agencies. Some
residents and workers alike expressed dismay and fear about the
changes, while others held great hopes that this was finally a
solution to joblessness and poverty.

In these meetings, several facts spoke loudly. The legislation
was an attempt to move welfare users to work and remove them
from state rolls. Yet, as a few in this city would attest, many of its
poor were already working, yet still poor. What would happen
when they were no longer eligible for assistance? Furthermore,
a quick glance around East St. Louis would lead anyone to ask,
What jobs? Much of the city appeared abandoned. Few trusted
that enough "good" jobs would be created to absorb those many
men and women in need of such employment.

I reevaluated my research agenda. How could I divorce the
experiences of men and fathers from the larger ecology of black
families? Men's experiences were linked to those of women and
children. How did black men, women, and families understand
their work and family circumstances and negotiate their lives?
But even such an interpretive approach would not suffice. How
could I separate out black families from the larger environment
of this physical space?

Thus, what began as a study of low-income noncustodial

fathers and other men quickly expanded into this larger project of studying an abandoned place and people. My first challenge was to access the people of East St. Louis. The usual hardships of qualitative research—such as arranging for interviews and commuting to meeting sites—were made even more complicated when in 2002 I accepted a position at Wayne State University, in Detroit, and then, two years following, moved back to Illinois, to the University of Illinois at Urbana-Champaign.

But those were not the only barriers to data collection. Residents, regardless of gender or age, were protective of their city and not keen on researchers or reporters. Many older residents recalled Jonathan Kozol's book *Savage Inequalities* and argued that his depiction of East St. Louis was not only harmful to the city's image but also unfair and inaccurate. Others felt that news reporters and researchers generally were interested only in making money or a name for themselves from the city's problems, and, according to one resident, "They only report the negative." Most contemporary stories on East St. Louis were about murders, rapes, welfare abuse, or AIDS; the only positive ones seemed to be about the city's high school football teams or written memories of the city's rich history. So it was this attitude of abuse and rejection that I was up against.

But the sense, at least initially, that I was just "another researcher" also inspired this project by putting me in touch with the hunger for a more affirming perspective. I traversed the broken and sometimes nameless streets of East St. Louis; I walked down the hallways of its magnet school during school hours and was overwhelmed from the stench of ever-backed-up sewers. As I did so, I pondered the links between these structural conditions and the everyday lives of residents who praised their city.

Meanwhile, plants throughout Illinois were closing and throwing a record number of men and women out of work; the rest of the state was looking more and more like East St. Louis. Even Granite City, Belleville, and Alton, Illinois, all predominantly white cities, were losing manufacturers, jobs, and population. Could East St. Louis be a precursor?

•   •   •

For this book, I have used a case-study framework and qualitative research methods to undertake a holistic investigation of the cultural aspects of family and work life while also examining the role of larger processes in shaping these circumstances. This allowed me to observe the impact of state policies and the economic and social trends that shaped East St. Louis over a particular period. Specifically, it provided a bounded system of study or a "case" to observe.

In social science terms, I approached the project as an "instrumental" rather than as an "intrinsic" case. East St. Louis was a good fit, because it illustrated the issue of abandonment of a place and a people. As a consequence, I could use multiple sources of information (interviews, focus groups) and ethnographic techniques, such as participant observation, as well as secondary sources of data, such as newspapers.

From 1996 to 2003, I met with over a hundred residents, observed city activities, and collected historical and contemporary data on the city of East St. Louis. I met residents at events we both attended, through word-of-mouth snowball techniques, or by simply approaching them in the supermarket, in the library, at the local fast-food restaurants, and at other shops and public places. Men and women were asked to talk about work, family, health, and their individual experiences with available services and amenities. They were also asked about their family's history in the city and their understanding of the past and contemporary circumstances.

The process could be frustrating, especially at the outset, because I was unknown. Many canceled meetings, or, once we met, they were reluctant to talk on audiotape or provide much detail. The project did not get a real foothold until scheduled focus groups were conducted through local churches. I, or an assistant, met with ten groups, each consisting of six to ten church members. I used responses from the interviews that had been conducted thus far to develop a shorter and more precise set of questions.

The most important of these focus groups was at Mt. Zion Baptist Church, on Bond Avenue. Most of the participants there were senior citizens who had spent most or all of their lives in East St. Louis. I met with a group of approximately sixty men and women, and then they separated and assembled themselves into smaller clusters for focus-group interviews. Their responses were slightly skewed to the past. They wanted me to know what the city used to be and how it and people's attitudes and behaviors had changed over time. It was in this round of research that I was able to distinguish myself as someone with a unique orientation and point of view. I was able to discuss with these respondents my own family's history in the area, my activities in the community outside the university, and local events and bits of news and to demonstrate a genuine appreciation for the neighborhoods and people of East St. Louis. And I could reassure others that my objective was not to produce yet another perpetuation of the negative stereotypes that they felt were generally reflected in social science and the media.

Consequently, some of these focus-group participants agreed

to individual interviews. They also directed me to sons, daughters, nieces, nephews, grandchildren, and friends. These contacts expanded my reach into the community and its networks of workers, the jobless single mothers, the married-couple families, the elderly, and young adults. This new round of interviews opened the door to participant observations in homes, at events and activities, and in workplaces and other spaces where I may not have otherwise been welcome.

Overall, this framework and these approaches enabled me to do two things: (1) to discover the values and attitudes of these residents regarding family and work; how they understood their circumstances and what they believed their life chances were; how they then made choices and negotiated their roles as parents, workers, and kin-care providers within the boundaries of an abandoned place; and (2) to situate the circumstances of this population in the broader urban social, cultural, historical, political, and economic processes. In the end, it was clear that the lives captured by their words reflected the role of ecology in creating the conditions of contemporary living.

CHAPTER ONE

In America's Heartland

These are hard times, and the struggle for American working-class men and women to maintain dignity, work, and family life is a national one. Nowhere is this struggle sharper than in America's heartland and especially in East St. Louis, Illinois. Life here is mired in issues of safety, damaged infrastructure, and poor prospects for the future. Acute distress defines every corner of the municipal landscape.

Located on the southwestern edge of Illinois, East St. Louis is part of the larger St. Louis, Missouri, metropolitan area. Five hours from Chicago and almost four hours from Indianapolis, East St. Louis—once a thriving industrial suburb—now leads as an example of how economic disinvestment sours a community and the lives within it. This is a city that reluctantly claims the highest unemployment, poverty, and high school dropout rates in the region.

Ninety-nine percent of the population is African American. Working-age youth and adults work as nurses, teacher's aides, shop clerks, cashiers, housekeepers, maids, janitors, barbers, truck drivers, and lawn-care specialists, among many other working-class occupations. Mothers and fathers commute by bus, train, and mostly older-model vehicles out of the city to work each day. Still, among those sixteen years old and older, almost 50 percent do not participate in the labor force, and of the 50 percent actively participating, about 10 percent are officially unemployed. Thirty-three percent of families and 56 percent of youth below the age of eighteen live below the poverty level of income.[1]

The majority of children in East St. Louis receive their education in a district where schools are now infamous for poor plumbing, dated labs and books, and poor retention rates. Bricks fall from the older buildings onto play areas below. Parents seek out the pitifully few outlets of family recreation and entertainment that exist. Residents must protect themselves and their loved ones from compound pollutants and toxins that fill the air, water, and ground soil. Fire-gutted and decaying buildings sit alongside more livable working-class quarters, and broken stoplights sometimes dangle precariously above tattered city streets. A smattering of more upscale and middle-class homes and vehicles sit here and there—but these only give nuance to a clearly devastated city.

Instinctively, the above description might be transposed with that of an impoverished community or neighborhood located in the inner core of one of America's large cities: New York, Chicago, Los Angeles, St. Louis, Detroit. Social scientists and popular media tell us that black people in *these* urban center spaces experience high rates of joblessness, poverty, tenuous labor, households headed by single mothers, dangerous streets filled with crime and violence, low academic achievement, gang activity, poor health, and dilapidated apartments and houses. We have all seen these characteristics of urban spaces popularized on television and in film—so much so that the public generally accepts that inner-city spaces are marginal to mainstream society. Contemporary African Americans are broadly understood as a monolithic population concentrated in the distressed cores of metropolitan areas.

East St. Louis, however, is not in the inner core of a metropolitan area. It is in the suburbs of America's heartland. This makes for a sociological brew that the nation as a whole and its policy makers would rather not confront. Yet confront it we must. The problems of places like East St. Louis keep deepening and getting more combustible. Even more pointedly, those problems are a lot more similar to those on the sunnier side of suburbia than we might think.

.   .   .

On a warm autumn day, my mother and I take a nostalgic journey together. Between 1996 and 2003, I spent many days, weeks, and months in this area, getting to know the people and the communities and collecting data for this study. But for Mom, the story is *really* personal: this region was once her home. She was born and raised in the smaller St. Louis suburb of Edwardsville, fifteen miles northeast of East St. Louis. Like many black women of her generation, she joined the army after high school. She later married, had children, and eventually settled in Texas. She returns to her hometown several times a year to visit and maintain ties to kin.

On this day, she and I are headed for the Red Door, a tavern located on the northern outskirts of East St. Louis. It is a small shop, off the Twenty-fifth Street exit of Interstate Highway 64— visible only if you know where to look and what to look for. Surrounded by empty lots and a few older homes, it is the only commercial enterprise on the block. Here, according to my mother, they prepare some of the area's best barbecued pig snoots (skin cut from the snout of a pig)—firm and crispy, smothered in a tangy orange-red sauce that marinates through the single slice of plain white bread that serves as a small platter for the meat. The memories of the soul-touching aroma is reason alone for this visit.

Our drive is otherwise uneventful. Forty years earlier, in my mother's youth, streetcar tracks stretched from East St. Louis into the surrounding smaller communities. People flocked to its downtown streets to shop for the latest styles of clothing, shoes, household furnishings, and entertainment. Sometimes they strolled the streets just to be seen in their Sunday best. Sears, the famous Majestic Theater, and Siedel's, among other institutions, peppered the downtown area. Today, Collinsville Avenue, historically one of the city's major thoroughfares, represents only a tiny fraction of what this business and shopping district used to be. In between vacant shops are the stores similar to those found in inner-city areas. African Americans who live here and in nearby communities often get hair service at Shear Magic and at Rodney's Barber and Beauty Salon, among the avenue's shops. Black women, who are unable to find their beauty products in predominantly white neighborhood stores, usually can locate them at Ace Beauty Supply, Illinois Wig and Fashions, or Collins Wig Shop. Or they may get their hair styled at the beauty school, two miles down on State Street. Collinsville Avenue also still boasts the presence of a few nightclubs and bars, such as Faces and Blackman's Terrace Cocktails and Steaks. And although one would be hard pressed to locate upscale furnishings for purchase in this city, discount stores such as Value Plus and Fay Furniture and Pawn sell beds, sofas, and other new and used wares for the home. In addition, other age-old "intimate" services survive on this city street and in the neighboring black towns of Brooklyn and Washington Park.

Visitors to East St. Louis are sure to notice closed storefronts. Many empty buildings are simply boarded up. Fire and other elements have left other structures to lapse into a dangerous state. According to some residents, the city officers are not doing their job. One, Elmer Middleton, noted, "They ain't doing what they was supposed to do, what they was elected for." As evidence, some residents say city officials do not demand that property owners maintain buildings and land. Others explain it in a different way: the city cannot afford to pursue absentee landlords or the cost of razing the many buildings and cleaning the lots that threaten the safety of city residents. Asked about these complaints, a city official admitted, "There is something to just about all of that."

My mother and I are staggered by the visual evidence of the disrepair of the streets; little sign remains of the industry that once placed the city on regional, national, and international maps. I avoid pothole after pothole, only to find another straight ahead. Most of the streets we pass do not have sidewalks, though many are quite wide. A few cars are parked in front of the 1940s-style, single-family brick homes. Most look as if they were once quite stately, and from a distance many still appear handsome in the shadows of the trees. Upon closer look, one can see that the roofs are discolored, and bricks are missing from porches and outer walls. An eyesore, yes—but forsaken lots also serve a purpose. These spaces offer a convenient resting place for old red bricks, concrete cinder blocks, tires, broken bottles, and miscellaneous other debris.

Yet this is not the complete picture. In almost any direction from the center of East St. Louis are blocks of well-maintained homes and yards, where the financed new cars of occupants soak up the warm sun in paved and edged driveways and where, on weekends, homeowners can be seen trimming hedges, planting gardens, and raking leaves in the fall. But many of these homes, though well kept, need repairs. Even new homes, such as those in the South End, are shoddy and overpriced, leaving the owners with high mortgage rates and property taxes and with costly feuds with developers and bankers—who profit regardless.

One of the newest housing developments is in the Emerson Park area. Homes here are offered for lease and, more recently, for sale. The housing was funded by a collective of investors whose interests, some say, seem to lie in pushing the "St. Louis, Missouri," agenda for East St. Louis, Illinois: discussion of sports stadiums and development of the Mississippi riverfront. Riverfront development, though, is controlled not by East St. Louis but by the Southwestern Illinois Development Association, a regional agency, run by mostly affluent whites, with the power of eminent domain. While Emerson Park Development now offers a few homes for sale, most of the newly developed property is for rent only. Some residents believe that this is so the property can be easily transformed to fit the long-term plans of state and regionally sponsored developers and contractors. Either way, it is a money-making resource for the outside, mostly white developers and construction companies.

Unlike larger cities with significant concentrations of poor and unemployed, the downtown streets are not interspersed with panhandlers, amateur musicians, and street artists. Some families with accumulated wealth and extra money to spend reside here, but they tend not to spend much time in the city's downtown area. There is also little to attract the wandering tourist with spare change in his pocket. There is almost none of the public-space interaction between residents and outsiders that you might find on the sidewalks of New York or on State Street and Michigan Avenue in Chicago.

The lack of racial diversity is discernible. What was once a majority white population is now almost 100 percent African American. Shops and restaurants in New York's Harlem attract racially and ethnically diverse visitors. Not true of those in East St. Louis. Other than the Casino Queen, a gambling facility located directly across the river from the St. Louis Arch, few businesses attract white consumers. They and others from outside East St. Louis are usually workers who arrive and depart by private car. On weekday mornings, they go right from car to office building, venturing out of their offices only to pick up lunch at Sandy's barbecue, Kentucky Fried Chicken, or Wendy's.

My mother and I notice that no graffiti exists on derelict properties except for occasional spray-painted "keep out" warnings. Though it is Friday and school is out for the day, only a few children are playing in their yards. Three young men look under the open hood of a car. Their T-shirts are grimy. Cans of Stag beer rest on the nearby porch wall.

Mom and I take the long route back to the highway—through the city and east. At the riverfront is the Casino Queen. This gamblers' haven brings in millions annually, yet somehow the riches have bypassed East St. Louis. If this is "trickle-down" economics, it isn't working.

The sights bring back a flood of memories for my mother: mothers and fathers, their children in tow, going in and out of stores; young lovers strolling down the sidewalks, the live music of Ike and Tina Turner flowing from the nightclubs; and she and her friends riding the streetcar for fifteen miles for the excitement of it all. But even her imagination cannot cloak the burned building that jaggedly edges the downtown skyline or disguise the tall weeds that grow ferociously in the empty lots behind the empty shops. It cannot regenerate the stockyards, chain stores, and factories that once made this a city dominated by blue-collar workers and families. It cannot conceal the poverty that seems to sit on every other doorstep, waiting for time to shoo it away.

. . .

George W. Bush's Council of Economic Advisors apparently didn't have the same view. In February 2007, the council's *Economic Report of the President* assured us all that America's heartland, as well as the rest of the U.S. economy, "continues to exhibit robust growth, with a strong labor market and moderate inflation . . . supported by rapid productivity growth that makes our economy one of the most dynamic and resilient in the world."[2] To be sure, in recent decades, central cities have witnessed increases in employment and have been less likely than in the past to be burdened with simultaneous population loss and increasing poverty. Suburban spaces are also part of the boom. Overall, these spaces are growing at much faster rates than central cities in terms of household income, business growth and development, falling rates of unemployment, and digital access.

Such rosy reports—which followed one after another right up to the moment of the near-universal collapse of financial markets in 2008—denied that immense fissures persist in the national economy. According to *The State of the Cities 2000*, a report commissioned by the U.S. Department of Housing and Urban Development, most of America's cities are participating in the "new economy," but a 1999 report focused on the string of small northeastern cities that have been left behind. A 2006

Brookings Institution report found that from 1999 to 2005, poverty rates increased in eighteen of twenty metropolitan areas in the South and the Midwest. Scholars have noted pockets of poverty elsewhere, as well. The suburban poor outnumber "their city counterparts by at least 1 million," according to the Brookings study.[3]

The first-ring and former industrial suburbs are doing worst of all. These are often the cities in between booming residential suburbs and recovering central cities and betwixt large cities and small communities. These are mostly working-class suburbs that once served as America's centers for industry and transportation. East St. Louis and Granite City, Illinois, Benton Harbor, Michigan, and even larger places like Gary, Indiana, and Flint, Michigan, have all lost industry and population and consequently suffer eroding tax bases. These have become showcases of midwestern decay. These are also the places where African Americans originally moved to escape the socioeconomic harshness of the South and the low quality of life in impoverished central cities.

Today, America is experiencing a demographic transformation. According to William Frey, of the Brookings Institution, "In 2000, 43 percent of blacks in major metropolitan areas lived in the suburbs, but that share increased rapidly to more than 50 percent by 2008."[4] No longer confined to the poorest parts of central cities, they are also now concentrated in the poorest suburbs in surrounding metropolitan areas.

Despite their growing numbers, we know very little about what life is like for poor workers and families in general beyond the central city limits, let alone for those of color. We know even less about the circumstances of suburban life and its meaning for African American residents in places as hard hit as East St.

Louis. How do they define their responsibilities as workers, parents, kin, and community citizens? How do they negotiate their lives and the lives of loved ones in these other urban spaces? Answering these questions is the mission of this book.

· · ·

Albert Haynes, sixty-five, could relate to my mother's nostalgia. "It didn't used to be this way," Haynes said in reference to the decaying buildings and streets. "There used to be stores everywhere. We used to go play in the park. We would ask Mama for a nickel to go to the show. We used to go fishing in the lake. I remember those days. Things were good then."

Taverns, stores, schools, churches, industry, and government all make up the atmosphere of a city. But its character is not accidental. It evolves and transforms over time. Its consistent transformation is the product of interactions among the city's residents, political entities, industry, and culture, as well as of regional and national trends.[5]

Despite its residential population, the city of East St. Louis actually was not designed with the capacity to serve residential men, women, and their families. Rather, it was established as an industrial suburb, with proximity to St. Louis on the other side of the Mississippi, and was developed to promote and protect particular industrial interests. As one researcher argues, "every major city needs a workbench, a trash heap, a washbasin, some kind of repository for the unattractive, yet essential, elements of urban life, such as the slaughterhouses, smokestacks, rail yards, and those who make them work. Philadelphia needed Camden, Chicago needed Gary, and St. Louis needed East St. Louis, conveniently located anywhere outside the city limits."[6]

Initially incorporated in 1859 under the name Illinoistown,

East St. Louis has survived many transitions over the last 150 years. In 1888, Illinoistown merged with the adjacent East St. Louistown and was reincorporated as East St. Louis. The prime location, untapped natural resources, and available labor helped the city thrive as both a commercial and an industrial center. East St. Louis has always capitalized upon its location for the transportation of goods. Early in the nineteenth century, the first ferry station was built in this area, allowing ferryboats and barges to use the Mississippi River. By the time the Eads Bridge was opened in 1874 and the Merchant's Bridge was opened in 1889, linking East St. Louis to the Missouri side, the city had established itself as a major transportation center. This accompanied the nation's demand for raw materials.

In the late nineteenth and early twentieth centuries, this region of Illinois, overall, was an appealing site for industry attempting to escape the high costs of doing business in the central city of St. Louis. The East St. Louis government operated primarily to protect investment and industry. Area industries influenced municipal governance and planning. Manufacturers impacted development, swayed land use, and manipulated demographics. Vast manufacturing activity provided thousands of job opportunities. The city attracted immense numbers of racial minorities and ethnic immigrants. In addition to southern Europeans, Croatian, Czech, Polish, and other eastern Europeans settled in the area, many in the city's north end.

The black experience in this part of Illinois is historically significant. A small population of African Americans has lived in the area since the birth of East St. Louis. America's first all-black town, Brooklyn, Illinois, shares a border with the city. It is one of a hundred or so communities organized by black Americans between the early 1800s to the mid-1900s and is one of a few that survive today. At the turn of the twentieth century, when most African American men remained part of the agricultural economy, most of those in this growing industrial and transportation center worked on the railroads and docks and in the stockyards, mines, and other industries offering low wages and requiring heavy labor.[7]

In East St. Louis the First Colored Baptist Church was founded in 1863. Lincoln School for Coloreds was built in 1886 on Sixth and St. Louis; for years, it was called Lincoln PolyTech. Education here centered on practical skills advocated by Booker T. Washington, such as piano tuning, band and orchestral instrumentation, carpentry, masonry, plastering, plumbing, electricity, cooking, and sewing. However, the majority of African Americans arrived after the turn of the century. Their inability to earn a decent living and their children's lack of access to education in the South motivated many to move into the Midwest. Black migrants were encouraged to settle in the area by industries, which viewed them as a source of cheap labor. Industries hired African Americans to do the work that whites refused to perform. Even this horrid labor was often better than what they had left behind, but it also meant these new midwesterners would encounter new forms of racial tension.

. . .

Among the first stream-of-consciousness responses to the prompt "East St. Louis" is "corrupt political machine" and "vice capital." These aspects of the city, too, have a deep legacy.

Noting that the primary purpose of a place like East St. Louis is to provide a political climate and regulatory freedoms that maximize the profits of industry, Andrew Theising wrote, "Industrial suburbs condone corruption and vice for purposes of profitability. By keeping everyone in the process happy, a measure of stability exists that ensures profitability of industry." Throughout the nineteenth and twentieth centuries, that corruption was pervasive. In the 1800s, a political machine created by elected leaders enabled them to merge personal prosperity with public gains. City mismanagement, nepotism, prostitution, gambling, and other forms of lawlessness were hallmarks of that period. The surge in the black population was a net benefit to the Republicans, the party of Lincoln.[8]

In the early decades of the twentieth century, as the population of African Americans began to swell (along with those of southern and eastern European ethnic groups), World War I–related industries boosted employment, and more workers migrated to the East St. Louis area. The labor force of both whites and blacks was augmented by industrial expansion, though whites were more likely to be hired than blacks. Eastern Europeans were the most represented group in the National Stockyards. American Zinc, in neighboring Fairmont, recruited workers directly from Mexico. Aluminum Ore and other manufacturers aggressively recruited southern black workers to replace white strikers. These tactics kept wages low for industry owners by pitting one group of workers against another. According to Elliot Rudwick, management maintained consistently large black proportions in their labor for two reasons: "Race differences among the employees decreased the possibility of unionization, and Negroes did not object to performing low-paying, dirty, unpleasant tasks involved in fertilizer manufacturing and hog-killing."[9]

In April 1917, black strikebreakers helped defeat the union effort at Aluminum Ore, and three months later that led to one of the deadliest race riots in American history. White mobs, instigated by a few political leaders and hopefuls, attacked black

men, women, and children. Forty-seven blacks and eight whites
were killed. In the aftermath, many black families fled East St.
Louis. Nonetheless, many remained, and still others continued to migrate into its borders. Besides contributing to the low
wages of a competing and diverse labor force, the labor manip-
ulations of the manufacturers prevented the development of a
pronounced middle class.[10]

The emergence of organized crime in the twentieth century
only exacerbated this element of city life. Thriving industries
remained passive in response to illegal practices so long as they
did not interfere with the industries' profits, and by 1920, East St.
Louis was a major industrial center. It had the cheapest coal in
the world, was the second-largest hog market, and was third in
the grain market. In 1921, Aluminum Ore was the world's largest
aluminum-processing center. The city also led the nation in the
production of baking powder, paint pigments, and roofing supplies. Industries planted within and outside city limits produced
a vast array of products for the nation's growing industrial manufacturing economy. Local historian Bill Nunes summarized the
immense list of products that included "acid, aluminum, barium,
barrels, beer, boxes, bricks, brass, cans, castings, cereal, coal,
creosoted timbers, dairy products, electrical supplies, elevators,
farm equipment, feeds, fertilizer, fittings, flour, foundries, fruits,
gas, glass, grin, heavy chemicals, ice, iron, lead, lumber, machine
tools, meats, oil, ore, paint and paint pigments, rail equipment,
roofing materials, rubber, soap, steel, shoes, syrup, textiles, tools,
utilities, valves, vegetables, wood, white lead, yearlings, and
zinc."[11]

Often referred to as the "Pittsburgh of the West," the city
had twenty-two railroad terminals and was the nation's second
largest rail center. The expansive coal mines of southern Illinois

shipped their product using the vast railway system, thus distinguishing East St. Louis from most other urban areas.

East St. Louis was a city on the move. A 1921 state report rated its schools the best in Illinois. But prosperity did not spread the benefits equally. Relative to other demographic groups, African Americans endured higher rates of infant mortality, tuberculosis, and other forms of morbidity. Black men toiled at the stockyards and on the railroads, while black women supplemented family diets by raising chickens, ducks, and pigs and tending small gardens on tiny dirt lots. Many also performed domestic work, cleaning the homes of the city's white residents. But during this period of great racial tension, they were forced to return to their neighborhoods by dusk.

And despite the presence of growing labor unions and abundant manufacturing, East St. Louis was the second poorest city of its size in the nation. Annual income per household was only about 24 percent of the average for the state of Illinois. The better-quality schools, open to white children, were closed to a black student body. The largest companies reaping the benefits of residential labor and the development of the city infrastructure were located just outside the city border in order to avoid taxes. Many of these companies even set up their own captive local governments.[12]

The Great Depression hit East St. Louis particularly hard before the industrial demands of World War II sparked a resurgence. By 1947, the population topped seventy-five thousand. Many African Americans were beginning to move solidly into the working class by moving into jobs previously held by white ethnics and by accessing government positions, but many others, left behind by the boom, lingered in poverty.

In 1943, the development of the federally funded, need-based

John Robinson Homes project began—ironically, the same year that stores and their profits were expanding. Sears department store moved into a larger and more magnificent building. A new bowling alley opened. In 1959, the city received the All-American City Award from *Look* magazine and the National Municipal League, and a new shopping mall opened. The next year, local businesses employed sixty thousand workers and paid $125 million in wages.

But trouble loomed. Population was declining from its peak of 82,295 in the 1950 census. In 1959, Armour Company relocated, and fourteen hundred jobs were lost. Between 1950 and 1964, eight other major industries and employers of African Americans left the area: Aluminum Ore, Walworth Valve, American Steel, Eagle-Picher Lean, Key Boiler, American Brake and Shoe, American Asphalt, and Excelsior Tool and Machine. Fifty-five miles of railway existed in the city, but the national trend of conversion from coal to gas as a fuel source drastically cut rail traffic. The Majestic Theater closed its doors after thirty-two years, and a new federally funded housing project, the Orr-Weathers Homes, was built to house the increasing number of low-income families in the area. White workers and families left the city for predominantly white towns on the periphery, such as Belleville, Sauget, and Fairview Heights, abandoning the debt and mismanagement that they had helped to infuse into the fabric of East St. Louis.[13]

Popular arguments mostly place blame for the economic and social decline of urban areas on the black and brown populations who generally live there. But the more accurate explanation is the migration of industry, heavy traffic, declining capital stock, and a concentration of low-income persons, all of which generate a need for higher municipal expenditures. For East St.

Louis, these problems reared collectively in the 1950s, prior to their appearance in many other locales.[14]

To address the fiscal crisis, the city instituted a strict budgeting system in the next decade, creating a deputy comptroller position to help implement internal efficiency and general control measures and tighter civil-service requirements for city jobs. Yet the crisis worsened. Other stopgap measures included new taxes on retail sales and utilities and on automobiles by requiring municipal auto registration fees, which just compounded the economic demands on working residents while failing to produce adequate additional public revenue. Still another creative, but failed, revenue enhancer was judgment-funding bonds. Payments on the judgment bonds were made out of a special property-tax fund. Over time, staggeringly higher proportions of property-tax revenues were used to service the ever-increasing debt.[15]

By 1970, almost half of the manufacturing jobs had disappeared. Five years later, more than half of the collected property taxes paid for local borrowing. But the use of property taxes as a source of stable funds was declining. Up until the late 1960s, the city had been responsible for collecting taxes that were extended to the county, with uneven results. The valuation of city property began to fall steadily in 1960. In addition to losing other tax revenues from the ongoing industrial flight, East St. Louis saw a significant portion of its land taken off the tax rolls thanks to excessive highway construction within its borders.[16]

An African American majority emerged. In 1960, the city was 55 percent white and 45 percent African American. By 1970, the black percentage had grown to 69. Whites were down to 4 percent in 1980 and 2 percent in 2000. Meanwhile, the total population plummeted from 82,000 in 1960 to 41,000 in 1990. Today,

East St. Louis is the city with the highest percentage of African Americans in the nation but has a population of just under 30,000.[17]

Just when many black Americans were gaining a foothold in the city's working class, core industries were well into the process of abandoning it. The losses overwhelmed basic municipal services to the point that the city could not afford regular trash pickup, plumbing repairs in public schools, or the demolition of abandoned structures.[18]

. . .

In just about every way, the history of East St. Louis varies significantly from the mythical suburbia of our literature and consciousness: just as poor areas of central cities have been cast as the primary living space for African Americans, suburbs have been perceived as white, middle-class, socioeconomically mobile, and affluent, homogenous residential retreats. These spaces were understood to offer these families respite from the harshness of city life—its dangerous streets and criminal kind, its loud noises and dense populations, its unpredictability, lack of personal space, pollution, and, yes, its dark racial element. Relative to suburban life in other nations of the Western world, American suburbs are said to be distinct in their reliance on the private automobile, the separation of daily activities into nuclear units, the upward mobility of residents, and the physical division that they provide between work and leisure time.

Perhaps the most damaging of the suburban myths, with respect to blacks, were those of the "pathology" of African American family culture and its corollary, a supposedly poor work ethic. The early history of blacks in East St. Louis confirms just the opposite. The family—and sometimes only the family, with a broad definition encompassing the extended family of cousins, uncles, aunts, and grandparents—is what ensured their survival in brutal conditions. And when it came to ingenuity and long hours, African Americans, by working several jobs and maximizing scarce resources, took a back seat to no other ethnic group.

Edith Taylor, ninety-two years old when I interviewed her, recalled how everyone in her family worked and harvested what was then farmland. Another elderly resident, Ida Fay, who also grew up on a family farm, explained, "But it wasn't enough, so my father worked, too." That is, her father worked as a full-time packinghouse employee while her mother managed the farm. The demands of the farm meant that the children were enlisted to pull weeds, till the soil, plant the seeds, and chop crops during harvest. After toiling at this monotonous work for years after school, another local resident, Oliver Fay, promised himself at a young age, "If I ever get grown, I'm not going to chop *nobody's* garden ever again."

Parents also demanded that children go to school and seek paid employment. "Otherwise we couldn't survive," Edith Taylor said. Consequently, she and her sibling also worked for wages in a local nut factory. To say the least, such anecdotes refute the notion that this was a culture deficient in work ethic. But such anecdotes fall into the historical cracks of the predominant suburban narrative marked by race and class.

Proletarian pluck and bootstrapping through education are major themes of recent revisionists, who have shown that in the early part of the twentieth century, suburbs attracted not just the white middle class but the white working class as well. The latter reluctantly followed industry and jobs, leaving behind cherished inner-city neighborhoods, neighbors, and extended kin. Somehow, the black working class gets omitted from that narrative. The appeal of owning a home and being surrounded by green grass, trees, quiet, and other similar things was not confined to a single group. Nor were a strong work ethic, a commitment to family, and a belief in the value of a good education.

East St. Louis native Clarisse James recalled that her father worked for Saint Louis Fixture, building cabinets for the growing number of department stores, businesses, and homes in this Midwest region. He also worked as a handyman, fixing roofs or basement-floor leaks. According to his wife, he began working at age ten with his father, "doing carpentry and acquiring some knowledge of building." Eventually, he built a new home for his wife and children on a piece of land inherited from his mother. With determination and patience, he constructed the house over a period of years, bringing spare lumber, nails, and roofing materials from the different construction sites where he worked and bargaining for discounts on the purchase of bricks and indoor fixtures. After school and on weekends, the children painted, carried lumber and bricks, and performed other tasks. His brother-in-law and uncle also participated in the project.

Once the family took residence, Clarisse James's mother spent mornings and afternoons "closing off" the back porch with wood posts and screening. "I wanted to use the porch like an extra room, so the children could sleep out in the summertime where it was so nice and cool," she explained. Her oldest daughter recalled coming home from school and seeing "Mama up on that stool with nails between her teeth and a hammer in her apron pocket." Such stories not only describe a culture with a dedication to the concept of work. They also capture that culture's specific ingenuity at assembling from scratch improved housing stock, its reliance on the skills developed in trades and in childhood, and its characteristic of communal participation by extended family members.

. . .

The 1979 election of Mayor Carl Officer, who for many offered a glimmer of hope, instead became a benchmark of the decline of East St. Louis. Officer appeared to have a chance to turn the city around and prioritize its needs. After all, he had come from a family of modest means: the Officers owned and operated a successful funeral home in the city, and they were well-known, respected, and trusted members of the community. Unlike past candidates, Officer was not beholden to the political machine of the Democratic Party.

But optimists underestimated the depth of the problems. East St. Louis was approximately $180 million in debt, and the same characteristics that had helped Officer win the election would prove to be barriers to his ability to network with politicians and legislators who could assist the city. When the debt further ballooned, state policy makers blamed the black mayor, who never hesitated to place blame on the white institutions and power structure that created and maintained a system of inequality for this predominantly black place. The Officer administration was accused of mismanaging money and federal grants, and with East St. Louis on the verge of bankruptcy, the city became the first to have its public housing managed directly from Washington, D.C. Consequently, mostly white policy makers, some of whom were angered by Officer's public charges of racism, assumed effective control.

In 1990, Governor James R. Thompson placed the city in receivership, establishing the East St. Louis Financial Advisory Authority (FAA) under the Illinois Financially Distressed City

Law. The FAA had the power to approve or reject the city's budgets, financial plans, new projects, and major purchases, among
other powers. Failure to comply with FAA requirements could
lead to the removal of the city's spending authority. The FAA,
for example, rejected the Officer administration's attempt to
use casino payments to the city to invest in infrastructure. The
white gubernatorial appointees on the board demanded that the
funds be used to pay down debt to outside entities.

Civil rights were a casualty of receivership, as residents lost
representation. Corruption lingered, especially in the form
of nepotism, with high-paying jobs and contracts consistently
going to elected officials' relatives and friends. Among the more
prominent scandals during my time in the city, in September
2004 Mayor Officer argued that the political opposition had set
fire to his campaign headquarters, the site where he had continued to hold meetings with supporters.[19] In 2006, four residents,
including Democratic Party leader Charles Powell Jr., were
found guilty of participating in a vote-buying scheme to get
Democrats elected during the November 2004 election.[20] Beer,
medicine, cigarettes, and cash were provided to those who cast
a Democratic ballot. In 2005, Kelvin Ellis, the former East St.
Louis director of regulatory affairs, pled guilty to evading more
than forty thousand dollars in federal taxes involving money he
primarily earned from his previous city employment.[21]

The fallout of these political woes benefits only outside commercial interests. In 2005, Schnuck's, one of two local grocery
store chains, threatened to close its East St. Louis location, cit-
ing high rent and declining profits. In response, the city council
agreed to pay a private developer $1.8 million to help buy and
renovate the supermarket building, for which Schnuck's got a
$1-a-year lease for five years. City administrators also consid-

ered a bond issue to create a similar deal for the expansion and renovation of the Casino Queen.[22]

The largest city in southwest Illinois, East St. Louis was also one of the nation's largest concentrations of poor at the time of this writing. About 40 percent of the population lived below the poverty line. Nearly half of residents age eighteen and older had not completed high school. . Fifty-six percent of East St. Louis individuals and families had annual incomes of less than twenty-five thousand dollars compared with 13.5 percent of individuals and families in the United States in general. Over half of the population depended on some form of government assistance.[23]

. . .

The goal of this study is to recast classic notions of the nature of American suburbs. These classic views are, at best, nostalgic, and they miss essential aspects of the African American experience there. Moving forward, what we need to understand is that suburban life has never been one of splendor for blacks.

We confront the problem not just as the first black president makes his mark but also as leading black intellectuals assess the comparative importance of structural explanations for black poverty versus the conventional "culture of poverty" thesis. Even the estimable William Julius Wilson struggles with this problem; in so doing, I believe, he downplays the key ingredient of this mix of structural explanations and conventional thesis. In his latest book, *More Than Just Race: Being Poor and Black in the Inner City*, Wilson reemphasizes his familiar theme that black America is really divided into two populations: poor inner-city residents and those who have escaped to the "middle suburbs." For black America (or America in general), it seems, race, poverty, and place primarily matter in urban settings, where structural inequities disproportionately affect minority populations. That notion is unassailable. However, Wilson misguidedly suggests that blacks contribute to or reinforce their own poor conditions of life by taking on unhealthy lifestyles and behaviors.

If the price that African Americans are paying for the ascension of the first president from their ranks includes a denial of the full extent of the legacy of racism in the persistence of black poverty, then that price is too steep.

. . .

Changing demographics and socioeconomic problems demand that we push aside outdated and inaccurate notions of suburbia. Suburbs are increasingly racially diverse, and first-ring and former industrial suburbs are experiencing crime, high school incompletion, and poor health at rates similar to many inner-city neighborhoods. The bedrock historical truth about East St. Louis is that, in many ways, it contradicts the American suburban ideal. Black people were never fully absorbed into the nation's cities or its suburbs. They were simply never fully absorbed into the paid labor force—particularly in jobs that paid living wages or provided for ideal "suburban-like" lives. In truth there was no golden age for black America. Andrew Theising summarizes the historical reality of East St. Louis: by the 1960s, over half of the city was black; about half of black families were surviving on annual incomes considerably less than the county average; a third of working-age adults were unemployed; blacks were not being integrated into union labor, nor did they find opportunities that would provide family wages and benefits. These trends have changed little in the decades since—for black urbanites or suburbanites.[24]

Still, those seniors, like my mother, wax nostalgic. While vividly recalling parents, uncles, aunts, and grandparents being out of work, looking for work, complaining about low pay and high prices, mistreatment by employers, and the lack of opportunities—just as many do today—they also recount other elements in scarce supply today: good times, happiness, and family. They remember children laughing, playing; women cooking, cleaning, tending gardens; and men at least having a fighting chance at jobs that demanded hard work and offered dignity.

"My daddy worked for Armour," said Alberta Cline. "Papa worked for the railroad for as long as I can remember," reported Marie Scott. This is also the East St. Louis described by white former residents. A former student of mine, Elmer Lynne, put it this way: "My daddy had a job. My uncle had a job. They really all of them did work. They would walk to work together. They would come home together. They would play cards on Friday nights. Drink beer together. That's how they enjoyed themselves. We children, that's all we saw was men going to work, our fathers going to work, coming home, resting, getting up. Going back to work. They were always tired, but that's what work was supposed to be back then."

For older black residents, the transition of East St. Louis from predominantly white to majority black corresponded with their increased local and national political influence and power and with a better standard of living and more buying power. According to seventy-eight-year-old Ohana James, "Back in the 1960s and 1970s I think it was coming along. You had black people in high places. We had black doctors and politicians. We had people that owned their own businesses. We had theaters and black-owned grocery stores. We had families that lived in the big houses—I know you've seen them. I mean mansions on Virginia Place. If we had a few pennies, then we could buy penny candy and bubble gum and pop. These are things that you can't do today with a few pennies."

Big names once called East St. Louis home: Miles Davis, Ike and Tina Turner, Jackie Joyner. People observed themselves or others moving up the economic ladder. They remembered working parents starting in a one-bedroom house and transitioning into larger accommodations as the family grew and the household income increased. Eighty-two-year-old Marian Mason talked of her parents' ascent: "Daddy started out on the railroad. Then somebody told him or somehow he got this job working over at the steel plant. I think, it seemed he preferred that, because he worked inside and he could get better pay. . . . Mama stayed home and took care of the house, the family. Daddy worked, and she stayed home until we was all in high school."

The full truth is not so romantic: East St. Louis could be harsh for many families. In the South End in the 1920s and '30s, the yards in which children frolicked had no grass; the streets on which parents marched to work were muddy. Morning, noon, and night, the stench of pollution from factory smokestacks and of death and manure from the stockyards sifted through the battered wooden lean-tos that many of the newest black immigrants called home. The stench of aerial smog and other by-products of Aluminum Ore, packinghouses, fertilizer plants, and paint manufacturers permeated the air. The raucous clackety-clack of moving railroad cars shattered the peace. Just as in the larger cities of Chicago, Milwaukee, and Detroit, homes for black families were largely the small and rundown ones abandoned by whites as they ascended the socioeconomic ladder. The gainfully employed found locations slightly farther away from manufacturers than the shacks of the poorest—but still, the properties sat at the edges of an industrially exploited landscape.

Olive Colter, ninety, moved from Mississippi to this area of the city in the 1930s. She remembered, "It was like living in the country.... To me, this city ain't never been beautiful." She qualified this by adding, "Now if you lived where most of them Caucasians lived then, some of them they lived real nice. But for us people, you know, brown skin, we was pretty much living right where I am now, in this part of town [Rush City/South End], and it has just never been pretty."

Whatever is either positive or negative about East St. Louis, past or present, is in the eye of the beholder. Popular images of a crime-ridden city, with prostitution, welfare queens, and lazy out-of-work men paint only part of the picture, for the city has produced many success stories, such as poet Eugene Redmond and the Hudlin Brothers filmmakers. The Officer family, whose funeral home has long been a staple of the city's commerce, and many others have achieved economic and social stability.

But certain grim facts of the contemporary plight are undeniable—not just the statistics about employment and income, but also the surrounding evidence of a deteriorating quality of life. For many East St. Louis households, something as basic as buying groceries can no longer be taken for granted. Construction of 40 percent of the city predates 1940, which contributed to some of the highest lead-poisoning rates in the region and to the designation of the city as a national "Brownfields" site—one of sixteen hazardous environments targeted for a monumental cleanup.[25]

With schools quite literally crumbling, young people are not preparing for college or planning for the prosperous careers that could follow. And with few entertainment or recreational businesses or sustained public cultural-arts programs, the task of parenting is unimaginably hard.

Theorists of the culture of poverty cite poor work ethics and morals and maintain that these traits carry across generations. Acting on this theory, recent changes in welfare policy concentrated on removing the poor from welfare rolls and forcing them into low-wage labor. The assumed dark color of welfare recipients and the assumption that these populations are dispensable burdens to the mainstream add up to the system that Kenneth J. Neubeck and Noel A. Cazenave have labeled "welfare racism."[26] The reality is that black families negotiate their activities in the context of a severely depressed environment. While social scientists and the media have begun to acknowledge the poor state of inner-city living, they have yet to make the connections to the past experiences of the middle classes in today's supposedly more tranquil suburbs.

The ways in which the history of East St. Louis deviates from the image of suburbia in our literature and consciousness are striking and instructive. Whether in inner cities or in suburbs, the African Americans who flocked from the South to the Midwest, like the white ethnic groups of the early twentieth century, sought gainful employment, access to education, and safe homes. But in East St. Louis, the erstwhile "All-American City," many blacks, unlike many white ethnics, have yet to find these things. What's more, in an age of environmental crisis and jarring economic transformation, even those inclined to write off the human fallout of industrial suburbs have an interest in understanding them. Casual employment, the crumbling of infrastructure, and the breakdown of community aren't threatening just the margins of suburbia. They are threatening the core of its idyllic vision.

IMAGES OF ABANDONMENT AND DECLINE
IN A BLACK INDUSTRIAL SUBURB

East St. Louis, Illinois, was once a major transit and industry center. It was a suburban city that witnessed rapid industrial growth and generally offered opportunity to the poor and the working class. However, for African Americans in particular, it became a suburb of stifled promise. By the mid-twentieth century, East St. Louis was experiencing considerable debt. Major industries were phasing out their local operations, which eroded the tax base, and the population of whites who were able to move began to leave the city, consequently further eroding the tax base and creating a population shift to a majority of African Americans. That remaining population was left with the task of maintaining and growing a city in financial despair. Nevertheless, relative to other places, the city remained a place of promise for many African Americans and those few from other racial and ethnic groups, both poor and professional, who continued to maintain residence within its borders. Still, as some of the following images reveal, today East St. Louis is a place in need of serious attention. Abandoned and deteriorating structures define the lives of those families who call this former industrial suburban city home. The photos in the first group that follows all come from the collections of the St. Louis Mercantile Library, at the University of Missouri–St. Louis.

Figure 1. Scene on Collinsville Avenue, circa 1890, when the primary means of transportation was streetcar, bicycle, and horse and buggy and the majority of the growing population was white.

Figure 2. In the early part of the twentieth century, thousands of African Americans made their way to East St. Louis in search of work. Armour and Company, Hunter Packing, Aluminum Ore, the National Stockyards, railroads, and other major industries offered low pay and often unsafe working conditions. For African Americans living here at the time, these opportunities presented an improvement on the employment options that had been available to them and their families in the South. Circa 1940.

Figure 3. In the wake of job loss, members of needy East St. Louis families line up for government surplus beans, butter, cheese, cornmeal, dried milk, rice, and flour. March 1958.

Figure 4. Public housing was a move "up" for many African American families in East St. Louis in the mid-twentieth century. It also represented the promise and expectation of greater prosperity. 1962.

Figure 5. Mr. Misker Williams, a disabled veteran, and his spouse were the first tenants in a newly completed East St. Louis housing project. They and their five children left behind a neighborhood targeted for urban renewal because of its deteriorated housing. In this photo, the couple is being welcomed by Mayor Alvin Fields and Goldie F. Orr (next to the mayor), the new East St. Louis housing commissioner. 1961.

Figure 6. By the mid- to late twentieth century, austerity further characterized the city's financial situation and complicated its ability to meet the
needs of families. While the riverfront continued to witness expansion on
the Missouri side of the Mississippi, attracting both tourists and commerce,
the same did not occur in East St. Louis. Here Mayor Carl E. Officer meets
with Senator Adlai E. Stevenson III, a Democrat from Illinois, to discuss
the drawing of redevelopment plans for the East St. Louis riverfront. The
expansion of the riverfront was perceived by many as a primary means of
attracting business, building a tourist trade, and generating revenue for the
city. 1980.

Figure 7.   Also in 1980, Mayor Carl E. Officer cut the city budget by
$1.6 million by terminating eighty-five city workers. In this photo, city
workers stand inside City Hall, waiting to be told details about the cut.
December 1, 1980.

Figure 8. In the 1980s, trains continued to move through the switching yard and still do today but at a volume far less than what was experienced in the early part of the twentieth century.

Figure 9. Goldie Dorsey stands in front of her home in East St. Louis, 1986. The city, at this time, consisted of a majority of African Americans. Poverty rates were on the rise, and housing quality was mixed. Many families lived in deteriorating apartments and homes; abandoned property and lots characterized the landscape. Nonetheless, many, similar to Ms. Dorsey, took pride in maintaining tidy multi- and single-family suburban homes. September 22, 1986.

EAST ST. LOUIS TODAY

Today, a range of housing remains in East St. Louis, from public low-income housing to pockets of well-maintained and modest working- and middle-class homes. However, abandoned or deteriorated businesses, multifamily dwellings, and single-family homes dot almost every block and neighborhood. Many are dilapidated beyond repair and, occupied or not, are potential health hazards for families with children in particular. The photos that follow were taken by Odell Mitchell during the summer of 2010.

Figure 10. Hazardous housing is characteristic of many East St. Louis neighborhoods.

Figure 11. Virginia Place, once a street occupied by middle- and upper-income whites, has since been occupied by African Americans. It is still a street of stately homes, but many of them are declining now.

Figure 12.   Many families must live in crumbling properties. Dwellings are often in need of extensive repair, but few family homeowners have the means of meeting the costs of refurbishing or even maintaining their homes. In addition, renters, especially those receiving state assistance, have limited housing options—many of which are homes and apartments that require renovation.

Figure 13.   Collinsville Avenue remains the major thoroughfare that it has been historically. But signs of decline are evident in the empty shell of the Majestic Theater (on the left), missing, broken, or boarded-up storefront windows, and piles of debris on the floors of closed businesses.

Figure 14. Views from most angles of the downtown are imprinted with blight and despair.

Figure 15. Inside one of many abandoned businesses. Empty buildings are generally neglected places that collect refuse, are fire hazards, and serve as unsafe dwellings for those without permanent shelter.

Figure 16.   The deserted Spivey Building and (to the right of it) the closed offices of the former newspaper, the *East St. Louis Journal*.

Figure 17. From 1961 to 1980 over ten thousand jobs were lost as industries closed their local operations. Seven hundred of those jobs were lost when the Hunter Packing Company, one of the last major employers to leave the area, closed its doors (its plant shown abandoned here). The city's population dropped by more than half from 1950 to 1964.

Figure 18. The East St. Louis riverfront today remains mostly undeveloped, and there seems little other than the presence of the Casino Queen.

Figure 19. Despite the tattered appearance of this shopping center off State Street, a few shops remain open here.

Figure 20. A view of the Metrolink, a Bi-State rail, with East St. Louis in the background. The abandoned Spivey Building and other past signs of prosperity can be seen in the distance.

ODELL MITCHELL

The renowned photojournalist Odell Mitchell Jr. spent twenty-five years working for the *St. Louis Post-Dispatch,* located in St. Louis, Missouri. His work has chronicled events from the daily news and sports to fashion. He has served as a freelance photographer and has traveled extensively in the United States and internationally. Today, he owns a photography studio and teaches at colleges in the St. Louis metropolitan area.

CHAPTER TWO

East St. Louisans
and Their Cars

Few, if any, accoutrements of American materialism embody the iconography of suburbia quite like the private automobile. The car represents freedom and spontaneity and is also a commodity and a status symbol in its own right.

When you start considering East St. Louis as an inner-ring suburb, rather than simply a small-urban collection of inner-city pathologies, the car problems of its citizens stop looking like the petty nuisances of poverty. Those nuisances magnify into Shakespearean agonies, torturing East St. Louisans twenty-four/ seven in their daily personal interactions, in their professional options, and in their sense of self-worth and full participation in the opportunities and benefits of national life. Their love-hate relationship with the automobile has an additional component that outsiders seldom notice: they are actually far *more* dependent on reliable private transportation than are more conventionally categorized suburbanites. That is because local employment is so scarce that East St. Louisans often need to travel long distances across the river, to St. Louis and its Missouri suburbs, for even the dead-end jobs for which their education targets them. An institutionally underfunded and inefficient public transportation system just reinforces this bitter state of affairs.

Curvis Shore, thirty-eighty, knows. On the day I met him, he had parked his 1980 Ford Fiesta in the Fairview Mall parking lot. He estimated it would take him about thirty minutes to walk into the shopping center, find and pay for the blue jeans he wanted, and then get back to the car. Time was of the essence. Not that he had a particularly heavy schedule that day; in fact, it was his day off work. But the starter, or perhaps the ignition switch, of his Ford Fiesta was balky. Curvis's strategy was that whenever he did manage to get the car going, he didn't turn it off until he had completed all his errands and returned home. He left the car's engine purring quietly, waiting in the most obscure section of the mall parking lot.

Often, he got a friend or cousin to tag along and sit in the auto while he took care of business. But this time he was on his own. His main concern was that mall security would be waiting for him when he returned and would ask for driver's license, proof of ownership, insurance. Scouting out the parking lot, he had seen only one security vehicle on the opposite side. He figured he had time to run in and run out of the store before they rolled around in his direction.

Although Curvis faced all these considerations in running a simple errand, he felt he did *not* have to worry about theft—and rightfully so. The vehicle's paint was yellow, the body rusted, and it had well over a hundred thousand miles and innumerable idiosyncrasies. The front-door lock had to be turned a certain way, just ever so slightly to the right to release and allow the door to open. The front seat would jolt backward if the driver did not have a brick placed just right underneath its adjustment lever. The blinkers had to be "blinked" up and down, up and down, up and down manually whenever the driver needed to signal a turn.

For months, Curvis's mother had been urging him to get the car fixed. Confined by a walker, she, like so many others, couldn't get far on accessible walkways, which in East St. Louis were few and far between.

Repairing the troubled vehicle was easier said than done. For a definitive diagnosis, Curvis would have to remove the parts and have them tested. The most economical way to replace defective parts was to do his own long, hot, and dirty search through junkyards.

And the car also needed tires, annual taxes and tags, insurance, gasoline, and certification in the state emissions-standards test. Fixing a starter or ignition switch had not yet crowned his priority list. Still, the car problem was a severe inconvenience, sometimes keeping him from getting to work on time or running his mother's errands or paying his bills or conducting his love life.

. . .

If having a mortgage, backyard parties, a career, socioeconomic mobility, and independence reflect the ideal suburban life, then it is the personal automobile that facilitates much of this lifestyle. Cars provide people with the freedom to live wherever they choose and visit friends and families. Minivans make possible the daily commute to employment and schools of family choice. SUVs allow for affordable family vacations, shopping sprees, and participation in multiple extracurricular student activities. Suburban residents from teens to seniors are more likely than people in urban centers to own vehicles and use them for many of these and other transportation adventures. Dependable private automobiles make the demands of parenting and aging more comfortable.

But automobile ownership is not spread evenly across the nation. A U.S. Department of Transportation survey suggests that those who rent, as many East St. Louis families do, are less likely to possess a vehicle than are homeowners. And households earning less than twenty-five thousand dollars annually, as this city's residents disproportionately do, are less likely than others to own a late-model auto or any auto at all. In other words, well-running cars are an elusive possession for the people of East St. Louis. For many in the city, however, owning a vehicle can be as burdensome as going without one. Besides the costs of upkeep, a car's absence or unreliability strains relationships, makes residents fearful of traversing predominantly white suburbs, and complicates already stressed working-class lives and households.[1]

The disconnect between the needs of citizens and the functionality of the public transit system has made buses and light rails a poor alternative. "If I take the bus," said Curvis's mother, "I'm likely to be waiting out there in the rain or anything. Then I got to get on for an hour to what would take me ten minutes by my own car." She also feared getting aboard a bus and handing over her life to people she didn't know. Safety was the number-one concern of surveyed public-transit riders, according to a 2007 passenger survey.[2]

Alberta Fisher agreed: "It's just easier to control your day when you can get a ride with somebody.... Taking the bus means that you have to get to *A* to *B* and back again before the kids get out of school. If *A* is in Belleville and *B* is in Collinsville, then there just ain't no way to take care of things that day. It's just what you live with when you got to take the bus."

East St. Louis's once elaborate and affordable streetcar system was developed for industries—to move workers to and from their jobs. Its latent function was to transport consumers back and forth from suburbs farther out from the metro center to downtown East St. Louis and St. Louis area shopping districts, restaurants, and clubs. As in other industrial cities, the streetcars were long ago dismantled and replaced by an emphasis on the ownership of private automobiles and, more recently, by limited public transportation. The loss of city amenities soon followed. The East St. Louis shopping mall and many of its grocery and retail stores, restaurants, movie houses, and clubs closed, leaving a shell of the cultural and consumer center that once was.

In 1968, the Kerner Commission, in its summary of American racial issues, concluded that the development of transportation routes to and from inner cities to the growing number of suburban jobs was an essential step to ending the high rates of unemployment in these urban communities.[3] Even earlier, private researchers had emphasized the link between proximity and joblessness and the relationship among transportation, commuting time, and jobs for residents in urban centers and their increased employment opportunities in the suburbs.[4] In the first decades of the twentieth century, streetcar schedules were coordinated around the shift schedules of factories whose low-wage earners commuted from in central-city neighborhoods to jobs in satellite cities. But today, there are few job opportunities within or near East St. Louis. Most residents search for employment in St. Louis proper and its predominantly white and outer-ring suburbs on both the Missouri and Illinois sides. Even this effort is challenged by middle-class suburban residents' protests against the establishment of bus and rail stations in or near their communities and the criminal element that they perceive will have access to upscale suburban neighborhoods.[5]

Policy makers assume that a public transit system will maximize employment opportunities for the central-city poor. But what about those in the suburbs? Of the approximately nine thousand East St. Louis residents sixteen and older who work elsewhere, about 15 percent traveled by bus during my period of research. This rate of usage was both significantly higher than that of the state and, if interviews with residents are any indication, a reflection of the paucity of private auto ownership. Bus patronage was higher among workers in East St. Louis (13 percent) than those in the state of Illinois in general (8.8 percent) and in the nation overall (5 percent).[6]

As the Curvis Shore story illustrates, getting from here to there in a personal auto is no small task either. Automobiles take a toll, both on the pocketbook and on relationships. A driver's license and access to a vehicle are veritable rites of passage in suburban America, a path to *independence,* but here they have been more like an unrealized necessity than a privilege, supporting only *interdependence.*

. . .

Alister Payne stayed at his sister Berta's on Friday nights. He had to be at work at 6:00 A.M. on Saturday mornings, and he knew he could count on her for a ride. She rose at 4:30 every day, got her kids ready for school, and herself prepared for work. She dropped him off at the Drury Inn in Collinsville, Illinois, and then drove on to her own job at the Holiday Inn a few blocks farther. If she ran late, he would ride all the way to her job and then walk back to his—which meant that he would arrive late.

Since she had children to care for, rent to pay, and a car note, he thought that was an appropriate sacrifice for him.

The car was a two-door Geo. Alister's long legs folded into his chest each time he squeezed into the passenger side. Afraid that he would get into an accident that would raise her insurance rates, Berta would not let him drive. Alister covered gasoline costs and was responsible for maintaining the car. Sometimes, car repairs and maintenance ate up nearly his entire paycheck.

One successful strategy was to "put a few dollars in the gas tank" to and from work; gas stations, other than the two name brands within East St. Louis, were both more convenient and more affordable in the surrounding area. In 2005, Doug Moore, a reporter for the *St. Louis Post-Dispatch,* found that in East St. Louis, the fuel costs averaged about ten cents more per gallon than just outside the suburb. Gas station owners argued that the cost of doing business in East St. Louis was elevated by higher sales and property taxes. Moore wrote, "The owner of a building valued at $50,000 pays $1,510 a year in property taxes. By comparison, a taxpayer in Belleville would pay $950.00, while the amount is even lower in St. Louis—$657.00." Many residents claimed that the stations colluded to keep prices artificially high. But Bill Fleischli, executive vice president of the Illinois Petroleum Marketers Association and the Illinois Association of Convenience Stores, disagreed, according to Moore. He explained, "A lack of competition kills any incentive to lower prices . . . and the lack of volume in the city compared with other places reduces the profit margin and gives East St. Louis owners less flexibility to adjust prices." Furthermore, the Illinois attorney general declared that the charge of collusion would be almost impossible to prove.[7]

The upshot was that Alister and his sister developed a reciprocal relationship. He watched Berta's children on Saturday evenings, when she liked to go out to a local club with her cousins, and he stayed at the house she rented at least two other nights a week, sometimes providing child care then as well. They clashed over whether his presence alone was a sufficient contribution. Berta kept expecting Alister to do more in return for her hospitality. This feeling on the part of a ride provider that his or her generosity was being taken for granted was common.

Finally, they had a blowup when Alister ate a package of hot sausage links she had purchased and planned to cook for the family meal. When Berta got home and discovered this, she angrily threw a plastic kitchen trash can at him, threw him out, and cut off his rides to work. He stayed a couple of days with his uncle, who advised him to make amends. Alister returned to Berta's house with several bags of groceries, and they reached a silent, bitter truce.

As we have seen, automobile problems affect a wide circle. Nancy Card, a fifty-eight-year-old grandmother, explained, "Needy people, they can irritate you in a way that rubs you the wrong way. I mean, you help out when you can, give a ride, give them a dollar, whatever the need is . . . but you know you encourage them in very blatant ways that they need to get up, do for self, and stop being so needy."

Jasmine Cord, twenty-six, said, "It's hard to always be asking people for help. But if you don't, then you gonna be pretty much trapped in the house or something. If I didn't ask for a ride to work, I couldn't work. If I didn't get a ride to the grocery store, I couldn't get my baby's cereal."

Every day found another East St. Louisan, Taneshia Wright, negotiating for rides from her mother, sister, cousin, or aunt. This was not something she enjoyed, admitting, "But sometime you don't have a choice." Herself a young mother who worked as a part-time home health care worker, she lived with her mother in a home that the family had leased for the past ten years. She believed that if she could save about a hundred dollars a month, she would be able at least to purchase a car of her own in a few years. No such plans were really possible on her combination of minimum-wage earnings, welfare assistance, and occasional funds from her child's father; they barely covered diapers and her share of the rent. When she asked for rides, they were not trivial: daughter Tria, age two, had heart problems, chronic sinus infections, and other ailments. There were times when she had to reschedule Tria's doctor's appointments around the availability of transportation, and when they got a ride, they might wind up tacking on the night at a relative's or Taneshia's boyfriend's place.

Her mother, Gladys, did not mind providing rides or even, occasionally, her car. "But 'Neshia don't always come back when she say," Gladys complained. It was a source of conflict. Once, Taneshia said she had to pick up medicine for Tria at Walgreens and left the little girl with her grandmother but didn't return for three hours, causing Gladys to be more than an hour late to her job at Barnes-Jewish Hospital in St. Louis. She felt used and taken for granted.

In this way and others, catching or borrowing rides adds to the cumulative frustrations caused by such obvious burdens of poverty as shortage of food or money.

· · ·

In the St. Louis metropolitan area during 2005–9, more men than women drove personal automobiles to work, and the same pattern held true in East St. Louis. Men were more likely to drive a personal automobile and less likely to use public transportation to and from work than women were, according to the U.S. Bureau of the Census.[8] Yet in East St. Louis, the general presumption has been that the women own the vehicles. This circumstance seems to have affected the self-esteem of the male population.

"Women can begin to think less of a man, 'as a man,' if he can't do for himself," said Tim Jackson, thirty-six. "On the other hand, a brother will understand 'cause he done usually been there. You can generally call on him." Recent research on the topic suggests that African American men have developed practices of manhood that reflect their marginal social and economic status better than hegemonic forms of masculinity do, the latter still tending to emphasize independence and autonomy.

Clearly, ideals of black masculinity have been linked to the automobile culture. Television and print ads told Curvis Shore, Alister Payne, and others that their manhood hinges on occupation and income and also on the size of their television screens, the price of their watches, the brand of their clothing, and the make and model of their vehicles.

The men in East St. Louis feel this pressure, where talking about cars is a favorite pastime. Men pick up their knowledge of classic and newer models, the costs, performances, and respective strengths and weaknesses from these discussions, as well as through observation and advertising. Those working as valets for upscale restaurants and hotels have firsthand experience that others have only vicariously.

Many of the male East St. Louisans I spoke with said private transportation affected dating in particular. Maurice Thomas told me, "These women nowadays, they expect a brother to come with something. If you ain't got no car, then that gives them a right to disrespect you." Ty Richard echoed that assessment: "If you want to take somebody out, then you got to have a job, you got to have a car . . . you got to be your own man."

Dominique Baylor also framed the issue in terms of power. "My girlfriend, she can be really, really sweet," he said. "She give me a ride to work, pick me up, take me over the river [to St. Louis], you know—as long as I don't get on her bad side. It's like she has some control over me because I need her for certain things, like transportation."

In comparison, women noted that they had multiple obligations toward work, children, and kin, many of which require the daily use of their cars. "I take my son to work to the Science Center in St. Louis," said Tara James, forty-two. "Then I'll double back and get some rest before I got to go work myself." Earlier, her son had used the car for a job delivering pizzas, but when Tara balked at all the wear and tear, he had to quit.

.   .   .

What most East St. Louisans want in an automobile is "something that you can count on," Vivica Blanchard, twenty-four, told me. She drove a 1986 Buick Regal, purchased from her uncle for $450, with the money from an income-tax refund, four years before we spoke. At the time of the purchase, the car's exterior needed minor paint repair, the muffler had a deafening rumble, exhaust poured visibly out of the leaky tailpipe, two tires were bad, and the engine needed an overhaul. Vivica factored these repairs into the price she paid her uncle and hired one of his friends to do the work.

Vivica could never have reached her goal of buying a new car. "All I wanted was something small like a little Pontiac Sunbird or a little Nissan," she said. But that would have required financing, which her poor credit ratings and minimum wages precluded. When she was enrolled in college, she had taken advantage of credit card offers but racked up bills of more than six thousand dollars in one year. She was nineteen years old at the time and, as she put it, "didn't know any better about money managing." Adding to her debt were three thousand dollars in federal student loans through the college.

Children of college age often rely on support from their parents, especially when it comes to large purchases such as computers, apartment rentals, and cars. Vivica's parents were in no such position. Both were born and raised in East St. Louis and had worked low-wage jobs for their entire adult lives. Her father had recently begun work as a security guard for a lumberyard. Her mother was a housemother at a transitional living facility for mentally challenged adults. The two had not shared a household in more than fifteen years, and each was caring for other children in their homes.

In her third semester at Southern Illinois University at Edwardsville, Vivica was in the school's work-study program and held another part-time job at an off-campus Domino's Pizza. It was difficult to keep her grades up with such a hectic work schedule. Access to private transportation would have made the schedule more manageable, but she had to commute by bus from East St. Louis to the campus at least four times a week. At times, waiting for a bus in the cold after a shift at Domino's, she felt as if someone were stabbing her feet with ice picks. When she walked through the front door of her home just before midnight, school homework could take a back seat to a few precious hours of sleep. But she needed to finish school, take care of her grandmother, and keep her debt under control.

Vivica's father called her prized Buick the "choppy jalopy." It always needed a part replaced, a hose mended, a plug made to spark again. Simply owning a car is not the same as having reliable transportation. Vivica's was one of the 69 percent of East St. Louis households reporting vehicle ownership in the 2000 census.[9] But that statistic says nothing about the cars' condition or dependability.

Carita Miles, mother of three children, owned a twelve-year-old Mazda. As a result of faulty wiring, the headlights abruptly stopped working one night when she and all three children were on the way home from dinner at McDonald's. For a month, she had to save money for the repair and drive only during the day.

Spontaneous breakdowns of used cars are so common in East St. Louis that many men make a living as uncertified mechanics. They have no formal business licenses or shops and pocket their fees "off the books."

Sean West, forty-four, could fix anything. His primary means of earning money in between jobs was car repair. "S. West at your service," he would say when answering his phone, silencing the *t* on "West" so that there was a rhythm and rhyme to the delivery: "S. Wes' at your service." Folks like Curvis, Hershel Gray, and Carita Miles would come to him from all over the city to have work done. Sean would diagnose the problem. The car owner would give him money for the part and then pay him an agreed-upon amount for his labor. This was cheaper than getting a muffler replaced at Midas Muffler or going to Sears or Pennzoil for an oil change. As long as a vehicle did not require complex electrical patch-ups, people like Sean could generally mend it.

Yet, as handy as he was with others' cars, Sean had problems with his own. Indeed, he had recently been fired from a job at Radio Shack because he routinely arrived late. His twenty-year-old Cadillac Eldorado routinely "quit" on him. He would then bum a ride from a family member or a friend. He would fix the car, but inevitably something else went wrong. And honestly, he spent more time working on other people's vehicles than his own. After all, it was in this sideline business that he made most of his income, not at Radio Shack.

．　．　．

Compounding these indignities has been the cost of insurance in East St. Louis. The residents there, one of the poorest city's in the state, pay the highest rates for liability and physical-damage coverage. In 2003, it cost an average of $396 for a married, thirty-six-year-old to cover a 2003 Ford Taurus with liability insurance. In neighboring Belleville, it was $341; in Bloomington and Champaign, comparably sized urban areas, it was, respectively, $270 and $246. The average expenditure for auto insurance rose 5.7 percent across the nation from 2002 to 2003, according to the Insurance Information Institute. During the same period, premiums in East St. Louis jumped 31 percent.[10]

It is therefore bitterly ironic that one of the biggest fears of African American East St. Louisans is that their car might break down after a late-night work shift and leave them stranded *in a white neighborhood*.

In the late 1990s, a group of white supremacists threatened to poison the East St. Louis drinking water. In the same period in nearby Glen Carbon, a predominantly white town, white youth burned a cross on the lawn of a black family. As I discuss in greater depth in a later chapter, questionable police beatings or killings of black males in the St. Louis metropolitan area occurred regularly. Word of mouth and local media carry accounts of other racial incidents that have occurred on both sides of the Mississippi River.

When Chester Miles could not get his car to start after working a late shift, he called his girlfriend for a ride. She couldn't pick him up because her sister had borrowed the car. Chester decided to walk home from the White Castle fast-food restaurant in Fairview Heights. "The police followed me real slow like for about, say, three blocks," he said. "Then they stopped, got out the car and asked me for identification, where I was going, why I was out here, that routine, patted me down, you know."

For Chester and other black men, these situations generate fear and a sense of emasculation and loss of control. "It makes you shake a little, especially if you by yourself . . . 'cause you just never know if they think you are guilty of something. You don't know if they going to assault you. You think, 'Okay, I can either run or try to be cool about this situation.' . . . If you run, then that just gives them the excuse they been looking for to arrest you, beat you, kill you, or whatever their issue is that day and time. Now everybody done heard of Rodney King. Well, I can tell you that all black men have had a Rodney King experience. They either know a Rodney King, or they are a Rodney King."

Weldon Williams had to walk home from work late one night from Fairview Heights. He stayed on the main roads for fear a shortcut could result in his being attacked. The police noticed him walking along the side of the road. They shone a bright light on him and then used their public vehicle to block his path. They waited for him to walk toward them. He thought of running, but there were two of them. "Besides," he said, "they got guns and all I got is feet." Additionally, this was a common occurrence. He figured they were just going to ask him some questions and look over his identification. The officers did all of this but in the process placed handcuffs on him and made him lie on the wet, muddy ground. After a time, they released Weldon and told him that they were looking for someone who fit his description. He walked home wet, dirty, angry, and disgusted with himself for not being able to do more about the situation. He said, "Sometimes you don't tell nobody when it happens."

Men and women in this region were very aware of racial profiling well before the term had traction with the general public or national policy makers. "My daddy'd tell me not to go in certain neighborhoods, like Granite City, you best not," reported Elmer Woodard, forty-three. "If you can prove you work there, then they more likely will leave you be. So I'm safer if I leave my uniform on after work."

This midwestern region of the United States has a history of reserving public space for use by white Americans.[11] Most black people know where they are not wanted, and the predominantly white population of the southern Illinois region makes its sentiments clear. In the late 1980s, an elite St. Louis organization influenced the local police to close a bridge connecting East St. Louis to St. Louis, with the explanation that this would discourage "East Side" gangs from traveling to rob attendees at a popular annual fair. In 2000, the adjacent predominantly white village of Sauget, Illinois, built a makeshift barricade across the major thoroughfare that connects its community to East St. Louis. This was a public road. Sauget's public officials claimed that the move was an attempt to prohibit speeding by traffic from entering its boundaries. However, they chose not to examine other possible solutions to the purported speeding problem, such as an increase in the presence of traffic police and ticketing. Instead, they found a "solution" that primarily targeted the African American residents of East St. Louis, who use the street for walking, bicycling, and driving to and from nearby shopping centers and other places in the area. East St. Louis residents protested, and the barricade was eventually removed. In the meantime, residents of East St. Louis had to find other, less convenient ways to get to where they needed to go.[12]

Through it all, African Americans, more than any other demographic group, are willing to travel widely to shop at new stores, especially for bargains. This makes sense, considering the few amenities available in predominantly black urban communities. The disparity amounts to yet another kind of unofficial tax on the minority population. East St. Louis has few decent clothing stores and zero bowling alleys or movie theaters. Until recently, there was just one chain supermarket. A second chain store then opened—directly across the street from the existing one, which meant that residents of the Emerson Park area, South End, and Virginia Place areas still had to travel considerable distances in order to shop at a grocery store with a wide selection and modest prices.

In these ways a public problem becomes internalized. Even in high-density cities, low-wage workers borrow rides, shuttle from one bus or subway to another for hours every day, and are frustrated by the absence of essential services in their neighborhoods. What has been unique about the East St. Louis experience is the extent to which the people there interpret their automobile woes as their personal failings. They fail to link the transportation problem with the cluster of issues surrounding their physical, social, and economic isolation.

Under the "spatial mismatch" theory posited by many social scientists and economists, high unemployment rates in black communities are a function of the geographical separation between prospective jobs and workers. While this helps us to understand where jobs are typically located for urban workers, it does little to explain why African American workers are some of the least likely to be employed. After all, white workers commute to East St. Louis for jobs. Black women have historically walked, bused, and carpooled to work in the kitchens, rooms, and hallways of affluent homes and hotels. Black men have commuted to restaurants, hotels, and factories by streetcar, bus, carpool, and on foot. Historically, most "good" jobs have been outside African Americans neighborhoods.

In the early decades of the twentieth century, African Americans who migrated to East St. Louis were isolated in the neighborhoods nearest the stockyards, railroads, and other industries and often lived within walking distance of these places of employment. But even this "spatial match" did not guarantee jobs for black men or women; unemployment rates for African American men have always been significantly higher than those for whites. A more accurate observation is that unemployment, underemployment, and poverty have been assured by job discrimination and segregation.

Access to consistent transportation, whether private or public, is the difference between better jobs and worse jobs, between the ability and the inability to meet familial emergencies and responsibilities, to maintain simultaneously a work schedule and the capacity to negotiate shopping, picking up children, caring for older kin, and having leisure time. These are the things that ease life's burdens—the things that, for most East St. Louisans, have remained beyond their reach.

CHAPTER THREE

Work and Meaning in a Jobless Suburb

For most Americans, voluntarily leaving one job for another usually is a mark of advancement. You expect your moves through the workforce to better your life in some important way: a raise, a promotion to a new title or set of responsibilities that in turn can be parlayed into another vertical breakthrough. But for Maxwell Lawson, and so many East St. Louisans whose stories I tracked, jobs were lifeless, dead-end things, passed around in meaningless lateral moves that added up at best to shuffling the deck.

Maxwell, a twenty-one-year-old cashier at the Chocolate Factory, considered himself a hard worker. Since the age of seventeen, he had held one part-time job or another. He had been working at this small candy store across the river for eight months.

Maxwell got the job on a lark. He happened to be window-shopping at the mall, on his way home from another job, when he noticed the help-wanted sign. It was his lucky day: an old high school friend was working behind the counter. She immediately gave his completed application to the on-site manager, who interviewed him on the spot. "They usually just talk to you right there in a corner somewhere," he said of his job-interview history. "People be going by, comin' up and askin' him questions. I'd say that's pretty much a typical way it goes." He had mixed feelings about the whole process, which didn't make him feel very valuable as a potential employee, but he wasn't complaining when he arrived home and found that the manager had already offered him the job.

Yet once the exhilaration wore off, he began to think about the work that went into training for a new job, getting to know his fellow employees, the work schedule, and the near-poverty wages. If he wasn't careful, he would find himself wondering, "What's the point?" before he even got started.

Maxwell was asked to report the following Monday. He decided to give his current employer one day's notice rather than the customary two weeks. "I wanted to give myself a little vacation before starting the new job. I like to celebrate whenever I get a new job."

What was he celebrating? For many East St. Louisans, finding a new job of any kind is worthy of a celebration. It provides a person with a stronger sense of control in his life choices. "It means," Maxwell said, "that I'm someone in demand." His personal bar for being in demand was set so low that he had not so much a career strategy as a repetitive scenario of tactics to help him cope, day to day, week to week, month to month.

Maxwell picked up his final paycheck from his former employer and then spent his "vacation" at his girlfriend's house. He relished the opportunity to be, albeit temporarily, a full-time daddy to the one-year-old daughter they shared. She stayed with him instead of going to day care. They sat around watching television, went for walks, and visited people he knew. He hoped that one day, he would land a job that would allow him and his longtime girlfriend to marry and raise up their child in a way he felt they all deserved. Whether that hope held any real promise was another question.

Bern Lawson, Maxwell's father, drove a truck for an ice company. Maxwell's mother continued to work in a local elementary-school cafeteria, a job she had held for fifteen years. His grandmother, who lived four blocks north, worked in the housekeeping department of St. Joseph's Hospital in St. Louis. His grandfather was one of her coworkers up until he died of heart failure, when Maxwell was a high school junior. Maxwell recalled his grandfather's calloused hands. "They was like hard and sandpaperish, but they was like working man's hands," he described with affection. "You know, from the hard work pushing them big brooms and mopping the hospital floors. People, when they walk on them floors and admiring how they're shiny, . . . they didn't know that it was my grandfather's hard work that made it that way."

He understood that his job options were limited in this place at this point in his life. Sometimes he made a move for marginally better pay and hours; other times, for a more hospitable work environment, which he described as "where I feel like I'm getting some respect." Still other times, his moves were either for easier or more challenging labor or "just for a change."

Maxwell's searches always began and ended outside the East St. Louis city limits. He was usually turned down. He handled the rejections in various ways. He recounted the numerous occasions when a job denial led him to sulk for weeks on end, "like a depression." His parents told him not to give up. At times, frankly, he did not get the source of their optimism: "They been working hard all their lives, and they still have it hard, real hard."

Maxwell admitted that sometimes he just felt lazy. "I just don't feel like going in to work all the time. What's the point? Sometimes, I just can't carry myself to the job." On these days, he slept in, cleaned house, watched television, picked up his daughter and visited with friends, and saw his girlfriend at her workplace.

. . .

Contrary to popular belief, many black men and women want to work and actually do. In a cruise through the St. Louis metropolitan area, we can see them here and there, working as police officers, store managers, sanitation workers, postal workers, sales clerks, and in various other occupations. Most black men and women do the work we hardly notice. They bag groceries and round up shopping carts. We hear them stirring in the kitchens of chain diners, punctuated by the clink of the dirty dishes they wash. The men open the doors and carry the luggage at hotels, responding to the whims of the clientele with a seemingly bottomless supply of warm smiles, "yes, sirs, "yes, ma'ams," and "Have a good day nows." The women, in uniform, vacuum the lobbies, remove the soiled towels and bed linens from guest rooms, and place mints on pillow tops. The men trim the oversized hedges that surround corporate and school campuses. The women watch over the children of the middle-class mothers in the corporate office suites. Others clean our Ameritech or university office buildings with an economy that belies the strength and sweat that is necessarily exerted for such a task.

Or maybe we see black men on a sunny Saturday morning in the service department of our local auto-service center, overalls smudged and grimy from changing our vehicle's oil, filters, and hoses. Or we see the women behind the customer-service counter. These tasks are mind-numbing and heavily supervised, offering little in the way of independence or growth, yet demand a usually underappreciated patience and proficiency.

Historically, joblessness, underemployment, and poverty wages have been the hallmark of inner-city neighborhoods, not the suburbs. In 2005, according to a Brookings Institution report, the poverty rate for the hundred largest U.S. cities (about 19 percent) was twice that of suburbia (9.4 percent).[1] So how to explain the high unemployment and underemployment of East St. Louis? Maxwell Lawson was part of a generation of thirty-five-and-unders who came to know, firsthand, that neither suburban living nor place is protection from low wages and marginal opportunities. The pay scale, the limitations on upward mobility, and the content of the work have conspired against this generation's goals of realizing their potential and living the American dream.

By any measure, jobs are difficult to come by for residents of East St. Louis. Throughout the Midwest since the 1950s, rates of joblessness in concentrated geographical areas have increased, especially for black males.[2] But they have also increased for women in urban geographical spaces predominated by African Americans. Tract data from forty-nine metropolitan areas show that in the poorest and predominantly black census tracts, male unemployment rose from 9.5 percent in 1950 to 21 percent by 1990.[3] When those who were unemployed and seeking employment were combined to create a single measure with those who are unemployed but no longer looking for employment, joblessness during this period rose from 25 percent to 44 percent among men of working age. Unemployment rates in East St. Louis were strikingly high well before the high profile of massive layoffs nationally at the beginning of the first decade of the twenty-first century.

There is no shortage of explanations for this. Most popularly, the argument has been that African Americans have attitudes and accompanying behaviors that demonstrate the lack of a strong work ethic.[4] These values are interpreted as a consequence of middle-class black flight from central-city areas, which were sent reeling into further economic despair, as housing, small businesses, and tax bases dwindled. A culture of poverty was said to have developed, because youth were raised without role models. High rates of school dropouts and crime ensued. All these factors inhibited the effectiveness of those left behind to seek and maintain upward mobility and stable employment.[5]

Other researchers have argued that the poor have values similar to those of other economic groups and that the culture-of-poverty thesis has become racialized. In making their way into mainstream terminology, labels such as "underclass" have sought to stigmatize African Americans. For Gans, the use of pejorative labels, which typically refer inaccurately to behavioral characteristics of those below the poverty line, has a pernicious influence on public policy and discourse. It is hard to disagree that stereotypes of black "welfare queens" and "lazy black men" made more palatable for white America the passing of the Personal Responsibility and Work Opportunity Reconciliation Act of 1996, which diverted attention from an economy unable to provide enough living-wage jobs.

The culture-of-poverty model was also powerfully refuted by the very history of East St. Louis, which in the mid-twentieth century was a destination for black middle-class teachers, social workers, nurses, office managers, supervisors, and other professionals, residing in proximity to factory workers and domestics. Their salaries, continued discriminatory practices by realtors, and the desire to live in diverse neighborhoods kept many tied to inner-city neighborhoods and to predominantly black suburbs.

The day-to-day reality of black poverty—as opposed to the competing academic theories—was well captured by Alford Young's 2004 study of twenty-six young men from Chicago's poor inner-city West Side. Within a system of racial and economic stratification, the most isolated African American men defined their employment prospects by blaming themselves. Contrarily, those who held jobs and, consequently, interacted with people from other racial groups were better able to articulate the multiple and structural forms of oppression that they encountered and that served to inhibit their economic and social mobility. These men did not react passively to their conditions but, rather, created worldviews that made sense of those conditions and gave meaning to their experiences.[6]

.   .   .

The East St. Louisans in this chapter were not familiar with William Julius Wilson, Reynolds Farley, or other celebrated researchers of the world of the working-class poor. Most, however, were clear and articulate about how their basic life circumstances affected decisions pertaining to jobs and work.

At the time they spoke with me, the city's top fifteen employers reported that they offered fewer than five thousand jobs. These employers ranged from School District 189 and the Casino Queen riverboat (each with about twelve hundred employees) on down to St. Mary's Hospital, Pfizer Pigments, and Locke Home Products. The makeup of their workforces did not reflect the city's native reservoir of human capital. The majority of the workers in these industries hailed not from East St. Louis but from surrounding cities and counties, in a phenomenon well encapsulated by the local quip, "The new mayor lives here, but the new city manager does not." Police officers and firemen have not been required to reside within city limits. Within thirty days of employment with the police department, for example, employees must establish residency within a one-hour drive of East St. Louis. Many of the public school teachers also lived elsewhere. Even many Casino Queen workers did not call East St. Louis home.

Residents noted ruefully that even when jobs exist, they do not go to the residents, or at least not the good jobs. The types of occupations available to locals have both diminished in number and changed in character. In 1970, 42 percent of the occupations held by employed persons age sixteen and over were crafts-men or foremen, machine operators, and unskilled laborers. By 1990, this number was only 25 percent. With low-skilled work-ers accommodating an expanding metro-area service industry, low-wage labor has become the city's primary export. Mean-while, the principal imports are the resulting low wages and the workers' need-determined government assistance. Statewide, Virginia Carlson and Nikolas C. Theodore found that in 1995, the statewide ratio of entry-level jobs to the population of low-skilled workers was one to five. In East St. Louis, they discovered, the ratio was one to nine.[7] There has been no improvement, and expanding a job search beyond the city limits is not necessarily the answer. A report by the Leadership Council Southwestern Illinois indicates that in 2008–9 alone, southwestern Illinois wit-nessed a significant decline in private-sector employment, losing approximately eight thousand jobs.[8]

What remained most prominently from the old days was a range of service and retail outlets on the main strip, Collinsville Avenue. These included furniture and pawn shops, high-priced off-brand clothing stores, beauty-supply stores, nightclubs, and Chinese and barbecue restaurants. These were by and large family owned and operated, many by Asian Americans. Few, if any, had significant black-resident employment.

People here share a definition of "decent jobs" and a desire for them. A decent job is not tied to long-term career goals or personal fulfillment, nor does it necessarily offer significant health benefits or even a wage sufficient to enable a single adult to support a household. A decent job probably does not mean nine-to-five work hours. Rather, it is, whether full- or part-time, simply stable and above minimum wage. Decent jobs are held by adults, not adolescents, so jobs as bag boys and McDonald's cashiers are less than desirable. Alister Payne put it this way: "Like, if I could get a job working for the city, cleaning streets, whatever, something that's secure."

The hospitality and chain-retail industries also fall under "decent job" opportunities. LaSasha Banks applied for a job at the Marriott Hotel in St. Louis: "I just, you know, clean the guest rooms, vacuum, clean the hallways, just clean." The worst part of this decent job, she says, is "sometimes the way the guests treat you" and "working on holidays." LaSasha would never call it fulfilling or enjoyable, but it was decent because she knew she could count on incremental raises and on sick leave and paid vacation time.

Decent jobs are found through personal networks. LaSasha found out about hers from a friend already at the Marriott, who in turn tipped off LaSasha's sister Macy and provided a reference to the hiring supervisor. Even with such strategies, decent jobs are not easy to find. Employers take liberties with the hiring process that work against many East St. Louisans—for example, asking applicants detailed questions about their means of transportation. Tamara Smith remembered a potential employer quizzing her about transportation. "The boss wanted to know if I would be driving my car to work everyday, since, you know, the schedule would be changing." She explained what the employer really wanted to know: "whether I had my own car or if I was going to be taking the bus or something." Tamara responded, "I've never had a problem getting to work on time, so you don't need to worry about that." In order to get and keep jobs, East St. Louisans go to elaborate lengths to keep prospective or current employers from knowing too much about their transportation struggles. One man, "Terrance," told of calling his wife from a pay phone at the end of the workday and arranging to be picked up at the back of the company parking lot: "That way, no one would know that my car wasn't working and count it against me."

Black job seekers reported that employers harbor stereotypical images of them. Black men are perceived as untrustworthy, black women as somewhat less so. For East St. Louisans, the issue isn't just a legalistic encounter with job discrimination; rather, as Vernor Green put it, "They don't really know anything about what it's like out there." The computerized job-search databases at large chain stores, to which applicants are routinely referred, have become yet another device to depersonalize and marginalize.

All of this contributes to feelings of instability about more than just work. East St. Louisans feel pressure to make money in any possible way, a feeling that continues even when they are gainfully employed. Work is understood to be not a career but simply "a job," which can be gone today or tomorrow. This understanding serves to protect workers by salvaging some of their dignity from a system skewed toward stripping it from them.

Stanley Evans, thirty-four, was a customer-service representative for a large company. He dealt with phone calls pertaining to customers' questions about their accounts. He explained, "I make pretty good money, $6.75 an hour. That's better than what a lot of people I know are doing." He rose every weekday morning at 5:00, ate a breakfast of hot or cold cereal, ironed his slacks and shirt for the day, and headed out the door. He walked three blocks to the bus stop, took the bus to the Metrolink station in downtown East St. Louis, and rode a Bi-State train into St. Louis. The office was another four-block walk from the Metrolink stop there. If the bus was running on time, the commute took an hour and a half.

Stanley had held many jobs. He once worked simultaneously for both the Dillard's department store and the Red Lobster restaurant in the Fairview Heights shopping area. He preferred the former job because he could wear a shirt and tie and get an employee discount on purchases. The pay was near minimum wage, but he felt he was on a career track. His model was one of the floor managers, also from East St. Louis. Later, Stanley learned that the reason this person had risen to a higher job classification was credentials: a bachelor's degree in business management.

He regularly worked multiple and short-lived minimum-wage jobs, for two reasons. First, he needed the extra money. Second, he was always looking for a better opportunity. He was naively confident, for example, that a job at the Pasta House might lead to a supervisory position, before he ran up against the blatant hierarchy of the white management. A position at a dry cleaner seemed to him the closest thing to being self-employed, because he ran the shop without a supervisor watching his every move. Unfortunately, he was fired when he failed to open the store on time one Saturday morning. "The guy was right to be angry," Stanley said, "but I think that firing me was going too far. He could have docked my pay or something, but I guess it was just easier for him to say, you know, 'The hell with you.' 'Cause, you know, it's easy to find somebody to work, really.... That's the attitude—no second chances."

Stanley had a diploma from Lincoln High School and had taken classes at the local community college in math, English, computers, and business administration. But progress toward a degree took a backseat to more urgent elements of his life. His divorce and his ex-wife's subsequent move to Cincinnati with their children set him back emotionally.

A friend of his mother's had helped him find his current job. Stanley was grateful, but he still wanted more. "I think at my age, I should be somebody's manager or supervisor. Don't get me wrong—my job is clean and all, and it brings in some money, but when you work all your life, you'd like to see yourself move up some, you know?"

Rodrick Jefferson, a married father with three children at home, worked two jobs, earning $8.75 an hour as a part-time parking lot attendant and a slightly lower wage at a McDonald's in Ferguson, Missouri, a St. Louis suburb. His days began at 3:30 A.M.; he had to be at McDonald's by 5:00. There he worked the grill and the fryers, unloaded stock from the delivery truck, rearranged the stock room, swept up and mopped, picked up trash from the parking lot, and kept both the dining area and the kitchen tidy. He didn't like breaks and took them only when ordered. He couldn't resist McDonald's bacon and French fries. His shift ended at 9:00. If the store was busy, he might stay a little longer.

Ferguson, Missouri, is no short distance from East St. Louis.

However, Rodrick learned over the years that businesses in the other suburbs tend to offer higher starting pay than those in East St. Louis or in the city of St. Louis—around $7.00 rather than minimum wage.[9] The drawback was the commute. When his car wasn't working, he could spend up to two hours on buses. Once the bus broke down, and Rodrick called in to say he would be late. He showed up four hours late, at 9:00. The supervisor sent him right back home. "And it wasn't even my fault. But I still showed up. . . . That's a sign of a good worker. I showed up, and they still didn't appreciate it."

Alberta Robinson represented some of the least alluring work of all, in the hospitality industry. The turnover was so high that, within three weeks, she was already training new hires: "I said, 'Shit, I barely know what I'm doing myself, and here I am telling other people what to do.' That's how it is, though. People just up and quit, and the next thing you know you may be the most senior person on your shift." The additional training duty did not mean anything extra in her paycheck. Alberta had worked for at least six different hotels in eleven years.

Though the characteristics of most of these jobs sound a lot like those of temporary work, many low-wage earners actually labor for temp agencies. Buster Tilly had a temp assignment at a mill in Alton, Illinois. The job was filthy and paid only $7.50 per hour, but it was relatively stable; he reported to the same supervisor and had regular hours for more than a year before the company declared bankruptcy and executed mass layoffs. Like Alberta, Buster was quickly training new hires, some of whom were full-time employees with union-enforced benefits. He told me, "They were making more money than I'd ever see there." So far, no permanent offers had materialized for Buster. Still, temp agencies give East St. Louisans a crack at work environments otherwise closed to them. These are usually in industries out-side the city with few African American employees.

The care field, in particular, uses temps. Herbert Phillips was assigned to nursing homes in predominantly white cities and communities. On his first night at the Tree Lane Nursing Home, Herbert recalled, the door was locked, and he couldn't get in. "They called the police. I had to go to my car and show them my ID. . . . I didn't feel like working then [after the situation was straightened out], because, you know, that was kind of devastating, you know. I'm here to work, and you treating me like this."

Despite that troubling start, the nursing home continued to request Herbert's services, and he returned again and again, appreciating the validation of his hard and competent work. He said he picked up his skills while caring for his mother, who had diabetes. He learned to administer both shots and comfort. "I kind of felt good being there with her, taking care of her; you need to do this. So you know, I went to school, and I been doing this for two years, and I love it. I'm like, this is my life. I go in there [nursing homes]—I kind of consider myself to be a Patch Adams. You know the guy that go in and make the residents laugh, feel good. . . . I figure if you can sit down and talk to 'em, get a laugh out of 'em, you done did somethin' good that day." He even went to the home on days off. After losing his mom, the work was therapeutic.

Still, Herbert would have appreciated better working conditions. The pay beat what he used to get at Church's Chicken, but he did not feel it reflected his value. After a decade, he was up to only $8.47 an hour. Disposable workers have a hard time accepting their lack of marketplace leverage. Men like Herbert stay in this line of work, despite little prospect of change, because they need the money, they are not sure they can do better, and they are tired of endlessly searching. And, finally and definitively, because the jobs have meaning for them.

. . .

Not everyone in East St. Louis is working-class poor. Nor do all East St. Louisans in the labor market move constantly from job to job. During 2005 through 2007, approximately 18 percent of households earned above fifty thousand dollars annually. Twenty-two percent of residents held managerial or professional positions. Fifteen percent had earned college or graduate degrees.[10] These people, of course, commanded superior pay, benefits, and work-related autonomy. Yet, even this subset minority of a minority had a hard time finding economic security in an environment of plant closings, across-the-board job losses, family tragedies, increasing costs of living, and accumulated debt.

Samuel Martin, fifty-three, benefited from the standard of living his grandparents were able to provide. In the 1970s, most students in East St. Louis attended the city's public schools. Samuel went to a parochial school in a nearby predominantly white suburb, one of the handful of black students there networking with teachers and more-affluent white students. These relationships opened doors to better jobs. He began factory work at sixteen for a small business owned by a white classmate's father. Later, he was a supervisor at American Steel and married and had three daughters.

His was a contented life until he developed a degenerative muscle disease called peripheral neuropathy. At age forty, he could no longer work, and without his job, he also lost his medical insurance. Equally devastating was the disintegration of his and his wife's dream of putting their daughters through college. Within a single year of Samuel's diagnosis, the Martins were in

economic peril. The declining health of Samuel's elderly grandmother, Mama Martin, further complicated the picture.

The Martin family found themselves scrambling to meet the
mortgage on their house and pay the groceries of two households. They had already taken out a second mortgage on their
home years earlier for a new roof and other repairs. And they
were paying high rates of 19 or more percent on credit cards. "It
was so bad—and this was embarrassing to me—we was putting
our groceries on credit cards, . . . and I had always told my daughters that credit cards are for major purchases," Samuel said. As
their finances spiraled downward, they reluctantly moved into
the modest home of Samuel's grandmother. This decision left
Samuel feeling inadequate.

Naomi Gibbs, who lost her job at Boeing in St. Louis, knew
the feeling. "When you can't take care of your loved ones, you
start to wonder what your purpose is . . . what are you here for? It
makes it hard to come home sometime," she said.

Without living-wage jobs downtown or on the riverfront waiting for their special talents, with no local redevelopment projects to incorporate their skills and no national policy to bring
economic relief to the region, and without well-placed friends or
hefty inheritances, the Samuels and the Naomis adopt awkward
and self-deflating strategies.

Although each of their children completed high school, the
years following were not what the Martin parents had dreamed
of. "I was planning on retiring early, buying a Corvette—red,"
Samuel said. "But you know, sometimes life don't do like you
expect. It turns a lot." Samuel's wife and mother-in-law also
had health issues. Ultimately, there were arguments over their
diminished resources, arguments that sometimes led Samuel's
wife to spend the night at her mother's or a sister's. He was hurt

by the sense he was letting her down, proving not to be the man she had married.

"I'm not saying it's anybody's fault or nothing, but sometimes it just doesn't seem fair," he summed up. "My mama and daddy [i.e., his grandparents] worked hard, I worked hard, my wife still works hard, and so do my girls. But I just think we are moving backwards. I mean, my girls are having a much harder time making a life for themselves than me when I was their age."

Mystic and Robert Garner each graduated from college with student-loan and credit-card debt. Explained Robert, "I had to get a student loan and Pell grants [federally funded student financial aid] to pay tuition, to buy books, and to just . . . well, live every day." Mystic concurred. Her parents, though divorced, tried to work together to pay for her to attend Northern Illinois University. They could accomplish this only with student loans, which she agreed to help pay back upon completion of her bachelor's degree. Her student-loan debt was not as great as Robert's, but she had managed to obtain three different credit cards during her academic years away from home.

After graduation, the Garners settled in East St. Louis and lived with Robert's mother until they were able to rent a two-story, newer home on the South End. By this time, they had jobs for the state, Robert a social worker and Mystic a caseworker, both in the Department of Family and Human Services. Together, they earned sixty-four thousand dollars annually, enjoyed adequate and affordable health care, paid vacation, and sick leave, and they could set somewhat flexible work hours.

But their jobs also required their own cars and professional attire, which had to be purchased on credit. These costs and the artificially high costs of car insurance and gasoline in East St. Louis affected the actual level of their financial well-being.

Owning a single-family home with a backyard, they had the appearance of upward mobility, but neither this mobility nor their material possessions reflected their true economic circumstances. Each month the couple worried that their family, which included two daughters, would have to skip a car payment, offer a partial payment to the utility company, or declare bankruptcy. "I don't know how people make it," Robert said.

He second-guessed his determination to make an adult life in the hometown of his youth. As a social worker, active in local politics and on his church board, he overestimated his ability to make a difference.

．　．　．

The failure of the Casino Queen to improve the lot of local citizens has layers of historical irony: from East St. Louis's very outset, it was a city infamous for vice. Every bit as much as its reputation as an industrial center, gambling, murder, prostitution, and corruption were what put East St. Louis on the map. In the 1950s and 1960s, officials made an effort to dispel that image, but it didn't take. The number of liquor and lottery stores dotting the spaces in between churches and residences could not be overlooked. Prostitution, strip clubs, and drug dealing were also woven into the East St. Louis fabric, especially where it bordered the towns of Washington Park and Brooklyn. Whites from the area and other suburbanites flocked there in search of illegal "action." In recent years, the tax dollars from not only the casino but also the liquor and lottery stores and the nightclubs were the focus of hopes for recovery; in Washington Park, strip-club owners even bought sorely needed vehicles and school buses for the city in an episode that attracted coverage by National Public Radio in 2003.

Velma Watts, forty-five, was elated when the Casino Queen began advertising job openings. She hoped she and her daughters and son would all benefit by what she called "solid" work, permanent occupations not in danger of leaving the community. Michael Stern, thirty-two, was another of the hundreds who stood in line to complete job applications during the grand opening. Their exhilaration didn't last. Few of the low-skilled workers who contributed to this book were ever interviewed, much less hired, for the available dealer, teller, and hospitality positions. The first people who found employment on "the boat" have at least high school completion. That prerequisite puts many local job seekers at a disadvantage.

Jobs in local, state, and federal agencies were once a staple source of work for low-skilled East St. Louisans, but no more. Both private- and public-sector jobs diminished in recent decades, and now the feeling persists that only those with connections have a chance. According to Sampson Smith, "Nepotism is in this whole area.... Even with a degree, you're still going to cross that road again and again. You have to be—if a white guy has his bachelor's degree, you have to have more than him, and you still won't get the job. It's difficult because you know that white guy is going to have it over you because he's white. But if you know somebody that works there, then that puts you at least even with the white guy."

Some tried the political game, volunteering in mayoral campaigns, for instance. But Reverend James said, "People who work in East St. Louis are 'cliqued up.' If you know somebody, most times a job is here." The reverend observed that, despite these select opportunities, most jobs for residents in the city have been those that often lead to little advancement or significant pay. He added, "Go to Belleville's unemployment office, and there are good jobs offered. Here it's cooks, truck drivers. Believe it or not, there are people in East St. Louis who are qualified to do great positions. We just don't get the good jobs."

The 2003 slogan of the re-elected mayor, Carl Officer, was "A Time for Hope, Healing, and Rebuilding." Yet, the new construction sites, on the riverfront and elsewhere, turned out to be managed and manned by outside companies and workers. When Raymond Moore applied at Emerson Park Home Construction, "They just flatly told me, they said, 'We don't need nobody ... we got it covered.'"

In 1991, Senator Kenneth Hall and Representative Wyvetter H. Younge, both state of Illinois congressmen from East St. Louis, secured a grant from the Illinois Department of Commerce and Community Affairs to convert an old Bi-State bus garage on Tenth Street into the Dawn Building Corporation, a cooperative development. The concept was to manufacture both jobs and homes. Neither the corporation nor its potential materialized. The only visible progress at the time of my research there was a handful of new signs at the dilapidated garage and the main office. By 2010 the space served as warehouse for a nearby local business.

The pattern of politicians and others with influence padding their own coffers at the expense of those who really need jobs and services has been like this for as long as James Tease can remember. He explained, "These people, they will come in here, they will talk about how bad it is in East St. Louis, how many things we need help with. Then they go and get big money from the government to build this building or make these jobs, but nothing ever happens. They just use the city's problems to make money for their own selves." Henry Moore, a long-time member of Mt. Zion Church and a neighborhood association activist, added, "All these university people and big people with money come in here saying that things could be different, but they really interested in seeing what they can get out of us. They don't want us to live any different, because then, you see, . . . they wouldn't be able to get all that money for doing absolutely nothing."

In 1998, East St. Louis was declared a federal Empowerment Zone. During a visit, President Bill Clinton said the designation would provide greater encouragement and tax incentives for private investors and, ultimately, more jobs for the people of East St. Louis. His words, "It's not a handout, but it is darn sure a hand up, and you are entitled to it," inspired many residents.[11] The new status and the presidential event renewed false hope that the city was at the cusp of a rebirth. To be sure, something of a redevelopment boon took wing, in the form of a strip mall built around a supermarket, off the Interstate 64 exit at Twenty-fifth Street. Residents, however, viewed the improvements with caution, fearing that they were part of a larger plot by regional planners and wealthy investors to shift property out of the hands of residents and make it more attractive to white tourists and gamblers. Whether low-income communities benefited on the whole from Empowerment Zone initiatives was questionable.

.   .   .

When the subject is job creation in East St. Louis and for East St. Louisans, little has seemed to work. Belleville, Collinsville, and Fairview Heights, on the Illinois side, and St. Louis, on the Missouri side, have each offered more potential employers in more industries.

But there are some jobs in East St. Louis. One can visit downtown and request an application from Fay's Furniture, Wendy's Hamburgers, Sandy's Barbecue & More, McDonald's, or KFC.

A job seeker can try his or her luck at the East St. Louis Center of the Southern Illinois University at Edwardsville, on J.R. Thompson Drive. The center provides "comprehensive program services and training in the areas of health, education, the arts, and social services." Fourteen categories of programs were offered from 2003 to 2005. These were funded primarily through state and federal sources and had a total of six hundred employees. However, many of these workers received low wages or were not East St. Louisans.

People in East St. Louis want good jobs and the good life these are expected to bring. Parents want their children to attend college and move on to successful careers. Mothers and fathers long for the days of empty-nesting and vacationing on retirement accounts. Adult children want to marry, own their own homes, and provide these things for their own young ones. Yet, by themselves, not even "decent" jobs can hold families above the fray of economic despair. Workers who were born and raised here are bound by the poverty that grips the whole city. At best, they get through higher education on student loans and have no accumulated wealth to shore up the wages that must be used for house notes, utilities, and medical expenses. Under these conditions, is the suburban American dream even possible?

CHAPTER FOUR

Hustling, Clean and Dirty

With only half of working-age East St. Louisans employed and 35 percent of the population below the federally defined poverty level, life is austere. Even though recent federal poverty guidelines specify that a family of four earning above $18,850 annually does not qualify for assistance, half of the city's households receive some form of public welfare assistance. But cash, food, and housing assistance generally provide less than the minimum requirements for family maintenance. For instance, the U.S. Department of Agriculture reports that families earning less than $40,700 a year spend an average of $6,000 to $8,000 annually on children,[1] but in Illinois the average cash grant is only $314 per month, although 63 percent of Temporary Assistance to Needy Families cases include a child under six years of age.

Conservatives and liberals alike tend to exaggerate how far welfare can be stretched. The truth is that many poor families cannot subsist on such income alone, and as a consequence, many heads of households take on multiple jobs. Others share lodging, vehicles, and other basic expenses. Still others use the food shelters and pantries of charitable organizations. They exhaust just about every sanctioned opportunity available.

But it is still not enough. So they seek other means. They "hustle." Merriam-Webster's online dictionary defines *hustle* in these ways as a verb: (1) to make strenuous efforts to secure money or business, or (2) to sell or obtain something through energetic and especially underhanded activity.[2]

For African Americans in general, the second definition is the more salient in the popular mind. The underground economy embedded in the neighborhoods and streets of the inner cities gets much attention, whether the focus is on peddling stolen or counterfeit wares on busy New York City sidewalks or shoplifting and prostitution in Washington, D.C. Hustling, in its varying forms, of course crosses racial lines. Ethnographic explanations for such practices among African Americans often link them to cultural deficiencies or high rates of joblessness or some combination of the two. Some interpret hustling as an act of resistance against an oppressive social and economic system; others add that actors in these arenas are culturally dislocated and lack the cultural capital to participate successfully in the legitimate world of work.

As this chapter reveals, people who hustle also work in the formal labor market. And the majority do not deal drugs, rob neighbors, or engage in other clearly dangerous pursuits. Furthermore, a close examination of what they do affirms that its focus is on meeting real personal and familial economic needs. Some men work as mechanics, setting up shop in driveways, for example, and some women sell homemade meals and do other domestic tasks.

For East St. Louis African Americans, hustling strategies have been rooted in the city's history—such as the discrimination that kept parents from earning living wages as well as the problems that arose when they assumed leadership of the city only after it passed its heyday. Once an "All-American City" with the best schools, shopping, entertainment, and jobs in the state of Illinois according to *Look* magazine, East St. Louis subsequently acquired public debt, a crumbling infrastructure, and a reputation that evolved from merely randy to thoroughly sordid, along with transitioning into vast residential poverty—all trends permanently affixed to black skin. People had to do something to survive, and they did.

Resident Wendell Collins broke down the categories. "There's different types of hustling. You can sell drugs, or you can do what you need to do to get by . . . like cutting grass. . . . I know a lot of guys with trucks, cutting yards, moving items. You can make a lot of money." As Wendell suggested, hustling ranged from the obviously illicit to the obviously benign, even useful. Some forms served a sordid demand from the outside; others focused on innocuous products and services within the community. More hustles in East St. Louis fit *Merriam-Webster's* first definition than the second; they are not all about underhanded activity such as swindling and thieving.

The East St. Louisans engaged in these activities reflect this reality. They may have chosen a hustle instead of, or in addition to, "approved" and reputable money-earning channels, but these decisions do not mark simply a turn toward easy street or a way out of the hurly-burly of a nine-to-five. Hustling requires enterprise, determination, and a commitment to work that may actually surpass what is expected within mainstream middle- and upper-class employment. In a poor place like East St. Louis, the decision to hustle is normal, having been reluctantly negotiated in the midst of large-scale economic and social abandonment.

Residents themselves distinguish "dirty" and "clean" hustles. The dirty kind involves what the public defines as vice or criminal: the sex trade and the narcotics industry, most notably. These hustlers manage the young men and women who sell sex to strangers or dance in strip clubs, or they sell sex directly. Others sell drugs, or they sell illegally acquired merchandise to legitimate retailers. Still others shoplift, burgle, commit robberies, or run scams.

Clean hustles consist of more routine "off the books" interactions, such as the unlicensed auto mechanics and food sales mentioned above. These particular hustling activities have emerged for a reason: they offer residents affordable access to everyday, practical services and products. Such activities are conducted by hustlers only because East St. Louis has been left to neglect by so many conventional merchants and institutions.

. . .

The primary hustle of Anthony King, thirty-two, was selling drugs. His best guess was that this phase of his life had begun when he was about fourteen or fifteen, the same time he stopped attending school. He was behind in his studies and got poor grades—"mostly Ds and Fs," he said, and "nobody cared anyway, not the teachers, not nobody."

His mother worked every day; there was little she could do about it. "I would tell him to go to school. I tried walking with him to school. I talked to his principal," she recalled. But she learned that her son was right: nobody seemed to care. "They kept telling me all the things I need to be doing. They said I ain't doing this and this."

Anthony's descent into dirty hustling was common. Many East St. Louis children move into the formal educational system through Head Start or kindergarten, showing early promise. Parents proudly display kindergarten artwork on refrigerators and living-room walls. They brag about their children's ability to count numbers and sing the alphabet. And then, as if a spell has been cast, a decline in academic performance hits, year after year, around the fourth and fifth grades. From the perspective of children, school becomes difficult. Teachers become mean. Class becomes boring, and children begin to believe what one fifth-grader told me: "I'm just not very smart anymore."

Anthony, like so many others, just was not worth the state's effort. Schools had become places where children were allowed to bide their time until they were old enough to drop out or move into the criminal-justice system or both.

Bill Cosby, among other popular critics, has fostered the belief that poor working-class parents have little interest in their children's education.[3] Anthony's and others' stories belie this. Frustrated and not knowing whom to ask for help, Anthony's mother reluctantly allowed him to stay at home, hoping that he would change his mind. Secretly, she understood and revealed that she herself had never had a good experience in a classroom. She had dropped out at fifteen, feeling strongly that her time in the classroom was a complete waste. "I just didn't understand how me being able to know about World War I, you know, was important. Or how come we had to learn about triangles."

But our conversation revealed that her thirst for knowledge was tempered by teachers who did not seem to have time to devote to those who struggled with coursework: "If you didn't know something, they didn't care. I don't think they didn't care all the time, but some of us needed extra help, and I don't think they wanted to give that, you hear what I mean?"

She thought Anthony would be okay without a high school

diploma. She actually encouraged him to "just get a GED" (a General Educational Development credential) and get a job working at a store. He was a big help around the house, keeping it clean and making sure his younger sisters went to school. She later learned that once her daughters were off to classes, Anthony just hung out on the streets. This was fine too, as long as he stayed out of trouble.

But this also meant he often visited with others like himself or older males who were no longer a part of the formal education system. His mentor was Vetty, an older cousin who lived just three blocks away. Vetty spent his evenings working on his GED. He was active all day on Sundays, playing in his mother's church band for weekly services. A couple of times a month, he earned cash by riding along with his uncle, a truck driver, on long-distance hauls. Most days, however, he smoked marijuana, watched televised sports and music videos, and sold drugs from the duplex he shared with his Aunt Jean. When Vetty was out of town or otherwise indisposed, he entrusted his business to Anthony, who got a share of the profits, respect from those around him, and the confidence to begin his own hustle.

Teachers, parents, and children grow frustrated with one another in a system of education that manages to push, or at least not to catch, those students who head toward the exit doors prematurely. Teachers did not remember Anthony King specifically, but they recognized his profile. According to one educator, "Parents need to do everything they can to keep their kids in school." For her, the primary issue is with parents who do not take enough time and interest in their children's education. That perception aligns with the public's. Yet, Ann Ferguson reveals in *Bad Boys: Public Schools in the Making of Black Masculinity* that low-income black parents have a variety of pressures and concerns that may inhibit the attention they pay to the circumstances of their children's education and schools. Further, the reported experiences of Anthony's mother suggest that the matter is even more complicated.

In conversation, Anthony conveyed that he had always wanted to stay in school; he thought he was pretty smart. He read magazines, and there was a time when he liked writing poetry. He spoke about his experience in the fourth grade: "I had a female teacher who liked what I wrote. She said, I could 'take any phrase and make it sound like a song.' She looked out for me. I did good in her class." That was his favorite and only positive memory of school, other than the time he won a contest for the most push-ups completed in one minute. Anthony did not limit his blame to others for his failed formal education, acknowledging that he should have made better "future-oriented" decisions: "I just think I took the lazy way out—that I should have been tougher and more resistant to my school situation . . . stuck it out . . . 'cause I think that I would be in a different place today." He was not sure that he would ever go back to school, but he felt it was his responsibility to keep others from following his path: "I always advise young people to stay in school. That's what I should've did, but I got caught up in the street."

What leads a youth to Anthony's predicament is a toxic combination: Adolescents from low-income families are not hired for jobs, yet remain part of the consumer culture. Girls and boys are both attracted to the better-dressed and fashion-conscious. They see advertisements for shoes, blue jeans, automobiles, and jewelry when they turn on their televisions, open a magazine, or glance at a billboard. They watch music videos and entertainers sporting fur coats and diamond earrings and living in large homes. When they take the bus, they pass McDonald's, Blockbuster video outlets, and Cadillac Escalades. When they get to the mall, they stroll by trendy shoe shops, pretzel stands, and people spending money on all of the above. There is little else to keep their attention after school and on the weekends. In East St. Louis, there are no bowling alleys or movie theaters, no science museums or zoos. Few parks or public pools. Even if these sources of recreation were present, they would cost money to attend.

Like middle-class teenagers in surrounding towns, Anthony wanted consumer power. He noticed that the popular kids in his school always seemed to have the hottest fashions. He observed the pitiable lives of so many in East St. Louis. "Man, even today you can see winos in the [abandoned] apartments, just a nasty way to live," he said. "We [he, his mother, and sisters] lived in a dump. No air-conditioning. No heat. Roaches everywhere you look. Leaks. Toilet never wanted to flush." He knew from watching television, visiting the mall, and observing those more affluent that he wanted something better.

"I didn't want to work for it. I knew I could just use my wits," Anthony said—though his experience demonstrated that this was only partly true. In the summers, he solicited lawn-mowing jobs. Business was interrupted when the lawn mower was unavailable or needed repair or he could not afford gas for it. He tried other ventures, such as collecting cans and cleaning out his uncle's shed at the end of each summer. In short, he had "clean" hustles as well as "dirty" ones.

Anthony had spent almost a quarter of his life in jail or prison. His first arrest, for possession of an illegal firearm, was at seventeen. His second, for possession and sale of marijuana and crack cocaine, came three years later. His arrests and incarceration tracked a statistical trend in St. Clair County. Between 1994 and

2003, arrests for all drug offenses more than doubled, from 631 to approximately 1,500. Arrests for the sale, possession, and cultivation of marijuana outnumbered those for all other illegal drugs, accounting for around half of all drug arrests. Unlike in most other counties in Illinois, crack cocaine was a substantial proportion (31 percent) of all cocaine seized by authorities. During the same period, the felony-filing rate in the county increased 53 percent, twice the statewide rate. And the number of individuals sentenced to the adult division of the Illinois Department of Corrections increased by 31 percent. Simultaneously, the high school dropout rate in East St. Louis continued its ascent.[4]

According to Anthony, hustling is savvy: "Being able to sell drugs and not get caught. Being able to steal and not get caught. Dealing with women and trick them, use them." These were the activities of others he would "hang with" at fourteen. "Everyone was drinking all night. We stayed in hotels. Ladies turning tricks, gambling, robbing, everything." This was an "easier and softer way" of making a living than "getting up in the morning and getting your hands dirty from digging a ditch," or so he thought at the time.

He once had a job sponsored by the Job Training Partnership Act (JTPA), enacted in 1982 to establish programs to prepare youth and unskilled adults for entry into the labor force. For Anthony's part in this training, he simply "dug dirt out of some swimming pool." After three days of seven-hour shifts of hard labor, he came home calloused, filthy, hot, tired, thirsty, and vowing never, ever again to pick up a shovel. "I didn't mind working, but they wasn't paying us anything for that type of work. It was like I imagine slavery was like."

Relative to professionals and middle-class workers, working-class workers often find less meaning in the activities of their

work and express less job satisfaction.[5] But the JTPA and similar programs are not designed to move youth into middle-class
work and lives. Rather, these government-subsidized jobs mostly
train youth, men, and women as workers in lower- to working-
class occupations.

Anthony noticed that some teens worked at the St. Clair Mall
in Fairview Heights. They cooked Hardy's hamburgers and
Chick-Fil-A chicken nuggets. They wore nametags and sold
clothes in J. C. Penney's. They measured men's inseams for tailored dress slacks in the men's department at Dillard's. There
was a time when he envisioned working in air-conditioned comfort, donning nice clothes, having regular hours—respectable
work. He applied for a few jobs but was never called back for an
interview.

Anthony observed that hustling did not require demeaning
physical labor. "You have to be slick. You use your mind. . . . After
time, you are making your way, wearing jewelry, nice clothes,
wake up at twelve in the afternoon, leave the house, and do it all
over again." The mental stimulation Anthony sought is not what
most people think of when they consider what young black men
seek in their daily activities, especially in the labor market. Yet,
there it was: a mind seeking inspiration, a body seeking opportunity, and a young man choosing from his options.

. . .

I first saw Edith Murray climbing out of the passenger seat of a
mid-'90s silver Lincoln Town Car at 6:30 on a Sunday morning.
The male driver had stopped the car and let her out on the corner of Baugh and Eighteenth streets, in the direction of Brooklyn, Illinois. She wore stretch, blue-denim, cropped pants and
a simple, clinging, multicolored, floral T-shirt that reached just

below her waistband and advertised her ample bosom. This was her usual drop-off point after a very late night or a very early morning with a customer.

There was a sidewalk here, and it was a public place, so it was safe. It was within walking distance of where she stayed, so it was convenient. It was out of direct sight of most residences, so no one could see what time she came in or whom she was with—this made it secure for male customers, who often wished to keep as low a profile as possible. Once a customer let her out of the car, he could easily turn and drive back onto the highway, to his suburban home, apartment, or university dormitory.

This morning was typical. From here, she would go to her place, clean up a little, and go to sleep. She had an "occasional" drug habit and would need to go visit the friend who kept her supplied. She would do this prior to heading home. Since it was Sunday, she was hoping to wake up in time to visit with her kids for a short time at her mother's home on the other side of I-64. If not, she would try to see them at some point during the week.

Even though female East St. Louisans are more likely than their male counterparts to complete high school, attend college, and avoid drug-specific trades, many young women also leave the formal education system and become immersed in dirty hustles. Many are adolescent mothers. According to Tiarra Gardner, "Women hustle like men, just in different ways. You may know somebody ho'in [prostituting themselves], but you may see [also] somebody trying to work at the club or get a man on her arm. That's all a hustle," or a way to get by. Many of the dirty hustles for women, of course, are variations of prostitution. They are activities begun in youth, burdened with little overhead, and offering plenty of opportunity and steady cash or in-kind gifts.

Prostitution was something that she just "started doing" at

about sixteen, Edith said. A girlfriend of the same age brought her along to stand outside or sometimes enter clubs. They "played" with the club patrons—talking, laughing, and just "looking sexy." They got passive support from the police, who cruised by and seemed to turn a blind eye to the young girls hanging on the arms of much-older men. Sometimes, club owners or bouncers shooed them away; other times someone might try to talk them into entering through a back door. The girls were young, easy to impress, untethered, inexpensive, willing to engage in a variety of sexual acts, and easily coaxed with promises of steady love, money, travel, and shopping sprees.

Edith had started having sex when she was twelve or thirteen with a neighbor man, forty-five or fifty, Kenneth, who plied her with candy, clothes, and money. She was not attracted to him at first, but he seemed to be in love with her. She liked the attention, and after a couple of afternoons of heavy petting, she thought she wanted to have sex. "I spread my legs for him and that was that," she said. "It hurt so bad every time he did it. I had a hard time with it at first," but she chose never to tell Kenneth of her pain. From then on, she realized that older men liked her.

When she started hanging out at clubs, she was not looking to sell sex to strangers but rather "for a man, like a boyfriend," who could take care of her, give her things. These relationships didn't last long, and she learned to get what she could "quickly" from any man who expressed an interest.

Edith had wanted a different life. In her youth at home with her mother, she shared a room and two beds with three sisters. Their sheets, blankets, and lamps had all been previously used and were damaged—retrieved from the back room of a local shelter or from a neighbor's trash can. She and her sisters covered most of the cracks in the wall with magazine miniposters of their favorite entertainers. They built a shelf of four stacked milk crates and two boards to store music tapes, books, and a vase of plastic flowers. The roof leaked, and blue plastic buckets caught the dribbling wetness from the cracks above. The room was stifling in the summer, and she found herself escaping to the mall or hanging out at McDonald's for the air-conditioning.

Like Anthony, Edith observed white teens her age shopping for all of the latest styles, using their parent's charge cards or pulling wads of cash out of their own pocketbooks. It just didn't seem fair. When she returned home, she would find the same food in the refrigerator, and she or her sisters had to do the cooking. The options were usually spaghetti, made with a jar of Ragu sauce, with bread and margarine on the side. Another standard option was cold cereal or scrambled eggs. She grew tired of these dishes. Her favorite meal was roast beef and potatoes, once a month, usually after her mother received her food stamps.

Her newest plan was to save enough money to go to school: "I think I know I want to be like, uh, you know those people who work with children who have disabilities, physical disabilities. . . . I think children like that need special attention." Edith herself was born with one foot smaller than the other. This problem with her foot was compounded by epilepsy, which she controlled with medication.

Edith stopped going to school when she became pregnant with her first child, Missy, at fifteen. But school was not especially appealing anyway. She had often skipped days here and there, staying home to watch a soap opera or to help her mother wash clothes at the Laundromat. She regarded herself as a pretty good mother, although her own mother had physical custody of the two children. Getting custody herself was a long-term goal. For now, she needed to earn money. Then she needed to "get a certificate or something" to get the job she wanted, then get a nice apartment, and finally petition the court.

Edith's only "regular" work had been as a teacher's assistant in a child-care center. She found the job boring and her supervisor unfriendly. She thought the people there looked down on her. Even then, she stayed out late at night, and she concluded that the sex-trade industry was better financially. Prostitution was a hustle, because you "got to be smart" and know how to "read a man," "read a situation—'cause it can be dangerous."

When she really thought about the work, she hated it: lying on her back on dirty sheets or often being asked to perform on her knees on the worn motel carpet or the gritty gravel of a dark parking lot, waiting for some man to "grunt and grunt" so that she could earn her fee. She said she tried not to think about it. She hoped her daughter would choose another way. Besides her major dirty hustle, Edith had a couple of clean ones. You could pay her to do your nails or "put a weave" in your hair.

Prostitution has a deep history in East St. Louis. Essie Rose, seventy-three, remembered that her uncle was part of something "like a black mafia" that operated in the 1950s and 1960s: "They would have these young girls working for them, selling their bodies, you know, sexual things. They all, every one of them, had guns. They had guns in their pocket, in their cars, and in their house. My uncle, he was one of them. I don't remember him doing anything else but running with them mafia."

The economies of neighboring villages of Brooklyn and Washington Park stay afloat with a bevy of strip clubs and gentlemen's entertainment. Both communities are predominantly African American and extremely impoverished, with 45 percent of individuals in the village of Washington Park and 35 percent in the village of Brooklyn living in poverty.[6] The children of these communities look up at local and highway signs that direct the public to view their mothers and sisters at work as "live female dancers" and "beautiful dancing girls." Zoning and licensing laws allow late-hour clubs and the sale of liquor near residential neighborhoods and parks.

In East St. Louis proper, the biggest employer has been the Casino Queen, an all-night gambling emporium parked on the riverfront and emblematic of the city's status as an adult entertainment center away from home. "I think this city is most interested in making gamblers happy," Iris Bamble observed.

. . .

A probing look at the drug trade debunks the idea that dirty hustles are "easy" money.[7] Lazy people who do not want to work cannot succeed in this industry any more than in a conventional one. "If you're a drug dealer," Sheba Parton said, "then that's what you are. You always on the job. Ain't no nine-to-five. Ain't no holiday. Ain't no lunch break. The minute you take your eyes off the game, let down your guard, that's when somebody gonna come in and take it from you."

Participants worried about robbery, bodily harm, and violent death, as well as about getting caught by the police. Marshall Hunter wore a bulletproof vest and carried a gun for three weeks until a personal threat was "taken care of." During this time, he made arrangements for his girlfriend, who also participated in the trade, and their daughters to move across the river to the home of a relative. He explained, "As it was, I just knew they lives was in danger. So you know, there're some things that you don't take no chances with."

Tres Mack summarized the stresses of the illicit drug trade by saying, "You got to always look over you shoulder around here. You have a nigga, maybe two, that you can trust but then that's it." Friendships and family relationships are dismissed or downgraded, even as drug dealers realize that their business endangers loved ones.

"It's sad, but people always gonna use this shit," Tres said. His own brother overdosed at thirty-five after years of drug abuse. On the day of the modest funeral, held at Officer's Funeral Home, Tres could not stop crying. This was the first time he recalled seriously considering the negative impact of the trade he had chosen. Yet as he spoke about the week he spent trying to think of a cleaner hustle or a legitimate job, he recalled, "I couldn't bring myself to get with it." A legitimate job would require some form of formal education, and he had never done well in school. Also, what "clean hustle" would afford him the type of income he currently pulled in by selling drugs? The persistent knocks of purchasers on his back door, combined with his own debts, spurred Tres back to hustling. He was realistic about his situation. He had tried the legal route before and was thwarted by both his poor education and his criminal record.

For Manny Larkin, a pimp, preparation was time-consuming: "Hustling is how you look, your appearance. You have to look right. Get up, want to look right, that is what is so strange. You get up like you are going to a job, and then you—it was always my nature to have handmade pants, handmade shoes, get a pedicure, manicure, make sure I was always just right, shoes polished, and then go right to the streets. Try to catch some girls, go to a bar, always trying to hustle someone or something. Do something like that."

Another East St. Louisan called it "like a job." Men involved in this trade described regular rituals that likely mirror those of

affluent aboveground businessmen: having manicures and pedi-
cures, buying tailored suits and dyed shoes. A good appearance
both announces success and attracts women. But these rituals
are only part of the list of requirements. Beyond those, managing the women under a pimp's protection involves meeting their
daily physical needs and "stroking" them to maintain emotional
stability and loyalty.

·   ·   ·

Herbert Gans theorized that those with few skills and little
access to high-income, legal job opportunities may respond with
illegal activities. By far, stealing and selling drugs bring in the
most money in the hustling fields. These and other choices seem
to be rational options given the hustlers' access to low-paying
jobs or no jobs at all.

Yet, when asked, men and women here said that they would
have much preferred a "normal" life—that is, a job that allowed
them to get up in the morning, take lunch at midday, and come
home in the evenings to their families. They wanted jobs with
decent wages, health benefits, and paid vacation. They wanted
to feel "ordinary."

Stan Roy compared his life with the lives of those legally
employed: "I was really gone streetwise. I didn't need a job,
because that was for squares. I didn't want to get my hands
dirty. They still look at it as square. But they are jealous of them
[squares] for what they have. I am in the process of getting a car,,
and I am hustling. I see the guy who earned it by working at a
job; I am envious because I know he has it, and he gets a paycheck every week. He ain't got to worry about the killers and
sneaks. You see him as one way, but you also know that he is
secure. In reality he'll live longer than you, because he isn't tak-

ing the chances you are taking and living the life that you're living. If you gamble, that could be it."

Another drug-trade participant agreed: "They got different kinds of hustling. The guy hustling, really hustling and making money off of dope, making ten thousand dollars a week. The risk is there. If you are working, the risk is zero. I believe sometime the guys see guys working, and they don't want to continue doing what they are doing, saying, 'I know I need to get out of this shit I'm doing. He's working, got a girlfriend, a house.' They might want to knock it, but they know there's a difference."

Stan Roy began hustling because he wanted to have money and a nice car and to be "somebody . . . like on TV." His parents had little to offer him; one was addicted to crack, the other an alcoholic. Both participated in illegal activities themselves. This did not prevent Stan from having his own dreams of wealth and prosperity. It did, however, make developing a realistic plan of achieving such goals quite difficult for him. He rarely attended school, and when he did, he often arrived late and with wrinkled clothing. The social worker was constantly visiting him at school, and the principal thought he was nothing but trouble. Stan was placed in foster care at ten, as a result of his mother's neglect, and again at thirteen, when his father beat him "senseless" with a heavily buckled belt. For him, the only way to improve his situation was to take control of his life. He was able to do this by helping his older cousin in the drug trade. By age fifteen, he was living in his mother's home but supporting himself and her with his illegal earnings. Yet, Stan remained hopeful that something would take him in a better direction.

Dirty hustling is not what most of the participants involved in it had intended to do for a lifetime. But the legal-job sector left something to be desired. Devin said, "I hate wearing uniforms. I think what would make it easier for people and keep them motivated to work would be if they raise the fucking minimum wage . . . it's $5.15. You get your check, and it's $200. Two hundred dollars!! Man, I know it has to do with the cost of living, but I would work it for $8.00. It would kill a lot of the bullshit and nonsense if they would. A lot of people want to work if they had somewhere that paid. Five dollars and fifteen cents an hour? I worked five hours and only made twenty-five dollars? And they gonna take some of that [for taxes]? Shit. On the street, you can make twenty-five dollars in fifty seconds, if even fifty seconds. Compare that to five hours. That promotes negativity. Ain't nobody stupid. Ain't nobody gonna bust their ass for nothing."

Carlos Stanfield explained why he chose hustling over a job at McDonald's. "When I was fourteen, it seemed like everyone around me had money. Everyone was doing it," he said. "I was living with my mother, and I was the oldest of five. I saw how she was always struggling and couldn't do for us. All of my friends always had things for themselves. So I just got out there and started hustling. I saw how much money could be made in one night. When I first started working [in the formal paid economy], I was only making $4.25 an hour. Then, I would think about how much money I used to really make, like between two thousand and three thousand dollars a night hustling. I thought, 'Why am I stopping all of this for $4.25 an hour?' I stopped that and went back to what I knew, the fast money, because I just couldn't deal with $4.25 an hour. I stuck with it [hustling], because the fast money outweighs the honest money. I was doing for my mama. Trying to help her, buy her things. I was showing off, wanting new things for her."

Dirty hustlers shared expectations similar to those with middle-income jobs. They wanted to earn a comfortable living. Still, illegal trades were problematic for them. These trades did not provide access to health care. They made participants vulnerable to arrest and incarceration. They offered little hope of social mobility. They never created the work record that would make it easier to transition into legal employment.

Of course, the similarity to legitimate employment is most pronounced in clean hustling, The elderly need their lawns cut in the summer and driveways shoveled and salted in the winter. Men need barbers, and women need beauticians. Apartment dwellers who hop from place to place need movers; their landlords need properties cleaned and readied for new renters. Car owners need affordable mechanics.

Some of the most interesting categories of clean hustles consist of community members who set up for-profit private services to fill in the gaps caused by the paucity of public ones—for example, cheap transportation to doctors, pharmacies, and grocery stores.

Rita Miles illustrated how clean hustling, like the dirty kind, requires an entrepreneurial spirit: fresh ideas, sharp evaluation of supply and demand, risk-taking. Rita was in her early fifties, heavyset, and round in the hips, with deep-set dimples framing her wispy smiles. She was in constant motion. All meetings with her were held in her kitchen, which doubled as her office. For more than twenty years, she had operated food services for East St. Louisans, many of them elderly. At one time or another, she had been a driver for women in her mother's network, cleaned houses, and cooked and delivered meals for shut-ins.

Rita charged modest fees. A two-serving meal of meat loaf, potatoes, and green beans, for example, ran about five dollars, she said. She could clean a two-bedroom house in two hours for fifteen dollars. Often, she was compensated "in-kind," with bartered clothes or household items. Rita had no health card or business license. But through a combination of money and gifts from these enterprises over the years, she was able to raise three children.

Trina Edwards, forty-one, specialized in child care, in addition to cooking, cleaning, and shopping. Like Rita, Trina was not formally trained or certified, nor did she list in the Yellow Pages. She was a tiny, dark-skinned woman who sported a short salt-and-pepper natural. Rain or shine, she wore skirts, brightly colored T-shirts, and flip-flop sandals. She lived in a two-bedroom, government-sponsored apartment community. The upstairs window had been smashed by a baseball three years ago and was still awaiting repair. The exterior grounds, cluttered with broken glass and some litter, mostly consisted of dark-brown dirt that sifted into the living room on hot, breezy days when windows and doors were left open. There was no air conditioner, although the heating generally worked well in the winter months. Her two daughters, ages ten and thirteen, shared one bedroom, and she usually had the other one to herself. A twenty-three-year-old son, who roved between her home and that of his paternal grandmother's, slept on her bedroom floor in front of the television. Upstairs and downstairs, the flooring was a dusty-colored linoleum with matured scratches and stains. Trina tried to hide the more discernible flaws with small colorful nonslip kitchen and bathroom rugs, which were scattered throughout the downstairs.

The house was cluttered with toys, videos, and clothing but sparkling clean. A white, metal portable crib filled a corner of the modest dining area. On any given weekday, the aroma inside this apartment was a merger of Campbell's chicken noodle soup for a meal and the Clorox cleaner Trina used to wipe the floors, floorboards, door handles, window sills, and every other part of the environment that could and would be touched by the tiny hands and bodies that played and napped in this living space.

This apartment had been Trina's home for eight years. She had been raised in these same housing projects along with four older siblings, and her goal was a house with three bedrooms, a fenced yard, a carport, and a full basement that could be dedicated to her child-care business. Parents found Trina dependable and good with kids. One explained to me, "She don't smoke, don't do drugs, no men hanging around."

The economies for both sides of this clean hustle are evident. Professional day-care services are expensive. Some families below the poverty line receive state subsidies to assist with day-care expenses. In 2001 to be eligible for subsidized child care, families of four could earn no more than $28,861 annually. Families below the level of poverty paid no more than 6 percent of their gross income for day-care copayments. A family of three with two children in day care and with an annual income of $15,275 to $17,456, for example, would have made a copayment of $147.32 in 2001. Theoretically, the state covers the difference in reimbursing the day-care providers, but in practice these providers have learned that reimbursement rates for subsidized children in Illinois are among the lowest in the nation. One recent report found that the state reimburses at the eighteenth percentile, far below fair market value.[8] Furthermore, Illinois's rates remain low in relation to those of some of its neighbors. According to the federal plans for the fiscal year 2008–9, the reimbursement rates for Illinois fell in the middle of the range for the rates of midwestern states. Its rates were higher than those set by Iowa and Michigan but lower than those of Indiana, Minnesota, and Wisconsin.[9] When reimbursements are low, child-care providers are less likely to accept the children of the poor, and families in this category must then seek alternative services. That does not even take into account the fundamental fact that working-class families resting on the edge of poverty are motivated to seek any edge they can get to hedge against the rising costs of professional child-care services.

The issue of affordable, quality child care is further complicated by the declining number of licensed child-care homes in Illinois. In addition, child-care centers have experienced a tremendous turnaround among qualified staff as a consequence of poor state compensation. Thus, the number of children these homes and centers can accommodate has been shrinking. In 2000, there were almost 900,000 children under the age of six and approximately 1.5 million between the ages of six and twelve in Illinois. However, licensed homes and day-care centers had fewer than 300,000 openings. Poor families were affected disproportionately. Poverty-level, working-class parents were less likely than those in more-affluent areas to find available licensed day-care services in their neighborhoods and communities. In 2002, just over 3,000 child-care centers and almost 10,000 family child-care homes were in operation in Illinois.[10]

Amaya Anderson explained that her day-care home, which serviced six or seven children, was operating just as it would if it were licensed. She saw no need to seek licensure from the state and perceived that the process would bring unwelcome scrutiny. State credentials require, among other intrusions, criminal-background checks and confirmation that no household members are delinquent in court-ordered child-support payments.[11]

Another popular clean hustle in East St. Louis is hair care. Nellie Bibbens, who lived off Tudor Avenue, would put a weave in your hair for twenty-five dollars. Erica Chambers and her boyfriend, Sam, ran a barbershop and beauty salon from the kitchen of their two-bedroom home. He cut, trimmed, lined, and shaped the hair of men and boys for five to seven dollars. She cut, shampooed, and styled hair for women and girls for fees far lower than those of the formal market. From Sam's point of view, converting to a legitimate practice would be an unnecessary hassle, entailing licensing tests and fees.

Lawn care is also a clean hustle with a good niche. Erica's neighbor, Mr. Roxdale, cut down trees, limbs, and hauled them away for a nominal fee. Requests for this service picked up during the storm season. Business could boom, but it could also get dangerous. Once he fell off a ladder and broke his hip, landing him in the hospital for weeks. He had no health-care coverage, no accident insurance coverage, and no paid sick leave, and he could not collect unemployment. At age fifty-one, he was far too young to receive retirement through Social Security, and the injury, painful and slow to heal, did not afford him any rights to federal disability payments. This is a problem that those who hustle full-time often face. They lack accumulated paid sick or vacation leave and unemployment insurance; there is no one to replace them if they have to miss work. Long illnesses devastate marginal pocketbooks. And such problems linger far beyond the working years: a full-time hustle contributes nothing to the Social Security benefits on which so many African Americans rely in old age.

· · ·

Early in the morning, outside Top Metal Buyers, a metal recycler on Walnut Avenue, out-of-work men and a few women often gather, waiting to cash in the cans they have collected over the previous twenty-four hours. At the time of my research, one of them was Marvin Gantt, thirty-seven. After seven years in a Mississippi prison for robbery, Gantt returned home to his mother in East St. Louis. He spent months job hunting unsuccessfully. Finally, he took up odd jobs, paid and unpaid, just to stay busy. He also scoured the streets and sidewalks for loose change and for aluminum cans, which could be recycled for cash. Marvin used his earnings to purchase cigarettes, toiletries, and beer.

Darshawn Williams, a former truck driver and armed-forces veteran, found it difficult to hold a job after his return from the Gulf War. According to him, "I came back with the shakes. I couldn't keep focused on anything." His formal diagnosis was depression, and the drugs that doctors prescribed did little to ease him back into the normal work world. He ended up trading his prescription drugs for cash and used the money to purchase beer, which numbed his daily and ongoing psychological turmoil. Collecting cans and bottles, cutting yards, and occasionally doing minor auto repair kept money in his pocket.

Oliver Simon, once a recovering alcoholic, relapsed after four months of sobriety. He had a violent relationship with an on-again, off-again girlfriend. He barely knew his children. And he had problems with his liver and both kidneys. Soothing grief and aches was his pastime. When he was in pain, vodka seemed the most cogent solution. "It's not like I got a lot of money to spend," Oliver said. Commenting on collecting cans and bottles, he explained, "It's better than me knocking somebody in the head or robbin' little ol' ladies, ain't it? I got habits, and this is how they get paid for."

Dirty or clean, hustling in East St. Louis is about survival. Charles was recently released from prison for selling drugs. For him hustling was an "extra"—something he did to supplement his legal, paid work activities. "I didn't make enough working," he explained. "When I started selling drugs, I jumped from making three hundred dollars a week to nine hundred a day. And the money just be coming so fast. Selling drugs is a game that is not hard to learn at all. You put yourself in the industry, and your money will come just like that, like clockwork. . . . Working at McDonald's [which was his legitimate job], you pay your bills an' ain't got shit. . . . I want nice clothes. I want nice jewelry. I want a nice car. . . . A lot of people do what they have to do to bring in extra money. . . . I'll keep my little job, and I'll keep a hustle. That will put extra money in my pocket, because I want nice shit, too, like everyone else. Just because I'm keeping a hustle, doesn't mean it has to be negative. You can have a bullshit ass job and cut grass on the side. That will give you the extra money. You've got to get it some way, because the job isn't enough."

Note, from this evidence, how hustling reinforces traditional gender roles. Men's clean hustles focus on the handyman, fix-it activities associated with husbands, and their dirty hustle activities often enable them to make more money than the women in their lives and also place them in positions of power over female family members, girlfriends, and prostitutes. Women are more likely to perform reproductive labor, that is, the everyday unpaid work that typically women do in the home, such as caring for children and the elderly and doing the cleaning, the laundry, the grocery shopping, hair care, and cooking. Their clean and dirty activities mirror the household work of wives and mothers.

Hustling allows fathers to approximate their ideal of masculinity, which includes providing for their families. The formal jobs that they may hold skew toward minimum wage, which is hardly enough for toys on Christmas and birthdays, cable television, telephone service, decent day care, dining out, and other luxuries that the more affluent take for granted.

Jasmine Leroy, a petite woman of twenty-five, kept her children in name-brand clothing and paid her mother's property taxes by working three different jobs, one of which was completely tax free. She was a part-time receptionist at Mercantile Bank in St. Louis, an exotic dancer three nights a week at a club in Washington Park, and an occasional call girl. The dancing and prostitution were far more lucrative than the bank job.

The male and female hustlers of East St. Louis share a belief in the American dream, using hard work and a strong will to climb the socioeconomic ladder. Ivan Miles summed it up: "There is one thing that I've learned about living in society: if you don't know how to 'Yank a chain,' you ain't gonna get it. I can stroke your ego all day to get what I want. That's why I say, living in East St. Louis, when you leave here, if you can't make it, you don't need to make it. You've been exposed to what it takes to make it. Even if you haven't done it, you've seen it. Utilize it in the right way."

CHAPTER FIVE

"Around here, women never get done workin'"

From whatever angle you examine them and with whatever terms you use, the lives of most East St. Louisans are distinguished by their desperation. They aspire to the same things middle-class Americans attain—stability, security, family—but at every turn, public resources and infrastructure fail to support them in that quest. In the face of these circumstances, the unorthodox strategies adopted by many represent rational economic decisions, even if equally doomed to frustration and failure.

How do these expectations get internalized and play out over the course of lives of poverty in a place that was long ago so systematically abandoned? Chapter 6 addresses how the lifelong burdens borne by the men of East St. Louis translate into their fears about a bedrock of their identity: their responsibility to keep loved ones safe and protected. In this chapter, we encounter the flip side of those stories: the seemingly never-ending demands on East St. Louis women for the care of others. These women bathe, dress, and nurture children, grandchildren, and even great-grandchildren. They take care of their boyfriends and spouses, who confront a dead-end job market and feel diminished by their inability to be better providers. And finally, the women administer to the sick and elderly in their families and communities—populations unnaturally swelled here by the inadequacy of access to health care and other resources. Sometimes, it seems that the only people these woman cannot find the time to care for is themselves.

These collective experiences have a distinct gender cleavage. The men and women of East St. Louis attack their challenges in ways that parallel, sometimes even caricature, the conventional images of the roles of sons and daughters, husbands and wives, fathers and mothers, uncles and aunts, grandfathers and grandmothers. These men and women also belie the canard that the African American population lacks the conventional capacities for commitment to family and work. Quite the contrary: the people backed into the corner of an abandoned place can exhibit resourcefulness bordering on the superhuman.

.　　.　　.

In television sitcoms and popular films, most elderly women characters are portrayed as enjoying their retirement years. On NBC's *Golden Girls* (1985–92), for example, four middle-income characters share a home in an upper-income suburb of always-sunny Miami, Florida, where they lead healthy, vibrant, and active lives. There are plenty of gentlemen suitors. They take tennis and dance lessons, eat at expensive restaurants, and never worry about health care costs, mortgages, or money for groceries. They represent a popular romantic stereotype of the aged. Middle- and upper-income retirees move to sunlit Florida; live in well-kept suburban homes or condos near warm beaches; and

purchase recreational vehicles, fill them with food and amenities, and travel across country, seeing all the sights that they
missed while they were tied to middle-class desks, offices, and
responsibilities for eight hours a day during their working years.
They drop in for annual visits with successful, healthy children
and grandchildren, bearing gifts etched with the name of their
most recent vacation adventure. These seniors may walk a little slower than the younger generations and share an outdated
sense of humor, but these minute matters are overwhelmed by
their zesty life spirit.

Indeed, sitcom and movie portrayals of seniors reflect a dra-
matic demographic shift: the U.S. population is graying as baby
boomers are reaching the age of retirement. Unlike the Golden
Girls, however, most African American women seniors are not
moving to the sands and suburbs of sunny Florida. Rather, they
are retiring "in place," many of them in their lifelong working-class suburban spaces. When Katherine Newman recently
examined the lives of aging African American and Latinos in
central-city neighborhoods, she found their senior years complicated by poor health, financial hardship, a ragged infrastructure, neighborhood violence, familial hardships, and despair. In
a summary of trends she suggests that the "good life" beyond
retirement age is mostly reserved for middle-class whites but
that racial minority middle classes have shared with them the
means and mobility to settle in the suburbs, experience financial security, and avoid the ugliness and hardship of inner-city
life. Newman explains, "Millions of Americans did not reap the
benefits of economic expansion and occupational mobility. They
did not decamp for the suburbs . . . They aged in place, and in a
very troubled place."[1]

Yet, as this chapter illustrates, life for African Americans in suburban space and place, historically and generally, has differed markedly from that of their white counterparts. As African Americans age, they reside in multigenerational households or, as one East St. Louisan reported, "just down the way a bit" from adult children and kin, in declining cities where neither they nor their offspring can afford even to think of moving elsewhere. The low earnings and obligations to those for whom these women care over their entire lifetime tie them to the workforce long after the age of retirement.

The most serious problems confronting aging Americans are health issues and financial instability, which are often invariably linked. Some seniors, though, fare far better than others. The most acute conditions for seniors exist in older, declining suburbs, which house not only a disproportionate share of the poor in general but also a growing number of seniors who are both financially disadvantaged and have severe disabilities. U.S. Census Bureau data for 2005–9 reveal that in East St. Louis 85 percent of women who shared households with grandchildren under age eighteen were also responsible for their care. One-third of all residents sixty-five years old and older lived below the poverty level, and 50 percent of all families with children were poor.[2] Sixty percent of them struggled with a disability.[3] Perhaps the most troubling dimension of their golden years was the way their jobs and multiple caregiver roles affected their own health, without any support or relief. Many of these women expressed the sentiment that, for them, age carried an increased obligation to kin. Thus, they found themselves tied to the low-wage, working-class labor market past the age of retirement and despite their own infirmities.

The effects of poverty on women's health are lifelong and cumulative. Poor women are likelier to confront breast and cervical cancers, diabetes, and high blood pressure and to be diagnosed with these diseases at later and less-treatable stages. A fifth of female African American female deaths every year are from the complications of high blood pressure alone, a major precursor of cardiovascular disease. This specific ailment is about 50 percent more common among blacks than whites.

Poor and working-class women generally and African American women in particular also suffer disproportionately from diabetes, or the body's inability to produce sufficient levels of insulin. Like high blood pressure, the symptoms of diabetes usually appear gradually and can easily go unnoticed. Consequently, the longer that one is not diagnosed with the disease, the more likely he or she is to have already suffered from many of its consequences. These include hypertension and cardiovascular disease, neuropathy that can lead to amputations, and retinopathy that leads to blindness and its related complications, such as increased susceptibility to illness and infections.[4]

The medical community encourages women of all racial and ethnic groups to participate in regular diagnostic screenings, such as mammography and the Papanicolaou test (Pap smear). But educating women about the need of such services and actually testing them are complicated tasks, especially in regard to those with low incomes. The factor that seems to influence women most significantly, regardless of race, in whether they utilize such services is having a regular source of care. And ultimately this factor affects African American women disproportionately, because they are more likely than women in other racial or ethnic groups to lack health insurance and to live in poverty—both of which contribute to lack of regular care.[5]

High blood pressure and diabetes are strongly associated with socioeconomic status and thus disproportionately evident among African Americans, Native Americans, Hispanics, and low-income women in general. Public-health experts point out that the management of these diseases should not be complicated; both require a modified diet, regular exercise, control of stress, and use of medications. Yet, researchers have found that health regimens to control high blood pressure are often abandoned or modified by almost half of all diagnosed patients.[6]

In these areas, the federal Medicare program is, at best, a threadbare safety net. Medicare provides only partial medical costs for physician visits and medications, and the remainder must be met through additional insurance or an ability to pay. Thus, low-income women are more likely than those of higher economic means to have unmet health cost needs. Additionally, researchers have noted that, at least among non-insulin-dependent diabetic women, African Americans are more likely than whites to report barriers to self-care, such as pain and financial constraints.[7]

While some seniors need or choose to work only part-time or seasonally to bring in extra cash, others find a steady paycheck essential. They must work, as they always have, to pay for the rising cost of medications, to pay rent and utilities, to purchase food, and to maintain the welfare of others, older and younger, in their household. Sociologist Barbara Butrica found that among married persons aged sixty-five and older, 29 and 20 percent of their household expenditures are devoted to housing and health care, respectively; for unmarried seniors, 39 percent of spending is consumed by housing expenses and 16 percent by health care. Most seniors spend almost all of their after-tax income on the most basic essentials. Worse yet, the incomes that approximately 20 percent of unmarried seniors retain after taxes are insufficient to meet their basic needs.[8] Another aspect of unmet health care needs is merely the location of services. Medical professionals are less likely to establish offices in low-income neighborhoods.

Though the overall data show a lack of access to consistent health care resources for African Americans generally, more pinpointed research suggests that women of color especially experience chronic stressors and hardships that accumulate over the life cycle, straining both physical and emotional health. Recent changes in social policy and in the economy have required many aging low-income women to negotiate health care needs for their own deteriorating health in the context of managing their low-wage employment and caring for and assisting adult children, young grandchildren, and disabled or elderly family members.

Here is what we find in East St. Louis: women make decisions about the care of others, work, and retirement, and their own health is caught in the middle.

. . .

Over the course of a lifetime, a woman undergoes several major transitions; for example, she may marry, give birth to a child, enter the paid workforce, and retire, though not necessarily in that order. Transitions are not isolated experiences but trajectories affected directly and indirectly by the lives of others. Family members are both expected to assume responsibilities and feel obligated to when a long-term illness or disability befalls another within a family system.

In these cases, an individual family member may have to assume the role of caregiver. This requires the adjustment of personal goals and living arrangements in order to accommodate the care of those in need. Likewise, if an adolescent daughter with little or no income produces a child, the mother of that adolescent may be expected to take upon herself the care of both her daughter and the new grandchild. These and other roles of obligation within African American family systems are what Carol Stack and Linda Burton define as "kin-work."[9]

Family members do not automatically assume such duties. Rather, kin-work is governed by "kin-scripts." Families develop these scripts, or norms, to guide the timing of significant life-course events. Kin-scripts also delineate the activities necessary to sustain a family system, such as the care of young children, the infirm, and elderly adults, as well as who is responsible for this care. If we think about our own family systems and observe others, we would probably note that, depending on the need, kin-work can be performed by men, women, or children.[10] Nonetheless, it seems that African Americans are more likely than whites to use kin-care systems to support the needs of their family system. That is, they are less likely to hire care services in the form of housekeepers, nannies, nurses, and nursing homes. And within these family systems, it is the African American women who carry a disproportionate share of caring work.

Additionally, health self-management may revolve around issues of employment and stresses related to living arrangements. In particular, demographic groups across racial and ethnic lines are living longer. Low-income women often simultaneously work and care for dependent children and other kin with perhaps little time to devote to their own growing health needs. These women, especially as they near retirement age, are increasingly pressed to care for the growing number of low-income seniors.

According to the U.S. Administration on Aging, the older black population (age sixty-five and older) was 3.1 million in 2007. It is projected to grow to close to 10 million by 2050, climbing from 8.3 to 11 percent of the U.S. older population. The starkness of the problems of aging becomes more apparent when you factor in the poverty that approximately one-quarter of the black elderly live in, making them likelier than whites to require economic and other assistance from friends and relatives.[11]

In East St. Louis, the pattern has been extreme. Decades after raising their children to adulthood, older women have found themselves as primary sources of care and support for multiple generations. Yet many are themselves older and ailing. Women generally accept the standard kin-script of caring for an aging spouse or a parent; as one put it, these are "typical life changes." However, few expect also to be responsible for the needs of grandchildren and adult children. The consequences of their life as part of the East St. Louis working class and the familial obligations that bind them to others in the city do not merely contribute to the definition of their last years; they overwhelmingly determine that definition.

Pearl Spence was one of those who saw the stress from work and home, paradoxically, expanding with age. At age sixty-two, her roles as mother, worker, and wife were compounded by the ill health of her mother, who required daily attention. Her mother joined the household following a debilitating second stroke. She had lived in a rented apartment for twelve years prior to her illness and thus had no savings and no assets, such as a car or home to share with her daughter's family. She had only small disability income and Social Security stipends, along with a body that had broken down from decades of scrubbing floors, cleaning carpets, and wiping windows. She needed help dressing and bathing. Her food had to be pureed or chopped into tiny bits because she had difficulty chewing. It was like having another child. Only this "child" was Pearl's mother, once one of the strongest women Pearl had known.

To see the mother reduced to frailty and dependence took a physical and psychological toll on both mother and daughter. The mother was susceptible to crying fits, for hours on end, in which she was inconsolable. Pearl tried to hide her own agitation, frustration, and sadness. She needed a brave, comforting face—this was her role as a mother, daughter, wife, and worker. The strategy that worked for Pearl was to treat her fatigue with endless activities as constant distractions: "I was tired when I got to work, when I got home, and while I was at work. Before I could even go to bed, I had to get all the kids ready for school the next day and most times do laundry. In the morning, get food ready for mother, lunch for my husband and children, prepare food for dinner."

Pearl assured herself that "the main benefit for doing the [paid] work was pay." But she could not forget that the pay had always been terrible. Nonetheless, as she saw it, "cleanup" work was one of very few labor options available to her. "A lot of women in here [East St. Louis] do what I do." She was never able to return to her full-time homemaker status and seriously doubted that she ever could. Hard labor defined her youth, middle age, and now her older years. A full twenty years after her mother's stroke, Pearl remained, at eighty-two, in the workforce and managing the life of her retired, ailing husband, her adult grandchildren, and her younger great-grandchildren.

She wished that she "could make thirty-five thousand dollars a year and some good insurance." She felt that she had acquired the requisite skills and knowledge after working almost all of her life, finishing high school, and completing two years of college. "But," she said with deep dismay, "I always end up doing some type of housekeeping work." In the past twelve months, she had earned about twelve thousand dollars. When asked to compare the present conditions of her life to her more youthful past, she offered the following analysis: "The only difference between today and then is that my children are grown, Mother is gone, my husband is very sick, the city has major problems now, and prices for everything are higher. I'm still taking care of children [great-grandchildren] and helping out my own kids. Taking care of my husband. I'm still tired. Morning, noon, and night, I'm tired."

Tired, bushed, worn-out—these were the adjectives Pearl and other low-income, working grandmothers used to describe their days working, raising grandchildren, and caring for kin. Each looked forward to the day when she could retire and enjoy the things she wanted to do, with no schedules, no commitments. This prospect did not loom in East St. Louis, where generations of low incomes wrote ongoing kin-script duties for older women.

Alberta Morgan, seventy, was another. "My daughter works hard," Alberta said. "She works at the Shop-n-Save. Then she works at the filling station. Sometimes she takes classes. She is a hard worker, and we all are. We help each other so that one day, we hope, none of us will have to go to work."

Francine Miller, sixty-six: "She [her daughter] lives here with me in my home, and we share the light bill. She gives me some money for groceries. I do what I can to help her and her husband. They are smart children, and they are trying to be independent—a good quality. Some people have grown children living with them that don't show them this kind of respect."

Delicia Moore, fifty-nine: "Sister is too precious to me to be anywhere else but here. There is no nursing home here that I would consider placing her. . . . What kind of sister would I be? If I cannot afford to put her in the best and cleanest and caring-est place, then she will stay here at home with me."

Missy Filmore, sixty-one: "We lived with my mother, and then my mother lived with us. Then my brother and his girlfriend lived with us, too. My sister and her sons live here, too. That is how we do things, good or bad."

Despite their rosy comments, the care work of these women wasn't purely altruistic and devoid of conflict; their relationships were rarely that simple. Kin-work was fraught with frustrations. Responsibilities often served as burdens, especially when these women had multiple commitments and roles. Caring for others was an obligation, a pressure, and a source of strain that few could ignore, particularly when these older women had so little, materially, to share. And many times, the strain of caring for and supporting others was an emotional and physical hardship for them.

Fredrica Mays, now sixty-eight and a grandmother, had had her first child at sixteen and married during that pregnancy. This trajectory was not uncommon. Girls "either did one of two things," Fredrica said. "They stayed in school, went to work, and then got married. Or they dropped out of school and got married, had kids." She could think of a few exceptions. Barbara Jennings, whose father owned a grocery store, went to school in Arkansas and later came back to East St. Louis to teach at Lincoln High School. And Esther Minton, whose mother was a teacher, joined the army. Fredrica heard that Esther had finally married at the age of twenty-eight or thirty-one and raised two children somewhere in the Chicago area, both of whom went on to college. Esther drove home to visit her relatives at least twice a year, always in a nice, fancy car.

It seems that even in those days, there were class differences in East St. Louis. You could live "on the wrong side of the tracks" even in the perception of other black people. Fredrica's family was poor and always had been. She was one of seven children. Her mother drank, smoked, cursed, refused to attend funerals, and carried a switchblade. Her father worked for the railroad and had two sets of children, one by her mother and another by his wife, who still lived in her house off Thirteenth Street in the South End. In Fredrica's memory, her father provided for both families. She remembered that on Friday nights, he would bring fresh fish home, and she would help her mother fry it. They had lots of company over on those evenings as well. The men would sit outside playing cards while women and children brought them beer and fish. Other than the weekends, he spent his time at work and with his other family. To this day, she resented her half siblings. From her perspective, they received the bulk of her daddy's attention, the bulk of his paycheck, the best food, the best clothes, and when he died, their mother got the insurance money and retirement fund.

Fredrica raised her children in the same three-room shotgun house in which she had grown up. The family home did not have running water or a toilet until the 1970s. She remembered using the outhouse during the day and a chamber pot at night. The family had a television before they had an indoor toilet. She could recall only one time when she had a new dress. Every item of clothing she ever wore was handed down from neighbors or cousins. She ate so many plates of beans and cornbread that she was sure she was going to start growing each out of her ears.

Her life was "a little better" than her mother's. Fredrica did not have as many children, and she saw this as a blessing. Her mother was on some form of aid for almost a lifetime. She would get "government cheese and things," Fredrica recalled. Fredrica, on the other hand, had gone on and off "aid" since the birth of her first child. She did not mind the assistance, but sometimes the jobs she managed to get pushed her just above eligibility requirements.

There were other near similarities between herself and her mother. Her mother buried three of her sons before she turned fifty. One was killed in the Vietnam War, and the others were victims of homicide. All of Fredrica's children were alive, though one was in prison in Joliet, one of the twenty-nine Illinois state prisons. For her, his arrest conjured mixed emotions of anger and relief. "I wanted him to stop messing around with them drugs," she said, because she feared either he would die of abuse or someone would kill him for drugs and money. She felt that his going to prison actually saved his life. "It got him away from the street. Because he was going to get killed one way or another." Her other three children lived in East St. Louis. A daughter, with three grown children, rented the house just across the street. A son currently lived with his "lady friend" elsewhere in the city and collected disability. He suffered from a severe hip injury at the age of twelve when he fell from a schoolyard monkey bar to the hard surface beneath. The injury healed at the time but later was aggravated by a workplace injury, when a forklift fell on him. Fredrica was never quite sure where her youngest daughter stayed at night. She worked at a club in Washington Park and gave her mother money whenever she came home. Her preteen children lived with Fredrica.

Women's care work was part of the family history. Fredrica's mother had taken care of one of her parents. Fredrica's grandmother had done the same. Now it was Fredrica's turn. "What choice do I have?" she asked rhetorically. She could try to place her mother in a nursing home, but she was uncomfortable with this idea. Ten years ago, she had worked in such a facility and knew that the elderly and disabled were treated very poorly.

"They just take their [the residents'] money," she said, "but they don't really take care of them like it should be." So she had vowed never to place her mother in a home, and she got her own children to make the same pledge. Bottom line, she cared for her mother, cashed her Social Security checks, and purchased her medication using Medicare and Medicaid. This personal care had some unexpected prices. Two weeks prior to our interview, Fredrica was trying to change her mother's undergarments. "She just hauled off and kicked me," Fredrica recalled, laughing mirthlessly. "Started cursing and fighting... I don't think she knew who I was that time."

Fredrica did the same work, part-time, for a family on Twenty-fifth Street. She tried to be as gentle, patient, and reasonable with her mother as she was with her client. But it was a lot easier to yell at her mother and ignore her than it was for her to do that to a paying employer. "See, I don't have to take the shit from her [mother] like I do from Miss Johnson [client]. Mama don't pay me. She oughtta be glad I'm here ... ain't nobody else coming around."

Talking about this led Fredrica to digress into remembering her childhood. Her mother's parenting, she said, had been abusive. "She would beat us. She would whup us with whatever, like a pot... a strap. Now, she wasn't no nice person." The beatings with leather straps "left welts up and down your legs and arms." She had a scar above her right eye from a kitchen chair her mother once threw. "Now, I don't remember that [incident], but my sister told me how it happened. She remembers that. We all [siblings] got it [beatings] when we was kids." Fredrica qualified the violence by asserting, "We was some bad kids. . . . Mama, she did what she had to, that's for sure. She had a lot of things on her mind."

Fredrica characterized her own parenting skills as similar to her mother's. When her children "got smart," they received a swift and stern smack. She always had a switch on the back porch, especially as the children grew older. She did the same with her grandchildren. Except, compared with the past, it seemed that she had a lot less energy to spend disciplining children—especially since they were her grandchildren. "I just leave 'em be sometimes.... If I got to get up to make sure they doing what they supposed to, then either they get it done, or they don't."

When she was tired, and this was a constant state, she was impatient with everyone, including herself. After ten years, taking care of her mother had become a burden. The Social Security checks helped with household bills, but they did not make up for the fatigue. The grandchildren were constantly walking in and out of the house, slamming the screen door, letting in gnats, flies, and mosquitoes. She had to hide her favorite foods and leftovers in a corner of the old refrigerator downstairs, because no one seemed to respect her things. Getting down those stairs was getting harder and harder, and no one seemed to notice her physical pain. She sometimes complained about her family as though they were strangers or very distant relatives. "They will eat everything ... and never say thank you.... Just gimme, gimme, gimme! That's all they know. Their parents, they do the same thing." She cared for her grandchildren and her children, of course, but often wished that she could have a house to herself, "just two seconds alone," she laughed.

For Fancy Burrow, seventy-two, taking care of her mother was a duty she did not question. Nonetheless, it sometimes elicited feelings of ambivalence. "I love my mother. I owe her, too, for all that she did for all of us when she was able," Fancy said. "Now it's my turn to take of her. I'm the one who is best able.

But . . . Lord knows, it ain't always easy to give of yourself. . . . It's hard on the body and soul."

Care labor as a form of kin-work is not always about physically caring for the sick and elderly. Many women feel the strain of supporting dependent adult children and grandchildren emotionally and financially. In East St. Louis, where jobs are scarce, and education is limited, financial independence has a minimal link to age. Aging women are often the ones who provide shelter, food, and clothing to unemployed and low-income adult children and grandchildren. Proximity contributes to the burden. When there are no jobs or educational opportunities to push and pull adult children from their childhood homes and communities, then, inevitably, they remain in place—near those on whom they can most rely for support.

Women seniors sometimes expressed to me a reluctant obligation to those they loved. These interdependent relationships brought considerable distress. According to Freda Robinson, sixty-nine, "Somebody ran up my phone bill, and it wasn't me. It had to be them [adult children]. But you don't know how hard it is to tell your own child she got to go. It's not easy. But there comes a point where a body just can't give anymore."

Flora Jones, fifty-six and a great-grandmother, said, "Young people are different today. They don't want to listen to their grandparents, but it is a grandparent's job to look over them. They don't respect. He [grandson] done about wore me to death. The school can't, won't help him. The police won't help. Ain't nobody. His friends are the boys you read about in the paper. They the ones that steal and rob people. He's gonna kill me [figuratively] along the way."

Joniece Miller also felt overwhelmed with her son, who had spent several years in and out of jail and on and off drugs: "When he [her son] got out of jail, he was just the same person but different. He started right back getting into the drugs and stuff. I had to keep my purse locked up, my cigarettes, my cell phone. Anything that was not nailed down he would take. It breaks my heart, but then you just got to be strong and tell yourself that you did your best. You support them as best you can, but there is a part of you that has to let your children go and make their way in the world, bad or good."

Without living-wage employment and opportunities to move ahead, childhood dependence is easily expanded beyond the age of eighteen. Adult children form families of their own, yet remain in their parents' households. Increasingly, aging women head these multigenerational units, all the while under the worrisome circumstances of their adult children's, nephews', nieces', and grandchildren's unemployment, incarceration, substance abuse, and diminished mental health. One such matriarch, Pearl Spence, said, "Sometimes when they doing wrong, then you got to find it in you to let them go. It's not an overnight decision, and, you know, it's a long-time, racking kind of decision. It's a painful thing for a mother to tell her child or grandbaby that you can't help him this time. It's a hurtin' thing."

.   .   .

Against the backdrop of all these hardships, the declining health of the primary-care women themselves can almost seem like an afterthought. Sadie Powers, seventy-three, learned that she had breast cancer two years ago, soon after her husband died following a long bout with colon cancer. At first, Sadie refused to believe her diagnosis. When she was much younger and first learned that her uncle had cancer, she thought it was infectious and superstitiously refused to visit him for weeks. Now, it was almost as if in those last months of touching her husband's hand and stroking his forehead, he had proven her earlier fears. Sadie's uncle, her sister-in-law, and grandmother all died of cancer as well.

She continued to work as a licensed vocational nurse (LVN) at St. Mary's Hospital. Helping others managed to take her mind off her treatments and her next visit to the doctor. "He never had any good news," she sighed.

A churchgoing woman, Sadie did not hesitate to share the Lord's word with anyone who would listen. She also found solace in Coors Beer, available at the variety of liquor and convenience stores that overrun the neighborhood. This gave her the nerve to cuss out her children whenever they came around asking for money or tapped into her cigarettes or beer. Sometimes, she did not want to be bothered with them or her grandchildren, especially on those days when she was feeling tired and weary from the illness and treatments. She loved her children, but they always needed something, and she felt she had done her part to bring them up as she did. They were grown now, and it seemed that it was time for them to start taking care of her.

Sadie had suffered for years from chronic hypertension. After the birth of her third child, a benign tumor was removed from her uterus. She had arthritis in her knees and left ankle and came down with the flu every spring. Although she worked at a hospital and in the medical field, she rarely visited the doctor, and the diagnosis of cancer came only after a visit to the emergency room. Hers had been a hard life, and most of her pleasure derived from her belief in God and her relationship with her husband.

A scan of the house revealed spartan material possessions. The kitchen housed mismatched plates, dented pots and pans, and jelly-jar glasses of varying shapes and sizes. Sadie's living room consisted of a black velvet sofa, television, and a rocking chair that had once belonged to her mother. The floor of her bedroom closet was filled with low-cost, worn shoes of assorted colors, heels run down from years of wear. Hanging above was a row of polyester printed blouses, flowery housedresses, and her Sunday best. Her most cherished possessions were a jewelry box filled faux-pearl necklaces, rings, and bracelets and a cuckoo clock that her deceased brother had mailed to her during his military service in Germany. She had never expected to grow sick with cancer, and she had hoped to have a lot more to give her children at this point in her life.

The closer Sadie got to retirement age, the worse her ailments became. Still, she continued her multitasked existence. "Working keeps my mind off of my problems," she explained. She might have added that she could ill afford to do otherwise.

Visits to the doctor are few and far between for the aging women of East St. Louis. The distance to physicians' offices, the lack of transportation, the chaos of work schedules, and the primacy of others' care put their own care at the bottom of the list and further endanger their health. In any given week, for instance, Dimple Lawson, seventy-six, might take her great-grandchild to school, drive her sister to a physician in Belleville, and spend a half day caring for an ailing neighbor. She earned fifteen dollars a day for this service and could not afford to pass up a day's pay. For Dimple, self-employed and without sick leave or paid vacation, any fragment of free time was like an oxygen tank on the moon, to be used only on the most desperately as-needed basis.

"I'll be lucky if I get to retire," said Lorraine Daley, sixty-eight. She had been a housekeeper at the Comfort Inn for twelve years. At the end of every workday, she had a backache and sore legs. She quit for a short while about five years ago when she began experiencing complications from her diabetes and hypertension. "My eyes were getting glaucoma," she reported. She also explained, "The doctor said my circulation was bad in my leg." But not having a regular work schedule made her feel old and decrepit. What really interrupted Lorraine's retirement, however, was taking custody of two of her grandchildren, a consequence of her daughter's poor mental health. The kids were a boy, seven, and a girl, ten. Lorraine got them ready for school, met with their teachers, disciplined them at home, and helped them cope with the incarceration of their mother for selling an illegal substance. Lorraine also had to purchase more and different types of foods at the grocery store and wash, dry, and fold more clothing, and she was constantly cleaning the mess her grandson left on the toilet seat and on the bathroom floor.

To make matters worse, the children constantly needed money for school projects and for the clothes they quickly outgrew. She felt the household could not survive on her and her husband's Social Security and the little bit of money provided through the Illinois Department of Human Services. She chose to return to the paid labor market.

Two decades after her initial diagnosis, Lorraine had a hard time following doctor's orders, especially in the area of diet. "I just—I would know that I wasn't supposed to eat that fried chicken, but you know, when you hungry, sometimes you don't really be as logical about things like that." She would often skip breakfast so that she could make it to work on time. "I have to get my grandkids ready for school. I got to get them to school and then get to work my own self," she said, "so it's hard to eat right." Lunch became whatever was available; the hotel did not have a restaurant, but it did have vending machines with chips and chocolate, and the boss supplied plenty of caffeinated coffee.

At home, Lorraine cooked the dinner foods that pleased every-one else in the family rather than suited her own health needs.

For women of this generation, their approach to food adds up to an easy and affordable, but ultimately dangerous, way to dem-onstrate care and affection. They think it is important to pro-vide children with the snacks they enjoy and their husbands with the meats, starches, and vegetables prepared the way they prefer them: greens drenched in bacon grease taken from a can stored under the sink; chicken legs and pork steaks battered and fried, the latter smothered in sautéed onions; potatoes mashed with butter and seasoned with salt. "Men get used to having things a certain way. . . . I fix him what he likes, because that what makes him happy," said Beatrice Manor, sixty-four.

The household food culture, driven by a limited budget along with the choices Beatrice identified, is high in carbohydrates, sodium, and glucose. The priority is foods at the low end of the cost scale, easy to prepare. The stock of food is heavy in canned, rather than frozen, vegetables and in beef roasts, hams, and whole chickens, which can be cooked in a crock pot over a period of hours and with little to no supervision, or it can be cut up and quickly fried in a skillet, accompanied with canned beans and instant mashed potatoes.

Lorraine found the strength to cook dinner regardless of how she felt. She longed to sit down, watch television, or fall asleep, but she pushed herself to finish the laundry and ensure that the kids had clothes for school the next day. And caring for the grandchildren wasn't the end of it. Lorraine also called her sister to see if she needed anything. "If she don't, then I just go on with what I'm doing. . . . If she do, then I need to make sure she get what she needs." She was on the receiving end of many phone calls from cousins, nieces, nephews, and others who knew when to call, because her work schedule was regular. If someone needed a ride, they called. If someone needed to borrow money, they called. If someone was upset "with this one here or that girl there," they called.

Fredrica Mayes relieved her stress by watching TV. In addition, she smoked at least a pack of cigarettes a day and drank beer the way a runner drinks water. Her children had the same habits, so there was always a supply of each on hand. On Friday and Saturday nights, the kids and other kin might visit for a game of pinochle or spades. These were good times, laughter, drunkenness, chips, and sometimes a cruel humor that family members can use only among themselves. Of course, sometimes under the mask of liquor, old, unaddressed hostilities and anger reared their heads. At least once a month, an argument or fight broke out between two or three houseguests. Still, this was cheap entertainment.

Fredrica had been diagnosed with hypertension and diabetes, and there were problems with her liver. She also had arthritis. But these diagnoses had been determined more than twelve years earlier, when she visited the emergency room following a minor stroke. The stroke paralyzed her left side temporarily. Upon her release, she was prescribed medication for high blood pressure and diabetes and was encouraged to follow up with her family physician. Unfortunately, she did not have a family physician. The visit to the emergency room was the first time she had seen a doctor since her oldest child's birth decades earlier. She neither trusted nor could afford doctors. Instead, she used home remedies for all of her ailments and sometimes her mother's medications if she felt her heart was "acting up."

·　　·　　·

The last casualty of these long lives of poverty is leisure in the broadest sense of the word—not just time off, per se, but mental freedom from the hour-to-hour demands on the women of East St. Louis. Fredrica rarely relaxed, and when she did, it usually involved activities that contributed to stress. She seemed to relish good gossip. It was like a soap opera. If there was something going on in the family or in the neighborhood, she generally knew, and she'd share the information. There was a steady exchange of scandalous hearsay streaming among her, her family members, and a few neighbors. They, after all, lived similar lives. Miss Evelyn, on the corner, stayed home and took care of her eighty-three-year-old sister. Mr. Parks, who owned the home next to the house of Fredrica's daughter, lived alone and had occasional company from a grandson who was frequently in trouble with the police.

"If I were rich, then I would take a vacation once a month at least," Pearl Spence daydreamed out loud. One of the usual hallmarks of suburbia is its smorgasbord of recreational, retirement, and family-oriented amenities. In nearby Edwardsville, seniors stay fit and relieve stress with regular visits to the YMCA for lively classes of water aerobics and yoga. They bike and hike on off-street trails and sidewalks. In East St. Louis, it is a different story.

Fredrica Mayes's front and back porches had the perfect view of most high jinks on and around her corner of the neighborhood. She could see when Mr. Parks went to work and when he came home. She knew all the juicy details of the fight between Pam Mathis and her boyfriend. Watching the people saunter in and out of her daughter's house at all hours, Fredrica suspected that her grandson was into selling crack and whatever else was available on this side of the city. The fifteen-year-old boy was too young to work, so Fredrica could think of no other explanation for the money he flashed around; just yesterday he paid a neighbor to pick up some spareribs from Sandy's Barbecue and More. The drama surrounding her everyday observations obviously did not calm Fredrica. They just made her even more anxious and worried about the next hammer blow her life was about to deliver to her.

But there was no other way. This was how Fredrica's mother had lived; this was how her own daughters would live. (In fact, Fredrica's mother helped raise the grandchildren while Fredrica went to work in clubs and truck stops.) What else could she do? She was a daughter and a mother. This was her kin-script. She was philosophical about her situation: "If you got parents, you got to take care of them. . . . If you got kids, you got grandkids."

Some grandmothers I spoke with were not so fatalistic. Freda Robinson kicked her daughter and grandson out of the house after they ran up phone bills, borrowed her car and "forgot" to fill it with gas, left food and dirty dishes in the living room, and didn't replenish toilet-paper rollers or soap dishes. Her daughter worked at a fish market in St. Louis, but her nineteen-year-old grandson was unemployed. On occasion, he collected cans and cashed in their deposits. At one time, he worked at a car wash on State Street, but she had heard rumors about the questionable business being run out of the establishment at the same time. Now, he spent his days asleep on the living room floor and his nights going out or watching TV. Reflecting on her decision to eject them, Freda said, "Family should stick together . . . but I don't know."

Ultimately, leisure time is a subjective concept. These women often counted as relaxation those moments on the phone with family and friends; gossip is a way of spreading news, but it is also a source of entertainment. Still, listening to gossip from those who are less able and less mobile can be taxing. "Some people, they just like to complain about everything.... Ain't nothing or nobody ever good enough," said Alberta Hatcher of the content of conversation from her mother. "She don't never be happy it seem. Always got something ornery to say about people." Other working grandmothers had similar reports. They said that answering the phone and listening to how the days of others went was anything but relaxing. "They say a mother is always a mother," observed Eunice Myers. "You worry when your children are young. You worry when they grown.... If they need you, you always going to be there."

Researchers suggest that married elderly women are happier and healthier than their single counterparts. However, a partner, especially one that is retired and ill, can sometimes feel like an added burden—someone else to take care of, someone else who complains, and someone else that takes away from the private time so many of these women crave at the end of a workday. Eunice Myers and her husband, who was seventy-one, were responsible for raising three of their grandchildren. He was quite helpful. He made sure the kids cleaned the house and did their homework. But he also seemed to sleep and visit "way more" than he worked around the house. She preferred that he stay busy doing something other than sitting around and complaining all day, especially on her days off work.

If the working people of East St. Louis want to relax after a long day or on days off, few points of leisure are within the city limits. In the summer, there is the front or back porch, and that is about it. According to a local librarian, Vera Daniels, she and her husband "can't even sit on the back porch anymore" because of the unseemly behavior in the neighborhood: "The language that you hear young people talk today. You can't sit outside, 'cause that's all you hear. Over there they be talkin' all that trash mouth. Then on the other side, these kids'll be up on each other [making out]. It's shameful."

Even church participation, a historical haven for African Americans, requires time and commitment that many working women have trouble giving. This is a setting, too, often replete with gossip. "You gotta go with your ear to the Lord. Otherwise, ain't no telling what you gonna pick up in the pews," said Gerry Taylor, explaining the stress of holding her tongue among churchgoing gossipers before and after Sunday services.

• • •

The "canary in the coal mine" analogy—the grim possibility that the woes of East St. Louis are precursors of problems in the United States at large—has special resonance in the structural depression in the lives of the aged in suburbia. Throughout the country, pockets of poverty persist in this demographic; the ones illustrated here are just extremes at one end of a scale. Relative to other Western countries, seniors in America are more likely than those of working age to live among the ranks of the poor. Additionally, among the elderly in America, racial minorities and women living alone are poorer than married couples, men of any race or ethnicity and poorer than whites in general, married or not. Women regardless of race, feel the pinch of poverty and health care costs in their old age. When medical out-of-pocket expenses are subtracted, their overall rate of poverty increases, for those without spouses, especially.[12]

The lifetime of low earnings for these women, coupled with their responsibilities for unpaid caretaking, often cement them in the workplace, even after retirement age. Their decisions to remain attached to the paid-labor market, offer them contradictory consequences. At one level, their paid labor brings much-needed money into their multiple-person households and family networks. At the same time, it seems to contribute to the deterioration of their physical health and to the ailments that beset their aging bodies. Care labor is not something that most East St. Louis women stop at the end of a paid workday or at the official age of retirement. Yet, paradoxically, the paid care these women provide for nonkin external to their household does not afford them the luxury of accessing this form of support for themselves or their own families.

But to call the socioeconomic situation of aging women in East St. Louis a microcosm of a national trend takes the conversation only so far. In the United States, most workers do not expect to reach retirement age only to be unable to retire from the paid-labor market. Older women in East St. Louis desire a life of earned leisure and comfort. But women here, pulled by familial obligations and a lack of savings (being disproportionately represented in low-wage work), often must continue working. Those who find themselves in this predicament often find that the type of work they perform and their low levels of accumulated wealth across their life span leave them in poor physical and financial health. Physical labor in the helping professions takes its toll on both bodies and minds.

Those with more accumulated wealth are able to relax, travel, and pay off their mortgages in their old age. The much poorer older women of East St. Louis are too busy fighting ailments and working and caring for spouses, adult children, grandchildren, and elderly kin, who also share life in the working class.

My mother's only sister, Aunt Sis, worked nearly every day of her adult life in the St. Louis metropolitan area. For decades, she was a housekeeper at the Jefferson Barracks veterans hospital. She swept and mopped. She wiped windows and tables. She did work similar to that performed by many women described in this chapter. She did all of this and raised eleven children, mostly on her own, and then helped raise and support her grandchildren. In her sixties, as cancer consumed her body, she continued to work and take care of others. Still, in her room, while she lay on her bed, waiting for death and relief to overtake her, I could not help but notice what she was leaving behind. For all of the decades of hard labor, almost everything that was hers fit into her ten-by-ten bedroom. Her closet burst with worn shoes and inexpensive clothing. Her dresser held pieces of faux jewelry and saved birthday cards and bills. She worried constantly about her mother, her sister, her brothers, her children, grandchildren, and great-grandchildren. I thought that for all she gave to others, at work and at home, she deserved a better life and a better end.

This sad and rotten truth about working-class poverty is a fact of life for many black working women in this metropolitan area and especially in East St. Louis. Relative to other demographic groups, low-income African American mothers in particular are more likely to provide parenting and caregiving in poverty and without the support of a spouse. While families tend to be the primary caretakers of both the young and old in poor communities, the women are the ones generally "caught in the middle," with primary and secondary responsibilities for the care and well-being of both their own children and their aged kin. Disproportionately caregivers and single parents, poor African American women are more likely to fall short of being able to meet the cumulative social, physical, and economic demands of both populations.

These trends do not disappear with time. Responsibilities to family do not end when children reach the age of eighteen. Nor do they dissipate when women reach the age of retirement in their suburban place.

CHAPTER SIX

"Gotta protect my own"

In May 2001, the following letter from a serial killer was sent to a reporter for the *St. Louis Post-Dispatch,* the major paper in the St. Louis metropolitan area: "Dear Bill: nice sob story about Teresa Wilson. Write one about Greenwade write a good one and I'll tell you where many others are. To prove I'm real here's directions to number seventeen. Search in a fifty-yard radius from the X. Put the story in the Sunday paper like the last."[1]

One month later, Maury Troy Travis sat in jail, charged with the kidnapping and killing of two women and linked to the deaths of at least five other women. At the time, East St. Louis police were struggling to solve the deaths of twelve women whose bodies had been found here and there, about the city and within the metropolitan area. They were killed in similar ways—a blow to the head or strangled. It was later determined that these killings and possibly more were actually the handiwork of not one but two independent serial killers. The dead had something in common—they were black, substance abusers, and according to police, most sold sex for money. It took the police years to link all the cases.

All told, the police linked six murders to this single killer (though he confessed to just five). These came at a time when the city's per capita homicide rate was the highest in the nation, and the city did not have the revenue to maintain an adequate police force. East St. Louis was borrowing police officers from the state of Illinois for daily police patrols.

October 4, 1989, was the date of the discovery of the body of Nicole Willis, a sixteen-year-old honor-roll student, in a vacant lot in the Parkside neighborhood area of East St. Louis and Centreville. She had been raped, mutilated with a stick, beaten on the head, and left for dead among the gravel and weeds. Earlier that year, six-year-old Aree Hunt had been murdered. He was outside playing with a cousin when a man convinced the boy to follow him to a nearby park. The next morning, his body was found. He had been brutally beaten, and once the murder was complete, the man had had sex with boy's body. These children were victims of a serial killer, Lorenzo Fayne of East St. Louis.

In 1992, fourteen-year-old Latondra Dean was raped and stabbed twenty-one times. A few months later, a gym teacher found nine-year-old Fallon Flood hanging from a belt inside the gym of East St. Louis High School, where she had attended the summer lunch program. She had clearly been left unattended by school officials.

In abandoned places, basic protection can be the first thing to go. Of the 284 murders from 1989 to 1991, most were adult men and women. But the Lorenzo Fayne cases demonstrate that not even the very young are spared the violence hovering over this city. In 2001, when Debra Powell was mayor, she was asked about the serial killing of the children. In her view, the area of Parkside became a different place after her election, safer than it had been before. She said, "I think what we've probably learned is to be more conscious of everyone's children."[2]

Fathers begged to disagree; they thought East St. Louis was no safer than it had been fifteen or twenty years earlier. Alvin Mooney argued that the city was more dangerous than in his youth. "We men here who is fathers, we just need to pay attention and protect our own," Mooney said.

. . .

For families relocating from cities to suburbia, safety—freedom from fear of violence and property crime—is a key motivator. Compared with central cities, suburbs and rural areas experience lower levels of both categories of crime. But the pattern of comparative tranquility for those in middle- and upper-income categories does not hold for the working class in poor suburbs.

In East St. Louis, newspaper headlines about body discoveries were common. The bodies were discovered among the weeds in vacant lots, on the floors of falling abandoned buildings, and on the pavement of fractured streets. According to one newspaper report, "The discovery of the first decomposed body in an abandoned house in November 1999 hardly seemed out of the ordinary." Dead bodies of mostly poor working-class black people were boldly dumped in full view of the city's residents—waiting patiently to be discovered by a passerby or a child at play.

Serial murders and other killings are, without doubt, extreme forms of violence. The seeming normality of murders demonstrates the acute harshness of living in this working-class suburb. Security and safety are measurable environmental characteristics, and like the degree of quality found in health care facilities, fully functioning schools, and supermarkets in East St. Louis, those measurements come up short. Relative to non-Hispanic whites, African Americans, regardless of their economic status and location, find safety elusive.[3] Where blacks reside, safety is a parent problem—especially one that concerns fathers.

Current family policy makes low-income fathers just as accountable as mothers for the health and safety of their children. However, what fathers do as parents is negotiated within a larger ecological context. Paternal behavior is influenced by, among other variables, men's relationships with others, their access to education, whether they work one or more low-wage jobs or are unable to find a job, the length and nature of their commute to and from work, their proximity to their children, and whether they have several sets of children. Stable employment and good relationships with the mother or mothers of their children can help men to maintain a paternal role, but the goal is hindered by such factors as divorce and the time it takes to continue higher education and to work at multiple jobs.[4]

But contrary to popular belief, good fathering is not limited to those who reside in the same household as their children. Many African American fathers, from all circumstances, maintain close relationships with their children, especially when those children are very young. Many men who live apart from their kids spend time with them, serve as role models, and give guidance and some form of financial support. Poor black fathers who have a hard time meeting financial responsibilities emphasize their social and emotional obligations to their children. Some low-income African American fathers respond to the growing incidence of the mothers' neglect or maltreatment of children or their incarceration, or both, by assuming the full-time care of their children. African American fathers are more likely than fathers of other races or ethnicities to be a full-time single parent. Overall, it seems that many black fathers believe it is their paternal obligation to provide support, security, and protection for their children.[5]

Children's exposure to violence in poor places takes three major forms: direct physical assaults by caregivers, assaults within the immediate family (often by the mother), and violence in the larger neighborhood or community.. But parents can mitigate the ill effects that poor neighborhoods have on their children. In a small study of ten African American women, researchers discovered that a group of mothers did not look to traditional institutions, such as the police or shelters, to rescue them or their children from potentially violent partners or community circumstances. Rather, they looked to themselves, peers, and neighbors to keep men at bay and to keep trouble from their doorsteps.[6] Similarly, fathers have developed strategies to protect their children from violent members of the community—by educating kids about safety, offering constant supervision, and directly confronting alleged troublemakers.

The traditional definition of violence against children in black neighborhoods starts from the false assumption that it originates primarily from their own mothers and fathers, or from African American men abusing and assaulting women, or from a criminal element within the community. Thus, proposed solutions emphasize the agency of individuals and individual households. But this definition of violence is too limited, for it fails to consider the everyday perils of the public sphere that jeopardize health and safety. It also fails to capture the experiences of the many parents who act to protect their children from the consequences of pervasive and large-scale state neglect.

No one has appreciated the harshness of life in East St. Louis more than its men. Regardless of their educational or occupational status, many men here have raised children and internalized the principle that it is their responsibility to provide for and protect them. Collectively, they expressed to me the belief that the most important element of their parental role is the time they take to guide their kids through a safe childhood and toward productive adulthood.

Above all, as the stories below illustrate, fathers strive to *protect*. They try to protect young ones from the everyday perils and violence associated with urban areas. They try to protect daughters from harmful sexual encounters and boys from the drug scene. But while some of their concerns fall into the categories of personal violence, others are more inclusive of the extensive dangers that make up the physical and psychological environment of this abandoned place.

. . .

Carlos explained that he was a man who used to like "young women." He sought them out in clubs, in the malls, or on the street after the Lincoln High School bell released the adolescents for the day.

He liked women who did not require deep conversation or a lot of time, had "tight" bodies, and were easily impressed by his "style." In those days, in his early twenties, he would drive around in his uncle's Cadillac. He lived with his mother and had no bills. Thus, he always had spending money in his pocket. And his job at McDonald's, and later as an office clerk at his uncle's law firm, enabled him to purchase the latest fashions in shoes and clothing. He'd say, "Girl, let me take you to Red Lobster," or "Let me buy you a new sexy dress at the mall." In East St. Louis, he explained, "These young girls eat it up. . . . They'll do anything for a brotha if you give them some food, buy them something, you dig?" He added, "It's easy for a brotha with a little bit of money in his pocket to get some play from these girls here."

So it was girls of high school age who captured his attention—that is, until his daughter became one. When she developed a shapely figure, he began to feel very protective, "overly protective," of her and her friends. "I know how these men be looking at these young ladies. That used to be me. I'm ashamed to say, but that used to be me. So I feel like me, better than anybody, know how to protect her from these niggas out here."

Other men agreed that seducing young women was "like a game here." Ty Johnson said, "Every brotha is constantly looking out for the sweetest young thing to come around. . . . Then you get her, and that's that [snaps his fingers]. Some wanna turn her out—you know make some quick cash off her. But some of us are just in it for the game. That's entertainment. Shit, we ain't got nothing better to do for free. . . . But really, that's one of the major ways that you can say, 'I'm a man.' Get these young things to open up to you." The men explained that a large part of the perception of masculinity is the ability to attract women—very young women who can make a man feel important and older women who can pay a man's way by buying him clothing, food, or maybe even a car and provide a place to live.

"The thing of it," Carlos said, "is that these girls, if they don't have nothin' else going for them, then they susceptible to men like that." From his experience, girls whose fathers are in jail or otherwise live outside the home are vulnerable. Girls whose mothers have full-time jobs and are away from home for lengthy periods of the day are vulnerable. Girls who live in impoverished households are vulnerable. In East St. Louis, one or more of these characteristics are represented in the bulk of households.

The behaviors of these men are hardly unique to either their locale or their socioeconomic conditions. White males search for prey in Internet chat rooms, movie theaters, shopping malls, and other public spaces. But here, where many men have few prospects for well-paid work, they stand outside their doorways daily, looking at young girls playing and walking by. Young girls attend school, looking for a way to have all of the nice things that mall stores offer and television entertainers seem to possess—no different from middle-class youth in urban suburbs.

In a community where, according to a 2001 U.S. Census Bureau report, nearly 70 percent of children are born to single mothers and 25 percent to adolescent girls, fathers take away from all these contradictions a simple lesson. First and foremost, they embrace the idea that parents must be on guard against predators. As one dad put it, high unemployment creates a population of men with "nothing better to do but hustle women" for food, money, lodging, and sex. Some of them so categorize their own activities. But in an echo of the popular blame game, they also finger mothers for lax discipline and morals. They blame church ministers for selfishly having relationships with young women in their congregation and taking money from poor households to line their own pockets with a "Cadillac fund." They blame fathers for not spending enough time with their children, for going to jail, and for not providing support to single parenting mothers.

Fathers worry about boys as well and have parallel protective strategies for them. The difference is that they identify deadly personal violence as the greatest danger to males. Dads are concerned that sons will get into fights at school or on the street. They are concerned that boys will hang around with the wrong kids and begin to make money in illegal and violent activities. The focus of supervision of boys is on making sure they are too busy to get into trouble. Damian Carver, for example, pressured his son to participate in the youth choir, ushering, and Sunday School at church. Prince Gerry used his unemployment as an opportunity to walk his ten-year-old son, David, to and from school every day. "Won't no bully mess with him, 'cause they see his daddy is going to be waiting for him after school," Prince explained. "When I'm around, that'll discourage any nonsense."

Supervision and extracurricular activities are not always successful. Nor do all fathers practice these methods. Adolescent boys especially seem to grow weary of their fathers lurking over their shoulders. One said of his father, "He has got to let me be my own man one day. At some point, I'm going to have to fight somebody. What's gonna happen if he ain't around then, huh? I'm gonna get my ass kicked, that's what."

Other fathers feel that offering advice, rather than supervision and intense engagement, is the best way to protect boys. Said one, "He's my son, so I gotta teach him how to be a man. I tell him how to back out of a bad situation, but when it come down to it, then he's gotta make a decision about what to do, you understand?"

. . .

On February 12, 2003, Clayton Harris Jr., twenty-four, was driving his vehicle along a street when a white police officer signaled him to pull over. Clayton was carrying 1.5 ounces of marijuana and seemed to decide to try evading possible arrest. He left his vehicle and fled from the officer on foot. In haste, he stole into a nearby alley and hid behind a corrugated-metal fence. The officer gave immediate chase in the patrol car, turned into the alley, and hit the iron fence where Clayton Harris was hiding. The young black man was pinned by the vehicle. He died before he could be rescued from the accident scene.[7]

News of the violent death spread quickly through the grape-
vine of the predominantly black communities in southwestern
Illinois. In the view of many African Americans in the area,
"it was definitely murder." This, after all, was not the first brutal death of a black male to occur at the hands of authorities.
Charges of police brutality rumbled from one block to the next,
from one resident to another. There were official and unofficial
reports that this was not the policeman's first violent encounter
with a civilian. However, after several weeks of sifting the pros-
ecutor's evidence, a largely white grand jury refused to indict
the officer. In response, many East St. Louisans marched around
the Madison County courthouse in protest. They voiced their
frustration, anger, and resentment with a criminal-justice system that did not seem to value the life of Clayton Harris and
other victims of brutality or the concerns of black citizens more
broadly. "If there ever was a case of police brutality without justice," asserted the Harris family attorney, "this is it."[8]

The scenario, all too familiar, highlights a bitter irony. One of
the most internally discussed categories of safety for black men
in East St. Louis is that of protection *from* the police.

This particular protest was briefly noted in local newspapers,
radio reports, and area television newscasts. But black residents
in southwestern Illinois, marchers and nonparticipants alike,
did not expect too much to come from it. Across the river in St.
Louis, Missouri, such public deaths had occurred at least once
annually over the past few years. And they had occurred many
more times across the nation, with little or no resulting change
in questionable police practices. Clayton Harris's mother, too,
held out little hope for legal redress or for reform of the justice system. A fellow protester told the *Belleville News-Democrat*,
"I think they [the public and criminal-justice system] heard, but

I don't believe they're interested because of the way things have gone on for years. The thing is that it keeps happening. This isn't the first murder."[9]

The Clayton Harris Jr. death chillingly encapsulates the meaning of abandonment. Disturbing police activities in black, urban, working-class communities and cities are often the subject of weekly news roundups on local and national television stations. Concerned citizens of New York City, Detroit, Cincinnati, St. Louis, and other cities have made attempts to establish citizen-control boards to oversee police activities. Yet, the majority of the public condones the common practices of law enforcement; nonblack, nonpoor citizens appear genuinely to feel that such tactics are necessary to maintain control of an alleged abundance of criminal activity in places far outside the orbit of their experiences.

Fathers in East St. Louis draw on their own experiences to emphasize to their children the perils associated with interacting with area police. They know that the surrounding communities maintain a fixed image of their town as a hotbed of prostitution, welfare mothers, unruly children, and drug dealers. In speaking with me, these men surmised that being a black man from East St. Louis also affects how people elsewhere treat them. "If you go to Target in Fairview, they gonna look at you funny; they gonna follow you around the store, make sure you ain't putting nothing in your pocket," reported James Hancox.

Josh Cowan's story reinforces the existence of lingering basic discrimination. When Josh was walking home from work from the nearby, predominantly white city of Collinsville, the police followed him three blocks, stopped him, pushed him down, and pinned him to the ground with the heels of their shoes. They then handcuffed him, frisked him, and demanded his identification. Josh was certain that they intended to kill him, but they eventually uncuffed him and told him to head home—apparently, they had the wrong suspect. Carlos, Josh, James, and others said such events were commonplace.

Josh advised his son not to move a muscle when confronted by police: he should not move. Men here feel that it is their responsibility to teach boys about these dangers. Many men here explained to me how they talk with their sons about what to do when confronted by police. Josh Cowan recalled that he advised his son to "not move unless the cop says to.... Do not reach for your wallet. Do not scratch your head. Do not move. Because, the next thing you know, they'll be saying you were reaching for a weapon and BAM! That's it."

Another man who had had unpleasant encounters with the police, despite having no involvement in a crime, made related points: "Never, if you can help it, be out by yourself in these small towns around here. The police will not hesitate to stop you, to take you in, to beat you. They will not hesitate. Always have an ID or something with your name on it. Don't be alone. And always tell somebody where you gonna be.... I tell my son to stay away from white women. Stay away from white neighborhoods. Those people will set you up. If you work for them, they are going to blame you if something is missing. If you having sex with their daughter, then they going to say you raped her. There's many a time that things like that happened."

Fear of becoming victims of police homicides is right at the top of the list of the concerns of East St. Louis men. It isn't that run-ins with law-enforcement officers can be entirely avoided; such episodes will happen, with or without cause, over the course of a lifetime. It is knowing how to handle them in ways that minimize the risk of the worst outcomes.

Work demands mean that no parent can watch out for his or her children around the clock. Moonie Johnson, a father of two grade-school boys, juggled much of his time between three out-of-town part-time jobs. Romeo Weeks supervised his preteen daughter in between his long commutes to two different jobs. Carlos did not allow his friends to come into the house when he was not at home.

Carlos also refused to admit anyone after 8 P.M., when his daughter was likely to be in her nightgown. Carlos tried to ensure that she came home directly after school. He kept track of her friendship network and her school grades. Like many single parenting fathers in this city, he lived with his mother and solicited her help in these areas. She monitored the girl's activities and telephone conversations. Many fathers acknowledged to me the limitations of these tactics and their sometimes-overbearing nature, but they considered them the best means to keep kids out of trouble.

While academic research underscores the value of parental supervision, the new insight from talking to the fathers of East St. Louis is how broadly they define the potential sources of harm to their children. Even the abuse and brutality of the police are just the most visible pieces of state-abetted violence.

•   •   •

Sandwiched between the city's State Street, Interstate Highway 64, and the area just west of the Schnuck's chain supermarket is a pocket of houses. Old, leaf-laden trees pepper the lawns of both the abandoned and lived-in properties. Abandoned properties are easily distinguished by their dilapidated porches, boarded windows and doors, or the lengthy grasses and weeds that seem to wave at passersby on windy, spring mornings. These were all

once stately homes. Many were two-story brick, with fireplaces
and large front porches. Before African Americans were the
dominant population, working-class and middle-income whites
owned and lived in these properties. Homes here were generally more impressive than those on the South End. But in East
St. Louis, no neighborhood, house, or family is spared the dearth
of services available or the sphere of pollutants that hang over
the town.

Arnie Millier, thirty-seven, father of two, knew all too well
that this was one of the reasons why safety is an elusive concept. He and his children lived with his mother in her home.
The house was on a small side street just off State Street. Few
cars came this way; their house and the one next door were the
only livable properties left on this road. Yet, somehow, trash and
debris found its way to their block, creating hazards for those
who ventured outdoors.

On a crisp school-day morning last year, Arnie's son slipped
in the grass of an empty lot and cut his hand on the jagged edge
of a broken bottle that lay hidden beneath the beauty of red and
yellow fall leaves. There was so much blood that a path of red
trailed behind the boy as he rushed home to his father. Arnie
thought a major artery had been cut.

"I didn't panic, you know, I got him to the emergency room
as fast as I could. . . . But you know it's those kind of times when
you wonder what your life would be like if you lived somewhere else. 'Cause then, you know, he could've fallen, but then
the glass probably wouldn't have been there in a nicer neighborhood. Here they don't really clean the streets, and people's
always tossin' their trash. It's dangerous for little kids here. You
think, 'What if some fiend leaves a used [hypodermic] needle on
the playground. Or what if somebody tricks your kid into trying

crack or something. Then you wonder if the doctors gonna give him the kind of attention he deserves. See, we on aid, so that means that we can't just get the best doctor; we can't pay for that. We got to get what they give us. And frankly, sometimes I don't think the city, the doctors, really care."

Arnie's mother had experienced a more severe trauma, breaking her hip in a fall to an ice-sheeted street. The city had not put salt on many side streets even after several days of harsh winter weather. Arnie blamed the city for the injury. From his perspective, he explained, "They should've threw salt on the street so old people don't fall and get hurt." A year after his son's accident, the scars from the cut and the four stitches, though barely visible, were aching reminders to Arnie. "You just feel vulnerable," he said.

Litter on the streets of East St. Louis is a common sight. On any given day, in just about any empty lot, a scavenger can likely find old tires, broken refrigerators, milk cartons filled with used automobile oil, ragged clothing, battered bicycles, and other trash. Pollution in East St. Louis comes in various additional forms. For decades, the air, water, and soil have been saturated with harsh toxins. City officials say this relatively small town has 153 hazardous waste handlers and no fewer than 26 businesses reporting toxic releases, many of them airborne. Contaminants include arsenic, lead, carbon monoxide, nitrogen dioxide, and other compounds known to cause cancer. A health hazard to all, the environment is a particular threat to young children, who experience high rates of asthma and lead poisoning.[10] The number of registered adult cases of psychosis, cancer, and intestinal and nervous disorders has been exceptional.[11]

With 40 percent of housing built prior to 1950 and 13 percent of all housing vacant, adequate living quarters are scarce. Vacant lots and fire-gutted buildings are scattered throughout East St. Louis. Almost half the residents pay rent to absentee landlords, who often provide insufficient maintenance. Adult men raise their children on streets even dirtier and amid a haze of pollutants even more choking than were known in their own youth.

"I think everybody should have the right to breathe good air, don't you?" said Brian Jennings. Six months earlier, Brian's oldest daughter, Trelise, was rushed to the hospital during a severe asthma attack. Brian's sister Mary had died of the same malady two years prior to that. "She was just sitting at home and then she couldn't breathe," Brian recalled sadly. "She didn't have any medicine, so we called the ambulance, but it was like there wasn't anything they could do at that point."

According to a 2011 report from the Center for Disease Control, from 2006 to 2008, 16 percent of the poor and 14 percent of the nearly poor and nonpoor children suffered from asthma. For non-Hispanic whites these rates were sharply lower.[12] The family was devastated by Auntie Mary's death, and when Trelise was diagnosed, Brian's concern led him to investigate numerous possible causes. He thought diet might have had something to do with it, because he had heard that too much fried food brought on asthma. Trelise's doctor informed him otherwise.

Continuing his spontaneous research, Brian learned that asthma disproportionately afflicts black children, who also are more likely to die from it. From these concerns, he developed a four-pronged strategy to prevent Trelise from experiencing a fatal attack. First, he kept their house spotless and dust free. To accomplish this, he got up early every morning to dust the furniture, wipe the cabinets, and sweep the linoleum floors throughout the house. Second, he banned smoking in the house or around Trelise. His mother, a smoker, wanted to know if he was scapegoating her. Brian said no, that he just wanted to keep his daughter clear of all possible irritants. Third, Brian always had Trelise's medicine on hand and made sure she knew how to use it in his absence. Finally, he watched over his daughter—and worried some more. "I don't like for her to be bouncing on the bed or running outside. I just worry. I think, 'If I'm not watching her all the time, then the time when I'm not there, that's when it's [a deadly asthma attack] gonna happen." So, he watched her and watched her, and he felt guilty every time he had to go to work or run errands. From his perspective, he couldn't "change the whole environment"; the solutions he devised were the only ones in his control.

Many fathers, like Brian, place their children's needs above their own. Brian himself rarely visited a physician. Lack of insurance and busy work schedules discourage working fathers from seeking health care. Additionally, many fathers just do not accept that doctors can "fix" most of their ailments. According to one, "If I'm tired, and believe me I'm always tired, that just mean I need more sleep. If I'm losing weight, like I did last year, then that just mean I need to eat more, take better care of myself. This stuff is common sense."

But these fathers are not cavalier, nor do they accept folk remedies, when the subject is their children's well-being. They want the best and most professional medical care for them. Nonetheless, in their isolation, they struggle to understand diagnoses and treatments, especially with respect to lead poisoning. In 2000, approximately twenty thousand children in Illinois showed hazardous lead levels.[13] Although the rates of lead poisoning for children in Illinois have been declining steadily, in 2008, East St. Louis zip codes remained high-risk areas contributing to hazardous lead levels among children.[14] The father of one child who had been exposed to toxicity said, "I'm not sure that there's anything wrong with him. They got to show exactly what's wrong, 'cause I just don't see it. . . . She [his son's teacher] told me I need to move to another house because of the lead thing . . . but I told her I can't do it. Then what? I don't love my son? I love my son, but I don't know what to do. Where do you move in East St. Louis that ain't just like the place you just moved from?"

Another father was also frustrated with his living arrangement: "I wish I could just pack up, move my kids to another city, another state—but—and you know I'm embarrassed to say this— but I can barely pack a bag full of groceries at the supermarket. I don't know where I'm gonna get the money to move out."

The limitations of the options of the fathers I spoke to led some to haphazard means to protect their children from continued poisoning. One father, who assumed his son had been poisoned by the many layers of old paint that were once peeling from the walls of his bedroom, brought his son's bed into his own bedroom. "So he's not in the room where the problem is," the dad said. He explained, "[When possible,] I let him stay with his grandmamma." If the culprit was the paint, the substance was never professionally removed, and it was likely still present throughout other parts of the house.

Many fathers are not quite sure specifically how or why their children have contracted lead poisoning. Still, they feel that their watchful eyes can help to prevent the illness. As one put it, "I just watch him so that he don't get into anything that may make him sick."

East St. Louis landlords in this city are notoriously absentee and slow to address issues of health and safety in their rental properties. Many of the renters I interviewed were reluctant to talk openly because they feared retaliatory eviction notices. "It just seems like we stuck sometime. Can't do right by our loved ones," said one with evident frustration.

Unquestionably, the city's environment as a whole is hostile to children's health. Many fathers have some understanding of the combined consequences of toxins, pollutants, and diminished public services but have resigned to further educating themselves the hard way—after an injury or an illness has already taken hold. The lack of resources also drives feelings of inadequacy about protecting their sons and daughters from health hazards. One father offered an analogy: "It's like all I can do is put a Band-Aid on his [son's] hurt. That takes care of the scar, but there's a whole 'nother sickness inside that I can't see to do nothin' about. You know . . . the Band-Aid just ain't enough, but it's all I got to work with."

A real prospect for homeownership, with a viable equity interest, might begin to alleviate problems such as lead paint. But the decrepit state of the East St. Louis housing has militated against that. Even owned houses—mostly handed down by parents—are in constant need of repair. Whether for rent or for mortgage payments, little is left from paychecks below a living wage (or no paychecks) for a fix-up budget. In nearby predominantly white towns like Edwardsville and Glen Carbon, families generally pay for major repairs and remodeling with special insurance, remodeling loans, credit lines, or cash. These are beyond the reach of the vast majority of East St. Louisans. Of the twenty-nine fathers discussed in this chapter, only three had bank accounts; others stored money "around the house" or in their "back pockets," if they weren't immediately spending it on bills, food, other essentials, and minor wants.

Troy Penelton, father of eight-year-old Justin, was standing next to a stack of mismatched roofing tiles when we first met.

He planned to replace the roof on the home he and his sister had rented for the past three years. The roof was aged and long over-due for repair. On rainy days, the floors of the house were scat-tered with pails and buckets. This was the family's attempt to catch the drips of water that splattered from the brown-stained ceiling. The landlord of the property was rarely available by phone and seldom visited his many properties in the area. He was earning substantial income from renting to Section 8 ten-ants, those below poverty level and receiving housing assistance from the federal government; property owners maximized their profits by choosing not to invest in upkeep. Renters often had to fix broken pipes, furnaces, and toilets themselves.

Troy was one of the fortunate ones, in the sense that at least his landlord did not complain when the accounted costs of minor fix-ups were deducted from monthly rent checks. Many tenants in this city have found this compromise a workable solution for small projects, such as a leaky toilet or sink. But it is hardly acceptable for more costly repairs, such as a broken furnace, a decayed roof, or leaking water pipes. Sometimes, these expen-sive projects require more imaginative solutions.

Troy's collection of roofing supplies and materials included gifts from neighbors. However, some were also plundered from active construction sites located in the St. Louis metropoli-tan area. That was how he replaced broken cabinets and pipes. When he wanted his son to have an enclosed space for playing in the yard, that was how he got the wire fencing and posts. This strategy of maintaining a livable space was a high-risk one: if he was caught stealing, it would not be his first arrest. Six years ago, he was arrested for lifting three furnaces from a newly built apartment community near Edwardsville. His black market in construction materials was lucrative, given the number of other

East St. Louisans in similar straits. This "hustling" business kept change in his pocket, though admittedly not the best way to make a living, especially since he was the primary caretaker of his son and a father figure to his sister's children. "I would hate to go to the pen because of what I do," he offered, "but there really . . . if you got people to look after, then sometimes you got to sacrifice yourself for them. . . . You just hope that they understand if something happens."

Other fathers I spoke with—several of whom had purchased appliances and other items from Troy—agreed. Manny Paul explained, "Well, if you wait for the landlord to come around, then you may as well forget that. You S.O.L. You better figure out a way to fix that roof yourself, or your children are just gonna get wet. You better figure out a way to do it yourself, 'cause your rent check don't buy nothin' from the landlord. That's just a fact."

• • •

When it comes to neighborhood cleanup, sometimes you just have to take matters in your own hands; as they say on the streets, "If the mayor won't do it, then I will." Galen, a father of three, decided to do something about the empty house next door to the home he shared with his aunt Merle. The house had stood abandoned for years, and phone calls to the city and the county had failed to get it razed. A couple of winters ago, a pack of dogs had taken to the spot. They went in and out through the missing front door and nibbled on the bits of food they scavenged from the garbage dumped on the property lawn. These dogs terrified neighborhood children and adults. Not long ago, across the river in St. Louis, Missouri's "black side" of town, a black child had been mauled to death by loose hounds such as these.

Ownerless dogs are a common problem in East St. Louis.

Catching them is a costly service, and the city no longer has the funds to undertake it in earnest. In St. Louis, it was the public killing of a child by wild dogs and the subsequent media attention that moved the county and city to confront the menace seriously—at least, these are the thoughts of many residents. The men I spoke with in East St. Louis thought that a similar scenario would need to occur in this city before the problem could be adequately addressed.

Like so many others, Galen was left on his own to determine a solution. He was one of two adult men who lived on his street, and sometimes the older women around here looked to him for protection. Early one Saturday morning, he got out of bed, grabbed his handgun and some ammunition, and headed toward the old house. Taking aim through a busted front window, he shot at as many of the dogs as possible while they slept. At least two escaped. (As if this were not enough, the dogs did not live alone. Mice scurried about the tall grass and the bags of trash as he made his way into the house to assess his work.) Galen told his young children to stay home and play until he could make sure that these dogs were no longer a worry.

More recently, Auntie, who always had her eyes to the window, noticed teenagers heading into the dilapidated structure. She was sure that this was the beginning of a crack house and asked her nephew to investigate. What he found instead was what appeared to be a space where young people sat, smoked, drank, and had sex. Empty cans of beer, wine bottles, and an old, brown-stained, worn mattress lay on the floor of what seemed to be the former dining area. Galen and his Auntie surmised that these rendezvous were simply preludes to collective drug use and dealings. Galen contacted the city, hoping that the owner of the property could be forced to clean it up.

He posted keep-out signs on the windows and, with the help of a neighbor, boarded up the doors. His next step was simply to tear the structure down himself, board by board. He said, "I think this is the difference between living here and living somewhere else like where white people live. You got to worry about the bad element. Your children count on you to protect them from this shit. If you don't watch for it, it'll be in your backyard."

Organized neighborhood cleanups and beautification projects temporarily improve the lawns and streets for children's play. Some arrange work schedules so that they can safely walk their children to and from school. Mostly, though, men in this city say that they generally act alone to protect their families. According to Mark Neil, "You can't really count on no one really . . . least not the city. They can't protect you from some of the things that's out here. You just got to do it yourself."

Robert Mooney summarized the thoughts of many others: "If you want something done around here, you got to do it yourself. Don't wait around for nobody. A man can't wait for somebody else to protect his kids and his family; he got to move on that his own self."

· · ·

Traveling west on Interstate 64, you will come to the Third Street exit into East St. Louis just before you cross the Mississippi River and move onto Missouri soil. From the exit, you can make one of two choices. The right turn leads straight to the Casino Queen riverboat and its waterfront hotel. It is by far the easiest place to get to in the city, with directing signs in full view, no stop signs or traffic lights to hold you up, and well-maintained street surfaces and overhead lighting. Workers, gamblers, and hotel guests take that convenient path to the city's second-largest employer. Paid security guards protect the spacious parking lot and walkway.

The locals comment on how all other traffic yields to the vehicles arriving at or leaving the casino. The exit leads to a three-way intersection with only two stop signs. Those leaving the downtown area must stop before they exit; those entering the downtown area must stop before they enter. But coming or going, casino patrons have no stops or yields. Some say the road signs are placed in this manner so that out-of-towners will not be afraid to visit the casino. Lore has it that white people especially fear that driving and hesitating anywhere in East St. Louis will invite a carjacking, rape, or murder. They say whites dread lawless, out-of-work black males who sit twiddling their thumbs waiting for an opportunity for easy gain. But these observations are not reserved for outsider gamblers. Residents say even white drivers who work in the city barely obey traffic signals. "They run stop signs, they run lights, they speed through here," all because they fear victimization by marauding black criminals— men looking for easy money—too lazy to work for wages.

The danger of the streets is commonly associated with dark-skinned, male gangs who presumably rob men of wallets, rape women and girls, and carjack unsuspecting drivers. But this danger has a much more literal meaning in East St. Louis: nonfunctioning stoplights, missing street signs, and vehicular traffic create hazards to city pedestrians and children, who often find their games rolling onto avenues and thoroughfares. Simply walking from here to there is a hazard in this town.

Though this view may seem merely anecdotal, the hard numbers confirm it. St. Clair County ranked in the top ten Illinois counties for traffic fatalities in 2006. The motor-vehicle fatality rate in East St. Louis that year was twice that of the state as a whole. "Don't nobody care about us gettin' hit by no car.... If they cared, then they wouldn't let it happen. The police could put a stop to it if they wanted to." Many men and women with whom I spoke felt that the city invested more in visiting gamblers than in its own citizens. According to one woman, "They do all this protection for gamblers carrying on, and that kind of policing is paid for by us tax payers, ... but they don't want to do anything to guarantee us some jobs. Hell, we can't even get the police to protect us, the people who maintain the city." Several police officers privately agreed. The municipal funds aren't there for effectively protecting the people. "Whereas now, you know, we need to have about twenty, twenty-four cars on the street at one time, we only have six," one cop said.[15]

The biggest complaints about the police here is that they are too slow to act, not around when needed, and do not prevent or solve crimes. Pedestrians here experience greater danger than in Belleville, Edwardsville, and Fairview Heights. Raymond Moore, whose daughter suffered minor injuries from a hit-and-run while riding her bike to school, explained what he believes is the reason for this: "Don't nobody care about the safety of the children here, or anybody. It's like the people that be living here ain't important." Residents juxtapose the police protection of tourists against declining local services, low wages, and diminishing jobs. Considered all together, these socioeconomic aspects of East St. Louis mean that people here matter very little to the world outside.

I would argue that black parents in the United States, today and in the past, have had to work hard to protect their children. The elements that challenge them may be experienced by parents of other demographic groups; for example, children's desire for independence and stranger predators are perils that cross racial and class divisions. But black parents are also confronted by issues of race that place their children in particular danger from white residents who feel threatened and from police officers who abuse their authority. My father was very strict with his children. He told us not to cut across the neighbor's yards, not to pick fruit from anyone's tree, not to go into friends' homes, and to be home before sunset. On the surface, it seemed that he was only teaching us good manners and how to respect the property of others. However, it was actually much more than this. He was protecting us from the dangers he had experienced and had observed as a sharecropper's son in North Carolina. Black children, we would learn, are not allowed to do the same things that many white children may take for granted. Whites in general and authorities in particular would not always act to protect black children, and so as a parent, in my father's mind, it was his job to do this duty overtime.

In East St. Louis, when it comes to the safety of children, even parents' overtime often isn't enough.

CHAPTER SEVEN

The Cost of Abandonment

The stories of African Americans in southwestern Illinois are contained in the history of my own family. My maternal great-grandfather settled in Pin Oak, a small rural community made up of mostly black farm families. His family's "Lewis Farm" grew tomatoes for the Brooks Ketchup company, located just a few miles west in Collinsville, a suburb of the St. Louis metropolitan area.

As agricultural life grew more difficult and greater educational and economic opportunities were evident in larger towns and cities, the Lewises did what so many African American families did during the early decades of the twentieth century: they migrated from agricultural to urban places. Historians have meticulously documented these mass moves. Many black families in Tennessee and Alabama settled in Chicago, Detroit, St. Louis, and Indianapolis. But while some moved to swelling inner-city neighborhoods, others found their way to smaller cities and suburbs outside the boundaries of these central cities. In these places, wage labor opportunities and education were superior to those in rural areas.[1]

The favorite destination of my mother's family, in the early twentieth century, was southwestern Illinois; jobs loomed in and around East St. Louis. Grandpa Lewis worked at Woodlawn Cemetery and as a cook at Catalina Café in Edwardsville. He also informally negotiated contracts with white families to haul away garbage and ash residues from their coal furnaces. He was exceptionally resourceful and successful. But the independence fostered by these new jobs did not ultimately eradicate unemployment, residential segregation, and social discrimination for many African Americans. Today, in these metropolitan-area small cities, African Americans are more likely than whites to live in poverty, to experience a high rate of school dropouts, and to be incarcerated. At a later point in the twenty-first century, a clear majority of African Americans will be living in the suburbs, not in either rural areas or inner cities. Yet, despite the efforts of my great-grandfather's generation to make a better life, the outcomes for subsequent generations have been mixed, to say the least.

• • •

In East St. Louis, African Americans have never known full employment, in the sense that racialized hiring patterns have funneled them to the lowest-paying, dirtiest, and most dangerous jobs. However, men and women who arrived before and during World War II unquestionably had greater economic chances than those who followed. In the 1950s, industry leaders began to merge, pack up, and move elsewhere. Their disinvestment from the region coincided with many African Americans' solid movement into the working class as they began moving into decent housing and sending their children to majority white schools with good resources and better records of academic success.

Left behind was a city with a shell of an infrastructure and a debt from which it has yet to recover. Left behind was a community of working-class black families whose financial limitations, experiences with housing and loan discrimination, and desire to live in and contribute to a place managed by black people tied them to a city that had become their own at precisely the moment when that status was transforming from a boon to a burden.

To be working-class and African American in America's suburban heartland destines workers and their families to be physically isolated from many jobs and from many cultural and life opportunities. It guarantees strain on health and kin networks as men, women, adult siblings, and grandparents test the boundaries of their relationships and sometimes exhaust them in the small city spaces that they share. It requires parents to work overtime to shield and safeguard their boys and girls from the concentrated dangers of violence, pollutants, and a crumbling municipal infrastructure. It limits the job opportunities that men and women have and the chances of upward mobility for themselves or their children. It ensures that those fortunate to have a steady job must wait every two weeks for a paycheck that does not cover the extraordinary cost of fuel, taxes, and groceries that plagues distressed and abandoned places. And it requires mothers and fathers to make choices about work, earnings, and the care of others that often compromise their own welfare, safety, and freedoms. Overall, the experiences of those in East St. Louis tell us that there is nothing particularly romantic about the deprivations of working-class suburban life in this space or place, especially for those at the outermost socioeconomic margins.

East St. Louisans occupy a city bereft of major industries, family-oriented leisure facilities, clean air, reasonably priced shopping outlets, quality schools, and safe and affordable housing. The most glaring lack is decent employment. "There ain't really no jobs here," Nathan Grey, thirty-five, told me, in what has become a local idiom. Old people murmur it. Middle-aged people know it. And young children recite it.

The people described in this book espoused the same hopes, dreams, and fears as their counterparts in white suburbia. The difference is that in East St. Louis, residents must cobble hopes and dreams together from aberrant everyday circumstances.

. . .

Government agencies and nonprofits have no shortage of proposals to improve human services. These range from testing lead levels in children's blood, to servicing invalids with home health care, to planting gardens and trees. A focus group of senior citizens who met weekly at Mt. Zion Baptist Church on Bond Avenue during my time in East St. Louis were suspicious of the programs of outsiders. The University of Illinois's Seed and Weed Project, for example, brought undergraduate students to East St. Louis to assist residents in beautifying parks and public spaces. A beautification project does not "pay our light bill," Chester Mays said. "But somebody's getting paid from those trees—it sure enough isn't me or none of us!" The consensus was that while the college students meant well, projects and grants tend to earn funding and prestige for those who manage them.

The George W. Bush presidency promoted the ideal of faith-based good works. In East St. Louis, the Morning Star Baptist Church was given a grant to build a banquet facility and day care, from which twenty jobs were created. The Shining Light

Baptist Church sponsored after-school help for children and computer training. Other church initiatives supported GED preparation for adults. Still others offered GED training and services. But deeply rooted socioeconomic problems that are products of government policies cannot be effectively addressed only through those programs.

For East St. Louisans, the struggle of daily life is a primal one, often coming down to the basics of staying warm in the winter and cool in the summer. As this book was being completed, the hallmarks of suburban living—space, peace and quiet, backyards, tall trees, single-family homes, two cars and a garage, leisure time, and upward mobility—were being threatened by a global economic crisis. But working-class suburbanites in East St. Louis have been feeling the pinch for a long time.

If the decline of this once-designated "All-American City" tells us anything, it is that men and women require living-wage jobs if they are expected to feed and clothe their children without entering illegal trades. Older women and men require a lifetime of quality, affordable health care if they are expected to maintain their own health and contribute to the kin networks and communities necessary in retirement years. Young men and women need an educational structure that prepares them for college-level training and available jobs. Without fixes of these problems at the root level, the spiral of distress and abandonment will continue.

Epilogue

Obama and East St. Louis

The historic election of Barack Obama, cause for euphoria throughout the American black community, had special poignance in Illinois. Previously, the state of Lincoln had produced the first African American elected to Congress in the twentieth century and two of the century's three black senators (Obama included). The Obama phenomenon simultaneously served as a potent role model for black youth and formidable proof that racial barriers cannot prevent African Americans from succeeding.

Yet, other contemporary developments are reminders that the story of American race relations will remain fraught and complex. On the eve of Obama's inauguration in January 2009, for example, the U.S. Supreme Court ruled that evidence gathered from an unlawful arrest based on faulty police record keeping may be used against a criminal defendant. In the metropolitan region centered by St. Louis, Missouri, where black residents complain of police harassment, the decision has had ominous implications.[1] In Oakland, California, in early 2009, the maelstrom surrounding the New Year's Day shooting death of an unarmed black youth by a white transit police officer graphically demonstrated the tense relationship that has persisted between black urban communities and policing agencies around the nation.[2]

Even after filtering out race—or at least viewing African Americans as the proverbial "canaries in the coal mine"—the economic crisis Obama inherited has had grim implications for the entire body politic. Business reporter Steven Greenhouse put his finger on a broad trend of the "decline in the status and treatment of American workers—white-collar and blue-collar workers, middle-class and low-end workers—that began nearly three decades ago, gradually gathered momentum, and hit with full force soon after the turn of this century. A profound shift has left a broad swath of the American workforce on a lower plane than in decades past, with health coverage, pension benefits, job security, workloads, stress levels, and often wages growing worse for millions of workers."[3] More recent symptoms of the great recession, such as the record levels of mortgage foreclosures and the overall devastated housing market, have known no class or income boundaries.

Against that backdrop, Obama's entry to the Oval Office seemed eerily analogous to the rise of black mayors in industrial hubs like East St. Louis, weakened by falling tax revenues, financial bankruptcy, declining infrastructure, and the dissolute practices of exiting white administrations. The disaster in New Orleans in the wake of Hurricane Katrina and the collapse of the Interstate 35 bridge over the Mississippi River in Minnesota combined to symbolize the treacherous deterioration of the nation's bridges, dams, levees, public transportation, and drinking water systems. (In a recent report, the American Society of Civil Engineers gave the nation's infrastructure a grade of D.)[4] The country at large has been feeling the pain long felt by East

St. Louis, where the Federal Emergency Management Authority (FEMA) has decertified the seventy-year-old levees, which have not been able to keep the overflowing Mississippi waters and heavy rains from annually flooding hundreds of area homes. (In 2006, the state gave East St. Louis access to grants to bolster its emergency-planning efforts, but the funding was contingent on the accreditation of a municipality's emergency services and disaster agencies—a hurdle this municipality could not clear.)[5]

In the wake of widespread corporate malfeasance and government irresponsibility, there was also general skepticism in East St. Louis that Obama's multi-billion-dollar economic-recovery plan would benefit the right people and entities. In 2009, the recently elected mayor Alvin Parks spoke hopefully of an alignment of national and state elected officials with some interest in and connection to East St. Louis.[6] These officials included the two Democratic senators representing Illinois: Richard Durbin, an East St. Louis native, and Roland Burris, Obama's controversially appointed successor. Will this alignment add up to anything more than the previous chapters of stops and starts in development, reform, and cleanup activities led by developers, faith-based organizations, politicians, and universities external to the city?

Mayor Parks touted the city's location. "The same thing that made this city the transportation and industrial center is what will bring it back to prosperity."[7] To be sure, some regional planners and land speculators have perceived potential in East St. Louis for upscale housing, recreation, and tourism. Meanwhile, however, the 2008–9 economic slump contributed to an expected drop in profits for the Casino Queen, the tourism model's biggest existing revenue generator. A new state smoking ban inhibited the Queen's ability to compete with neighboring Missouri casinos.

Some suggest that a significant portion of Casino Queen revenues have not been directed at improving city infrastructure because they are being used to support oversized police and fire departments. The city cannot afford to replace equipment or purchase fire trucks or police cars. However, police and firefighters were, at the time of this study, still operating at personnel levels similar to those dating from when the city boasted a population of eighty thousand rather than adjusting to the current thirty thousand. The heated disagreements over solutions—between unions and city officials and among city officials themselves—played out while the fire department building itself, ironically, remained boarded up, with fire trucks parked along the curb behind the Municipal Building. The department had no ladder truck, and consequently, Mayor Parks said, "When we have a fire in a tall building, then we've got to call St. Louis, Missouri, to help us put out the fire."[8]

In July 2010, Mayor Parks announced that the city was shrinking its police force by 30 percent, from sixty-two to fifty-three officers. "The blood is on your hands," officer Michael Hubbard yelled in response to the mayor's public announcement. He was one of many concerned about what the cuts would mean for safety in the city.[9]

Real-estate taxes have continued to be the steepest in the state of Illinois, and foreclosure rates have been high. The East St. Louis population is steadily declining. If current trends continue, it may be below twenty-five thousand within the next few years. For residents, their numerical decrease jeopardizes the amount of money the city receives from the state and federal governments as well as its status *as* a city. Its numbers are moving it closer to the category of "village."

It must be added that the city government (at the writing of this book) was scarred by familiar allegations of nepotism and corruption. The mayor's sister, as an example, was his executive assistant. The mayor's brother-in-law, as another, directed emergency planning. On March 26, 2009, the FBI raided East St. Louis City Hall offices to investigate charges of liquor license violations. In August of that year, the former deputy liquor commissioner Walter Dortez Hill was indicted on federal charges of extortion, "including seeking cash, liquor, and sexual favors" from East St. Louis liquor license holders.[10]

At the time of his appointment, the current city manager, Robert Betts, was the sixth city manager in sixteen months. In September 2009, the city's former financial oversight director, Ken Gearheat, publicly declared that the city was broke and in a $2.7 million deficit, because city leaders, in addition to managing finances poorly, had "refused to rid themselves of the culture of corruption and entitlement that are so deeply inbred in city government."[11] Sadly, at the same time, the city had recently laid off fourteen employees, including eleven firefighters, and had instituted furloughs for nonunion employees—part of an effort to balance the budget before the end of the fiscal year.[12] Yet, despite the charges of nepotism and corruption, one would be hard pressed to find an East St. Louis city administrator or official who did not express a genuine personal interest in bettering the city to which he or she was professionally obligated.

The truth is often difficult. And the truth is that, as a nation, we have neglected the welfare and potential of large segments of our population. Worse, we have privileged certain places over others and left behind our most vulnerable. Still, the circumstances of East St. Louis provide us an opportunity to reconsider our core values and direct our attention to building equity and creating a just America.

The problems of East St. Louis are national ones and warrant both a state and national response. Given the depth of the city's social and structural problems along with the imminent threat of its loss of city status, East St. Louis has increasingly begun debating the option of annexation by a richer adjacent suburb. But annexing East St. Louis also means absorbing its problems, and the prospects of this solution may be slim. Nonetheless, its consideration may lead to discussion of the responsibility of regions for municipalities. Suburbs are decentralized municipalities. As such, each is responsible for addressing its own set of ills. Regional governance and strategic planning involving the leveraging of the combined resources of more affluent communities seem certain to emerge as an issue for Obama policy makers managing the economic recovery.

Recovery, though, remains distant for many people across the nation. In April 2010, there were 5.5 job seekers for every job opening in the United States,[13] but unemployment has not been evenly experienced across all races and ethnicities. At the close of 2009, 16 percent of African Americans were unemployed compared with 13 percent of Hispanics and 9 percent of whites. In fact, in the year prior, the unemployment rate for black Americans had risen much faster than that of either of these other demographic groups, and African Americans were three times as likely to live in poverty. In terms of wealth, African Americans remain behind whites, possessing ten cents of net worth for every dollar held by whites. In East St. Louis, one-half of working age adults remain absent from the paid workforce.

Recovery for many suburbs is equally distant. Not all suburbs are experiencing distress, just as not all suburbanites are living with severe hardship. Some places are flourishing, while others, like East St. Louis, are in deep despair. In the view of several board members of United for a Fair Economy, such disparity demands aggressive and targeted policies. I agree. Federal and state governments, they argue, must privilege those communities and populations in greatest need. Targeted national policies must create jobs, and they must produce living-wage job opportunities. Funded job initiatives should be strictly tracked to ensure that funds are awarded to and directed toward those critical places and people. Targeted policies must emphasize the rebuilding of devastated city infrastructures and provide for improved roads, schools, and other public spaces. Targeted policies must also immediately facilitate the ability of families in working-class poor cities to maintain quality housing and increase their wealth.[14] Targeted policies should support the development of regional planning in which wealthier municipalities share resources to create a more equitable metro area.

According to recent news reports, the nation is experiencing an improved domestic economy and is slowly rising from its latest recession. The consensus of presidential watchers is that President Obama's ability to sustain his popularity level will depend largely on the success of his policies in Iraq and Afghanistan. His domestic achievements will be measured by the rebound of national employment numbers and the overhaul of the banking and credit systems. Lurking mostly out of sight, as they have been for the last half century, are abandoned places like East St. Louis, Illinois. Their fate, and that of their residents, will go a long way toward determining the depth of the promise of change from the first African American occupant of the Oval Office. The question, though, is not whether we are able to address the marked poverty in our new suburbia. Rather, it is whether we have the will.

NOTES

PROLOGUE

1. There is a popular assumption that inner-ring or first suburbs are homogenous. However, see Bernadette Hanlon, "A Typology of Inner-Ring Suburbs: Class, Race, and Ethnicity in U.S. Suburbia," *City & Community* 8, no. 3 (2009): 221–46, for a detailed discussion of types of suburbs. Hanlon analyzes a sample of 1,742 inner-ring suburbs nationwide and identifies five different types: vulnerable, ethnic, lower-income and mixed, old, and middle-class—all differentiated by race, ethnicity, and class composition. The poor, minority, working-class populations are "often excluded from elite suburbs close to and well beyond the city, and segregated into specific inner-ring suburbs" (242). East St. Louis is a "vulnerable" suburb.

2. "Working class" is arguably the category that is best applied to the paid labor of the majority of American men and women. According to Michael Zweig, "class" is a category related to power, not income. It is determined by how "the person got the income, what role he or she plays in society, how he or she is connected to the power grid of class relations." For Zweig, working-class workers are "skilled and unskilled, in manufacturing and in services, men and women of all races, nationalities, religions. They drive trucks, write routine com-

puter code, operate machinery, wait tables, sort and deliver the mail, work on assembly lines, stand all day as bank tellers, perform thousands of jobs in every sector of the economy. For all their differences, working class people share a common place in production, where they have relatively little control over the pace or content of their work, and aren't anybody's boss" (Zweig, *The Working Class Majority: America's Best Kept Secret* [Ithaca, NY: ILR Press, 2001], 3).

Using this standard, we find that the majority of the U.S. working population, especially in "new suburbia," have historically been and continue to be part of the working class. But "working class" is not a monolithic categorization. Some workers and their families are better economically situated than others within this category. Those employed in heavy-manufacturing industries, such as Granite City Steel or American Steel, for example, both located in nearby Granite City, are likely to receive greater pay and benefits than those working as cashiers for the East St. Louis Walgreens store or as delivery drivers for Domino's Pizza. The former are likely to earn compensation that often characterizes the middle class, while the latter tend to earn lower wages, often no more than minimum wage.

3. Nell Irvin Painter, *Exodusters: Black Migration to Kansas after Reconstruction* (New York: Knopf, 1976); Bryan M. Jack, *The St. Louis African American Community and the Exodusters* (Columbia: University of Missouri Press, 2007); Charles L. Lumpkins, *American Pogrom: The East St. Louis Race Riot and Black Politics* (Athens, OH: Ohio University Press, 2008); and Jack S. Blocker, *A Little More Freedom: African Americans Enter the Urban Midwest, 1860–1930* (Columbus: Ohio State University Press, 2008).

4. Carole Marks, *Farewell—We're Good and Gone: The Great Black Migration* (Bloomington: Indiana University Press, 1989); James R. Grossman, *Land of Hope: Chicago, Black Southerners, and the Great Migration* (Chicago: University of Chicago Press, 1989); Blocker, *A Little More Freedom;* James W. Loewen, *Sundown Towns: A Hidden Dimension of American Racism* (New York: Simon and Schuster, 2005); Elliott M. Rudwick, *Race Riot at East St. Louis, July 2, 1917,* Illini ed. (Chicago: University of Illinois Press, 1982); William M. Tuttle, *Race Riot: Chicago in the Red Summer of 1919*

(New York: Atheneum, 1970); Lumpkins, *American Pogrom;* and Malcolm McLaughlin, *Power, Community, and Racial Killing in East St. Louis* (New York: Palgrave Macmillan, 2005).

5. For other works that demonstrate these dynamics, see, for example, Camille Charles Zubrinsky, "Socioeconomic Status and Segregation: African Americans, Hispanics, and Asians in Los Angeles," in *Problem of the Century: Racial Stratification into the United States,* ed. Elijah Anderson and Doug Massey (New York: Russell Sage, 2001), 271–89; Reynolds Farley, *The New American Reality: How We Are, How We Got There, Where We Are Going* (New York: Russell Sage, 1996); William E. Jackson III, "Discrimination in Mortgage Lending Markets as Rational Economic Behavior: Theory, Evidence, and Public Policy," in *African Americans and the New Policy Consensus: Retreat of the Liberal State,* ed. Marilyn Lasley and Melanie Jackson (Westport, CT: Greenwood Press, 1994), 157–78; John R. Logan, "Ethnic Diversity Grows, Neighborhood Integration Lags Behind," American Communities Project, Brown University, www.s4.brown.edu/cen2000/report.html (accessed November 1, 2009); and Joe T. Darden, "Residential Apartheid American Style," in *The Black Metropolis in the Twentieth Century: Race, Power, and Politics of Place,* ed. Robert D. Bullard (Lanham, MD: Rowman and Littlefield Publishers, 2007), 67–86.

6. Robert D. Bullard and Beverly Wright, in *Race, Place, and Environmental Justice after Hurricane Katrina: Struggles to Reclaim, Rebuild, and Revitalize New Orleans and the Gulf Coast,* provide substantial evidence of discriminatory practices. For example, the National Fair Housing Alliance released a report documenting high rates of housing discrimination against African Americans (180); some predominantly white Louisiana parishes adopted emergency ordinances that limited the number of families that could reside in mobile parks and took other actions to keep African Americans from settling temporarily or otherwise near their property following the storm (180–81). Also, the government suspended the Davis-Bacon Act of 1931, which required businesses with federal contracts to pay the average wages in the region and relaxed federal rules that required federal contractors to hire only properly documented workers. Consequently, tensions rose between African

Americans and Latino immigrant workers, though both groups earned less than minimum wage under these waived rules (181). Even under the Federal Emergency Management Agency, African American business owners were less likely to receive loans, and those who received loans received smaller amounts on average than white business owners (181).

7. ". . . Why East St. Louis Needs to Be a Demonstration City," Public Administration and Metropolitan Affairs, Southern Illinois University–Edwardsville, Illinois, January 1967, an advisory and consultant study: Report No. AC-10, 39; Hubert O. Williams, "The Central City Blight Study," Public Administration and Metropolitan Affairs Program, Southern Illinois University–Edwardsville, Illinois, October 19, 1967; Jane Altes, "Employment and Unemployment in East St. Louis," Public Administration and Metropolitan Affairs Program, Southern Illinois University–Edwardsville, Illinois, 1964.

8. ". . . Why East St. Louis Needs to Be a Demonstration City"; U.S. Bureau of the Census, 1960 *Census of Population and Housing*.

9. Robert Mendelson, "Housing: An East St. Louis Challenge!" Public Administration and Metropolitan Affairs Program, Southern Illinois University–Edwardsville, Illinois, 1966.

10. See Alexandra K. Murphy, "The Suburban Ghetto: The Legacy of Herbert Gans in Understanding the Experience of Poverty in Recently Impoverished Suburbs," *City and Community* 6, no. 1 (2007): 21–37; Herbert J. Gans, *The Levittowners: Ways of Life and Politics in a New Suburban Community* (New York: Columbia University Press, 1967); Thomas M. Stanback Jr., *The New Suburbanization: Challenge to the Central City* (Boulder, CO: Westview Press, 1991); Kevin M. Kruse, and Thomas J. Sugrue, eds., *The New Suburban History* (Chicago: University of Chicago Press, 2006).

11. Kenneth T. Jackson, *Crabgrass Frontier: The Suburbanization of the United States* (New York: Oxford University Press, 1985), 6.

12. Sylvia Fleis Fava, "Suburbanism as a Way of Life," *American Sociological Review* 21 (February 1956): 34–37.

13. Gans, *The Levittowners*. Murphy, in "The Suburban Ghetto," shows how suburbs are perceived as homogenous and affluent. Jack-

son, in *Crabgrass Frontier,* discusses the physical division between spaces associated with work and leisure time. Fave, in "Suburbanism as a Way of Life," highlights suburbia as a lifestyle with a unique cultural connotation.

14. Murphy, "The Suburban Ghetto"; Maria Kefalas, *Working-Class Heroes: Protecting Home, Community, and Nation in a Chicago Neighborhood* (Berkeley: University of California Press, 2003); Andrew Weise, *Places of Their Own: African American Suburbanization in the Twentieth Century* (Chicago: University of Chicago Press, 2004).

15. Weise, *Places of Their Own, 5.*

16. Kenneth Kusmer, "African Americans in the City since World War II: From the Industrial to the Post-Industrial Era," *Journal of Urban History* 21 (1995): 458–504.

17. Mark J. Stern, "Poverty and Family Composition since 1940," in *The Underclass Debate: Views from History,* ed. Michael B. Katz (Princeton, NJ: Princeton University Press, 1993), 220–53.

18. J.L. Hochschild, *Facing Up to the American Dream: Race, Class, and the Soul of the Nation* (Princeton, NJ: Princeton University Press, 1995); Dalton Conley, *Being Black, Living in the Red* (Berkeley: University of California Press, 1999); Peter Blau and O.D. Duncan, *The American Occupational Structure* (New York: Free Press, 1967).

19. Childtrends Data Bank, "Estimated Life Expectancy of Newborns by Race and Gender (in Years), Selected Years, 1970–2004," www.childtrendsdatabank.org/tables/78_table_1.htm; National Center for Education Statistics, *Status and Trends in the Education of Race and Ethnic Minorities,* figure 26.1: Percentage of Adults Ages 25 and Over with Bachelor's Degree or Higher in Their Highest Level of Education Attainment by Race/Ethnicity: Selected Years, 1990–2005, http://nces.ed.gov/pubs2007/minoritytrends/figures/figure_26_1.asp, and figure 17, Percentage of 16- to 24-Year-Olds Who Were High School Status Dropouts, by Race/Ethnicity: 1989–2005, http://nces.edu.gov/pubs2007/minoritytrends/figures/figure_17.asp.

20. David Schwartzman, *Black Unemployment: Part of Unskilled Unemployment* (London: Greenwood, 1997).

21. Barry Bluestone and Bennett Harrison, *The Deindustrialization*

of America: Plant Closings, Community Abandonment, and the Dismantling of Basic Industry (New York: Basic Books, 1982), 6.

22. Ibid., 25.

23. The U.S. Bureau of Labor Statistics (www.bls.gov) defines a "mass layoff" as that which affects fifty or more employees, regardless of the duration of the layoff.

24. U.S. Department of Labor, Bureau of Labor Statistics, News, "Mass Layoffs in October 2003," USDL 03-762, 1, Washington DC. Also available at www.bls.gov/news.release/archives/mmls_1126203.pdf (accessed February 5, 2011).

25. This summary of seasonally adjusted mass layoff totals for 2007–10 is provided in U.S. Department of Labor, Bureau of Labor Statistics, "Mass Layoffs—February 2010," Economic News Release, Mass Layoff Summary, posted March 23, 2010, USDL-10-0362, www.bls.gov/news.release/mmls.nro.htm.

26. In December 2009 and December 2010 Illinois led the Midwest in mass layoff events and seasonally adjusted jobless claims. Its seasonally adjusted unemployment rates in December 2009 (11.0 percent) and December 2010 (9.3 percent) were above the Midwest average: 9.9 and 8.8 percent, respectively. The December 2010 rate was slightly below the national average (9.4 percent). United States Department of Labor, U.S. Bureau of Labor Statistics, "Midwest Economy–Labor Force Statistics," www.bls.gov/xg_shells/ro5xgo2.htm#ro5xgo2rate.f.P (accessed February 5, 2011).

27. Bluestone and Harrison, The Deindustrialization of America, 11.

28. Other academic institutions such as the University of Illinois at Urbana-Champaign and Washington University, St. Louis University, and the University of Missouri in St. Louis (among others) also had relationships with the city that provided research-grant opportunities.

CHAPTER ONE

1. American Community Survey, U.S. Bureau of the Census, "East St. Louis City, Illinois, Selected Economic Characteristics: 2005–2009 Data Set: 2005–2009 American Community Survey, 5-Year

Estimates Survey," www.factfinder.census.gov/servlet/ADPTable?_
bm=y&-geo_id=16000us1722255&-qr_name=ACS_2009_5YR_G00_
DP5YR3&-ds_name=ACS_2009_5YR_G00_&-_lang=en&-_sse=on
(accessed February 6, 2011). The current means of calculating unemployment disguises the considerable level of joblessness in East St.
Louis. Labor market participants are those sixteen years old and
older who are employed or have searched for employment in the
past twelve months. Those sixteen years old and older who have not
searched for employment in the twelve months prior to the survey are
not counted in official unemployment calculations. Poverty data can
be found in "East St. Louis City, Illinois, Selected Social Characteristics in the United States: 2005–2009 Data Set: 2005–2009 American
Community Survey 5-Year Estimates Survey," www.factfinder.cen
sus.gov/servlet/ADPTable?_bm=y&-geo_id=16000US1722255&-qr_
name=ACS_2009_5YR_G00_DP5YR2&-ds_name=ACS_2009_5YR_
G00_&-_lang=en&-redoLog=false&-_sse=on (accessed February 5,
2011).

2. Edward P. Lazear, Katherine Baicker, and Mary Slaughter, *Council of Economic Advisors, Economic Report of the President* (Washington DC:
GPO, 2007), 17.

3. U.S. Department of Housing and Urban Development, Office of
Policy Development and Research, *The State of the Cities 2000: Megaforces
Shaping the Future of the Nation's Cities,* 4th annual report (Washington
DC, June 2000), www.huduser.org; U.S. Department of Housing and
Urban Development, *Now Is the Time: Places Left Behind in the New Econ-
omy* (Washington DC, 1999), www.hud.gov/library/bookshelf18/press
rel/leftbehind/menu.html; Alan Berube and Elizabeth Kneebone,
Two Steps Back: City and Suburban Poverty Trends 1999–2005, Living Cities
Census Series Report (Washington DC: Brookings Institution, 2006),
1. The last source documents the existence of poverty beyond inner
cities. Often-neglected small-city poverty is also a focus of Paul A.
Jargowsky, *Poverty and Place: Ghettos, Barrios, and the American City* (New
York: Russell Sage, 1997); and Mark D. Partridge and Dan S. Rickman,
The Geography of American Poverty: Is There a Need for Place-Based Policies?
(Kalamazoo, MI: Upjohn Institute for Employment Research, 2006).

4. William Frey, "Race and Ethnicity," in Brookings Institution, *State of Metropolitan America: On the Front Lines of Demographic Transformation* (2010), chapter 2, 50–63, quote from 61, www.brookings.edu/metro/stateofmetroamerica.aspx (accessed February 5, 2011).

5. Jargowsky, *Poverty and Place*.

6. Andrew J. Theising, *Made in USA: East St. Louis: The Rise and Fall of an Industrial River Town* (St. Louis, MO: Virginia Publishing, 2003), 8. For a detailed description of the evolution of the planning of the city, see Mary Edwards and Laura Lawson, "The Evolution of Planning in East St. Louis," *Journal of Planning History* 4, no. 4 (2005): 356–82.

7. Sundiata K. Cha-Jua, *America's First Black Town: Brooklyn, Illinois, 1830–1915* (Urbana: University of Illinois Press, 2000).

8. For East St. Louis history, see Theising, *Made in USA*, 133.

9. Ibid.; Elliot Rudwick, *Race Riot at East St. Louis, July 2, 1917*, Illini ed. (Chicago: University of Illinois Press, 1982), 22.

10. Ibid.

11. Ibid.; Theising, *Made in USA*; Bill Nunes, *East Saint Louis Remembered* (Glen Carbon, IL: self-published, 1997). East St. Louis Action Research Project, University of Illinois at Urbana-Champaign, "The IBEX Archive: East St. Louis Action Research Project's Social History Project, Timeline," www.eslarp.uiuc.edu/ibex/archive/nunes/timeline/192029.htm (accessed May 3, 2011).

12. Rudwick, *Race Riot at East St. Louis, July 2, 1917*.

13. Ibid.; Theising, *Made in USA*.

14. Rudwick, *Race Riot at East St. Louis, July 2, 1917*.

15. Ibid.

16. Sally S. Ferguson, *East St. Louis Area: A Changing Population* (Edwardsville, IL: Southern Illinois University Center for Urban and Environmental Research and Services, October 1981); Theising, *Made in USA*.

17. U.S. Bureau of the Census, "East St. Louis City, Illinois, American Community Survey Demographic and Housing Estimates: 2005–2009, 5-Year Estimates," www.factfinder.census.gov/servlet/ADPTable?_bm=y&-geo_id=16000US1722255&-qr_name=ACS_2009_5YR_G00_DP5YR5&-ds_name=&-_lang=en&-redoLog=false (accessed February 5, 2011).

18. Robert L. Allen, *Black Awakening in Capitalist America* (Trenton, NJ: Africa World Press, 1990). A central thesis of Allen's work is that the experience in America for the majority of African Americans is similar to that of colonized peoples in third world or developing countries—their labor restricted to unskilled work and to activities that would prohibit their competition with the white middle class. Simultaneously, a small middle class of African Americans is allowed to develop as a means of controlling the larger black population and maintaining the image of a meritocracy and fairness in a white-dominated society.

19. Carolyn P. Smith, "Fallout from ESL Five Continues," *Belleville News-Democrat,* September 24, 2004, Local/National section, 1A.

20. George Pawlaczyk, "Ex-ESL Worker Pleads to Tax Evasion; Ellis Refuses to Testify against Others," *Belleville News-Democrat,* August 27, 2005, Regional/Business section, 3B.

21. Mike Fitzgerald, "ESL Votes to Keep Schnucks Open; City Council Approves Funding Plan for Store," *Belleville News-Democrat,* June 14, 2005, Local/National section, 1A. See Theising, *Made in U.S.A.,* for a detailed discussion of the political development and corruption of the city.

22. Fitzgerald, "ESL Votes to Keep Schnucks Open; City Council Approves Funding Plan for Store."

23. U.S. Bureau of the Census, "East St. Louis City, Illinois, Selected Economic Characteristics: 2005–2009, American Community Survey 5-Year Estimates," http://factfinder.census.gov/servlet/ADPTable?_bm=y&-geo_id=16000US1722255&-qr_name=ACS_2009_5YR_G00_DP5YR3&-ds_name=ACS_2009_5YR_G00_&-_lang=en&-_sse=on (accessed February 5, 2011); U.S. Bureau of the Census, "United States, Selected Economic Characteristics: 2005–2009 American Community Survey 5-Year Estimates," http://factfinder.census.gov/servlet/ADPTable?_bm=y&-geo_id=01000US&-qr_name=ACS_2009_5YR_G00_DP5YR3&-ds_name=ACS_2009_5YR_G00_&-_lang=en&-redoLog=false&-_sse=on (accessed February 5, 2011); U.S. Bureau of the Census, Factfinder, "East St. Louis, IL, 2005–2009 American Community Survey 5-Year Estimates, Data Profile Highlights," http://

factfinder.census.gov/servlet/ACSSAFFFacts?_event=Search&geo_
id=&_geoContext=&_street=&_county=east+st+louis&_city
Town=east+st+louis&_state=04000US17&_zip=&_lang=en&_sse=
on&pctxt=fph&pgsl=010 (accessed February 5, 2011).

24. Theising, *Made in USA*, 195–97.

25. According to the U.S. Environmental Protection Agency, "Brownfields Showcase Community Fact Sheet," "Brownfields are abandoned, idled or underused industrial and commercial properties where expansion or redevelopment is complicated by real or perceived contamination." In May 1997, Vice President Al Gore announced a Brownfields National Partnership to bring together funding from various federal agencies to coordinate the cleanup of hazardous waste sites. The partnership pledged support to sixteen Brownfields showcase communities, of which St. Louis, Missouri, and East St. Louis, Illinois, together, were designated as one showcase. See www.epa.gov/brown fields/success/showcase/sc_stlouis.htm (accessed February 5, 2011).

26. Kenneth J. Neubeck and Noel A. Cazenave, *Welfare Racism: Playing the Race Card against America's Poor* (New York: Routledge, 2001).

CHAPTER TWO

1. U.S. Department of Transportation, Research and Innovative Technology Administration (RITA), Bureau of Transportation Statistics, "Household, Individual, and Vehicle Characteristics, 2001," www .bts.gov/publications/highlights_of_the_2001_national_household (accessed January 30, 2011).

2. Missouri and Illinois share a bi-state public transportation system, Metro: Bi-State Development Agency, which offers an annual survey of consumers. See the June 2007 Survey: Comprehensive Market Research Analysis of Metropolitan Bus and Rail Passengers, available on-line at www.metrostlouis.org/ResearchRidership/MetroOnboard Survey_Spring2007.pdf (accessed September 20, 2009).

3. U.S. National Advisory Commission on Civil Disorders Report, *The Kerner Report: The 1968 Report of the National Advisory Commission* (New York: Pantheon Books, 1988).

4. Graham Romeyn Taylor, *Satellite Cities: A Study of Industrial Suburbs* (New York: Elibron Classics, 2005).

5. There is little empirical basis for the popular notion linking rail transit to increased criminal activity in suburbs. A 2003 study by Keith R. Ihlanfeldt in the *Southern Economic Journal* linked rail transit to increased crime in central-city neighborhoods and to reduced crime in suburbs ("Rail Transit and Neighborhood Crime: The Case of Atlanta, Georgia," 70, no. 2 [October 1, 2003]: 273–94).

6. U.S. Bureau of the Census, "East St. Louis City, Illinois, Selected Economic Characteristics: 2005–2009, American Community Survey 5-Year Estimates," http://factfinder.census.gov/servlet/ADPTable?_bm=y&-geo_id=16000US1722255&-qr_name=ACS_2009_5YR_G00_DP5YR3&-ds_name=ACS_2009_5YR_G00_&-_lang=en&-redoLog=false&-_sse=on (accessed February 5, 2011); U.S. Bureau of the Census, "Illinois, Selected Economic Characteristics: 2005–2009, American Community Survey 5-Year Estimates," http://factfinder.census.gov/servlet/ADPTable?_bm=y&-geo_id=04000US17&-qr_name=ACS_2009_5YR_G00_DP5YR3&-ds_name=&-_lang=en&-redoLog=false; and; U.S. Bureau of the Census, "United States, Selected Economic Characteristics: 2005–2009, American Community Survey 5-Year Estimates," http://factfinder.census.gov/servlet/ADPTable?_bm=y&-geo_id=01000US&-qr_name=ACS_2009_5YR_G00_DP5YR2&-ds_name=ACS_2009_5YR_G00_&-_lang=en&-redoLog=false&-_sse=on (accessed February 5 2011).

7. Doug Moore, "East St. Louis Poor Get Squeezed at the Pump; Higher Gasoline Prices Don't Mean the Stations Are Taking Advantage of a Vulnerable Market, Says One Station Owner," *St. Louis Post-Dispatch,* December 4, 2005, Metro section, C2.

8. U.S. Bureau of the Census, "St. Louis, MO–IL Metro Area s0801, Commuting Characteristics by Sex, American Community Survey 5-Year Estimates," http://factfinder.census.gov/servlet/STTable?_bm=y&-context=st&-qr_name=ACS_2009_5YR_G00_S0801&-ds_name=ACS_2009_5YR_G00_&-tree_id=5309&-redoLog=false&-_caller=geoselect&-geo_id=31000US41180&-format=&-_lang=en (accessed February 5, 2011); U.S. Bureau of the Census, "United

States, s0801, Commuting Characteristics by Sex 2005–2009, American Community Survey 5-Year Estimates," http://factfinder.census .gov/servlet/STTable?_bm=y&-qr_name=ACS_2009_5YR_G00_ S0801&-geo_id=01000US&-ds_name=ACS_2009_5YR_G00_& -redoLog=false (accessed February 6, 2011); U.S. Bureau of the Census, "East St. Louis City, Illinois, s0801, Commuting Characteristics by Sex 2005–2009, American Community Survey 5-Year Estimates," http:// factfinder.census.gov/servlet/STTable?_bm=y&-context=st&-qr_ name=ACS_2009_5YR_G00_S0801&-ds_name=ACS_2009_5YR_ G00_&-tree_id=5309&-redoLog=true&-_caller=geoselect&-geo_ id=16000US1722255&-format=&-_lang=en (accessed February 5, 2011).

9. U.S. Bureau of the Census, "American Factfinder dp-4, Profile of Selected Housing Characteristics: 2000, East St. Louis City, Illinois," http://factfinder.census.gov/servlet/QTTable?_bm=y&-geo_ id=16000US1722255&-qr_name=DEC_2000_SF4_U_DP4&-ds_ name=D&-_lang=en (accessed February 5, 2011).

10. Illinois Department of Insurance, "Illinois Personal Lines Premium Reports," March 2003 and February 2004, www.insurance.illinois.gov/; Insurance Information Institute, "Facts and Statistics, Auto Insurance," www.iii.org/media/facts/statsbyissue/auto/; and interviews with staff, City of East St. Louis Department of Regulatory Affairs (interviews conducted in 2004, 2005).

11. Rebecca Stanfield, Robert Manning, Megha Budruk, and Myron Floyd, "Racial Discrimination in Parks and Outdoor Recreation: An Empirical Study," in *Proceedings of the 2005 Northeastern Recreation Research Symposium,* ed. and comp. John G. Peden and Rudy M. Schuster, April 10–12, 2005, Bolton Landing, NY, Gen. Tech. Rep. NE-341 (Newtown Square, PA: U.S. Forest Service, Northeastern Research Station, 2006); J. Dwyer and P. Gobster, "Black/White Outdoor Recreation Preferences and Participation: Illinois State Parks," *Proceedings of the 1991 Northeastern Recreation Research Symposium,* USDA Forest Service, Gen. Tech. Rep. NE-160 (1992), 20–24; J. Dwyer, "Outdoor Recreation Participation: An Update on Blacks, Whites, Hispanics and Asians in Illinois," in *Managing Urban and High Use Recreation Settings,* USDA Forest Service, Gen. Tech. Rep. NC 163 (1993), 119–21.

12. George Pawlaczyk, "Barricade Is Racially Motivated, Some Say," *Belleville News-Democrat,* October 26, 2000, Local/National section, 1A; Doug Moore, "Blocked Road in Sauget Draws Complaints," *Saint Louis Post-Dispatch,* November 2000, D1–6.

CHAPTER THREE

1. Alan Berube and Elizabeth Kneebone, *Two Steps Back: City and Suburban Poverty Trends 1999–2005,* Living Cities Census Series Report (Washington DC: Brookings Institution, 2006), 4.

2. Gerald D. Jaynes and Robin M. Williams, *A Common Destiny: Blacks and American Society* (Washington DC: National Academy Press, 1989); Neil Smelser, William Julius Wilson, and Faith Mitchell, eds., *America Becoming: Racial Trends and Their Consequences National Research Council Commission on Behavioral and Social Sciences and Education* (Washington DC: National Academy of Sciences Press, 2000).

3. Lincoln Quillian, "The Decline of Male Employment in Low-Income Black Neighborhoods, 1950–1990," *Social Science Research* 32, no. 2 (June 2003): 220–50.

4. William Julius Wilson, *The Truly Disadvantaged: The Inner-City, the Underclass, and Public Policy* (Chicago: University of Chicago Press, 1990).

5. Variations on the culture-of-poverty thesis appear in such works as Elijah Anderson, *Code of the Street: Decency, Violence, and the Moral Life of the Inner City* (New York: Norton, 1999); Oscar Lewis, *The Children of Sanchez* (New York: Vintage, 1979); Daniel P. Moynihan, *The Negro Family: The Case for National Action* (Washington DC: U.S. Department of Labor, 1965); Wilson, *The Truly Disadvantaged;* David Blankenhorn, *Fatherless America: Confronting Our Most Urgent Social Problem* (New York: Basic Books, 1995); and E. Franklin Frazier, *Black Bourgeoisie: The Book That Brought the Shock of Self-Revelation to Middle-Class Blacks in America,* 1st paperback ed. (New York: Free Press, 1997).

6. Alford Young, *The Minds of Marginalized Black Men* (Princeton, NJ: Princeton University Press, 2004).

7. Virginia Carlson and Nikolas C. Theodore, *Are There Enough*

Jobs? Welfare Reform and Labor Market Reality, Illinois Job Gap Project (DeKalb: Office for Social Policy Research, Northern Illinois University, 1995).

8. Leadership Council Southwestern Illinois, "Labor for/Employment in Southwestern Illinois," 2010, www.siteselection-il.com/employment-labor-force.html (accessed January 1, 2011).

9. At the time of this interview, 2003, the federally mandated minimum wage was $5.15 an hour. This was increased to $5.50 in 2004 for the state of Illinois. The Illinois minimum wage was increased to $8.25 an hour in 2010.

10. U.S. Bureau of the Census, "Fact Sheet: 2005–2007 American Community Survey 3-Year Estimates: East St. Louis City, Illinois," http://factfinder.census.gov/servlet/ACSSAFFFacts?_event = &Active GeoDiv = geoSelect&pctxt = fph&_lang = en&_sse = on&geo_id = 16000US1722255&_state = 04000US17 (accessed August 2009).

11. Jo Mannies and Mark Schlinkmann, "Clinton Urges End to Racial Hatred—He Notes Diversity of Crowd at His Stop in East St. Louis—City Deserves 'Hand up,' He Says," *St. Louis Post-Dispatch,* Wednesday, July 7, 1999, Five Star ed., News section, A1.

CHAPTER FOUR

1. See Mark Lino, *Expenditures on Children by Families, 2003,* Miscellaneous Publication No. 1528–2003, 2004, U.S. Department of Agriculture, Center for Nutrition Policy and Promotion, 3101 Park Center Drive, Room 1034, Alexandria, VA 22302. This annual report on expenditures on children by families breaks down ranges of total expenses for housing, food, transportation, clothing, health care, child care, education, and miscellaneous items such as personal care, entertainment, and reading materials. The $6,000 to $8,000 range for families below $40,700 in annual income is for children from birth to age seventeen. Families with higher incomes spend more on their children. Those earning between $40,700 and $68,400 spend an average of $9,510 to $10,560 per child. Those earning more than $68,400 spend an aver-

age of $14,140 to $15,353. All income categories tend to spend slightly more on older than on younger children.

2. Merriam-Webster Free Online Dictionary, www.merriam -webster.com/dictionary/hustle (accessed February 5, 2011).,

3. "Bill Cosby Blasts Black Parents for Not Getting Involved in Children's Lives," Fox News, Sunday, October 29, 2006, www.foxnews .com.

4. Illinois Criminal Justice Information Authority, *Research and Program Evaluation in Illinois: The Extent and Nature of Drug and Violent Crime in Illinois' Counties*, (Chicago, December 2004). Total drug offenses are those that violate Illinois's Cannabis Control Act, Controlled Substances Act, Drug Paraphernalia Control Act, and the Hypodermic Syringes and Needles Act. African Americans are disproportionately represented among those arrested for drug offenses in St. Clair County, the state of Illinois, and the United States.

5. Jennifer Johnson, *Getting By on the Minimum: The Lives of Working Class Women* (New York: Routledge, 2002).

6. U.S. Bureau of the Census, "Washington Park Village, IL, Factsheet, American Factfinder, 2005–2009 American Community Survey 5-Year Estimates, Data Highlights," http://factfinder.census.gov/ servlet/ACSSAFFFacts?_event=&geo_id=16000US1779085&_geo Context=01000US%7C04000US17%7C16000US1779085&_street=&_ county=washington+park&_cityTown=washington+park&_ state=04000US17&_zip=&_lang=en&_sse=on&ActiveGeoDiv=&_ useEV=&pctxt=fph&pgsl=160&_submenuId=factsheet_1&ds_ name=null&_ci_nbr=null&qr_name=null&reg=null%3Anull&_ keyword=&_industry= (accessed February 5, 2011); and U.S. Bureau of the Census, "Brooklyn Village, IL, Factsheet, American Factfinder, Data Highlights," http://factfinder.census.gov/servlet/ ACSSAFFFacts?_event=&geo_id=16000US1779085&_geoCon text=01000US%7C04000US17%7C16000US1779085&_street=&_ county=washington+park&_cityTown=washington+park&_ state=04000US17&_zip=&_lang=en&_sse=on&ActiveGeoDiv=&_ useEV=&pctxt=fph&pgsl=160&_submenuId=factsheet_1&ds_

name=null&_ci_nbr=null&qr_name=null&reg=null%3Anull&_key
word=&_industry= (accessed February 5, 2011).

7. Elijah Anderson, *Streetwise: Race, Class, and Change in an Urban Community* (Chicago: University of Chicago Press, 1990); Sudhir Venkatesh, *Off the Books: The Underground Economy of the Urban Poor* (Cambridge, MA: Harvard University Press, 2006); Phillip Bourgois, *In Search of Respect: Selling Crack in El Barrio* (Cambridge: Cambridge University Press, 2002).

8. Kathy Stohr, Susie Lee, and Sessy Nyman, "The Illinois Child Care Experience since 1996: Implications for Federal and State Policy," Day Care Action Council of Illinois, 2002, www.clasp.org/admin/site/publications_states/files/0006.pdf.

9. Ibid.

10. Ibid.

11. A complete description of licensing standards is provided by the Illinois Department of Children and Family Services, "DCFS Rules: Title 89: Social Services, Chapter III: Department of Children and Family Services, Subchapter E: Requirements for Licensure, Part 411, Licensing Standards for Secure Child Care Facilities," June 2000, www.state.il.us/dcfs/docs/411.pdf.

CHAPTER FIVE

1. Katherine S. Newman, *No Shame in My Game: The Working Poor in the Inner City* (New York: Knopf and Russell Sage, 1999), 2.

2. U.S. Bureau of the Census, "East St. Louis City, Illinois, Selected Social Characteristics in the United States: 2005–2009, American Community Survey 5-Year Estimates," http://factfinder.census.gov/servlet/ADPTable?_bm=y&-geo_id=16000US1722255&-qr_name=ACS_2009_5YR_G00_DP5YR2&-ds_name=ACS_2009_5YR_G00_&-_lang=en&-_sse=on (accessed February 6, 2011).

3. U.S. Bureau of the Census, American Factfinder, DP-2, "Profile of Selected Social Characteristics: 2000," http://factfinder.census.gov/servlet/QTTable?_bm=y&-geo_id=16000US1722255&-qr_

name=DEC_2000_SF3_U_DP2&-ds_name=DEC_2000_SF3_U&-_
lang=en&-redoLog=false&-_sse=on (accessed February 6, 2011).

4. Mary T. Bassett and Nancy Krieger, "Social Class and Black-White Differences in Breast Cancer Survival," *American Journal of Public Health* 76, no. 12 (1986): 1400–1403; Dionne J. Blackman and Christopher M. Masi, "Racial and Ethnic Disparities in Breast Cancer Mortality: Are We Doing Enough to Address the Root Causes?" *Journal of Clinical Oncology* 24, no. 14 (2006): 2170–78; U.S. Department of Health and Human Services, "Minority Women's Health: African Americans," Office on Women's Health, www.4women.gov/minority/africanamerican (accessed November 10, 2008).

5. R. Bernabei, G. Gambassi, K. Lapane, F. Landi, C. Gatsonis, R. Dunlop, L. Lipsitiz, K. Steel, and V. Mor (SAGE Study Group), "Management of Pain in Elderly Patients with Cancer: Systematic Assessment of Geriatric Drug Use via Epidemiology," *Journal of the American Medical Association* 279 (1998): 1877–82; A.M. Epstein, J.Z. Zyanian, J.H. Keogh, S.J. Noonan, N. Armistead, P.D. Cleary, J.S. Weissman, J.A. David-Kasdan, D. Carlson, J. Fuller, D. March, and R. Conti, "Racial Disparities in Access to Renal Transplantation," *New England Journal of Medicine* 343, no. 21 (2000): 1537–44; B.D. Smedley, A.Y. Stith, and A.R. Nelson, eds., *Unequal Treatment: Confronting Racial and Ethnic Disparities in Health Care* (Washington DC: National Academies Press, 2002).

6. Epstein et al., "Racial Disparities in Access to Renal Transplantation"; Smedley, Stith, and Nelson, eds., *Unequal Treatment*.

7. Blackman, and Masi, "Racial and Ethnic Disparities in Breast Cancer Mortality"; N.E. Schoenberg, and S.C. Drungle, "Barriers to Non-Insulin-Dependent Diabetes Mellitus Self-Care Practices among Older Women," *Journal of Aging and Health* 13, no. 4 (2001): 443–46.

8. Barbara Butrica, Dan Murphy, and Sheila Zedlewski, "How Many Struggle to Get By in Retirement?" working paper, Center for Retirement Research, Boston College, 2007. Also see Barbara Butrica, "Older Americans' Reliance on Assets," Urban Institute, publication 411632, 2008, www.urban.org.

9. Carol B. Stack and Linda M. Burton, "Kinscripts," *Journal of Comparative Family Studies* 24 (1993): 157–70.

10. Ibid.

11. U.S. Department of Health and Human Services, Administration on Aging, "A Statistical Profile of Black Older Americans Aged 65+," www.aoa.gov (accessed September 2009).

12. Smedley, Stith, and Nelson, eds., *Unequal Treatment.*

CHAPTER SIX

1. Bill Bryan, "Suspected Serial Killer Is Found Hanged in Jail—Ferguson Man Was Charged in Deaths of 2 Prostitutes; Court Documents Connect Him to 5 Other Slayings," *St. Louis Post-Dispatch,* June 11, 2002, Five Star List, A1.

2. Denise Hollinshed and Michael Shaw, "He Killed Five Children Here and You've Probably Never Heard of Him," *St. Louis Post-Dispatch,* Sunday, March 12, 2000, Three Star ed., News section, A8.

3. Lauren J. Krivo, Ruth D. Peterson, and Danielle C. Kuhl, "Segregation, Racial Structure, and Neighborhood Violent Crime," *American Journal of Sociology* 114, no. 6 (May 2009): 1765–802.

4. Jennifer Hamer, *What It Means to Be Daddy: Fatherhood for Black Men Who Live Away from Their Children* (New York: Columbia University Press, 2001).

5. Ibid.; Jennifer Hamer and Kathleen Marchioro, "Becoming Custodial Dads: Exploring Parenting among Low-Income and Working-Class African American Fathers," *Journal of Marriage and the Family* 64, no. 1(February 2002): 116–29.

6. Wanda K. Mohr, John W. Fantuzzo, and Saburah Abdul-Kabir, "Safeguarding Themselves and Their Children: Mothers Share Their Strategies," *Journal of Family Violence* 16, no. 1 (2001): 75–92.

7. George Pawlaczyk and Beth Hundsdorfer, "Former Brooklyn Police Officer Cleared a Second Time at Coroner's Inquest," *Belleville News-Democrat,* Thursday, June 12, 2003, Local/National section, 1A.

8. Ibid.

9. Jayne Mathews, "Decision by Jury Protested," *Belleville News-Democrat,* May 8, 2003, Local/National section, 1A.

10. According to the U.S. Environmental Protection Agency (EPA),

high levels of lead can produce brain and nervous system damage, hearing loss, slow growth, and behavior problems. People can get lead in their bodies if they ingest it, touch objects or soil covered with lead dust, or breathe air with lead particles. In 2008, the EPA issued a rule that requires the use of lead-safe practices to prevent lead poisoning: "Beginning in April 2010, contractors performing renovation, repair and painting projects that disturb lead-based paint in homes, child care facilities, and schools built before 1978 must be certified and must follow specific work practices to prevent lead contamination." U.S. Environmental Protection Agency, "Lead in Paint, Dust, and Soil: Basic Information," 2008, www.epa.gov/opptintr/lead/pubs/leadinfo .htm#health.

11. According to an EPA chemical report, "TRI On-Site and Off-Site Reported Disposed of or Otherwise Released Chemicals (in Pounds), for Facilities in All Industries, for All Chemicals, Zip Code 62201 in Illinois, 2007" (www.epa.gov; accessed January 18, 2008), approximately 1,618,491 pounds of disposed of or otherwise released chemicals were released in the East St. Louis zip code area in 2007. Also, visit www. epa.gov to see the Resource Conservation and Recovery Act (RCRAInfo) report on East St. Louis (zip code 62201) for a list of seventy-seven reported corporate hazardous waste releasers, updated September 2009; and Illinois Department of Public Health, *Health Statistics* (Springfield: State of Illinois, 2002).

12. Jeanne E. Moorman, Hatice Zahran, Benedict I. Truman, Michael T. Molla, "Current Asthma Prevalence—United States, 2006–2008," *Morbidity and Mortality Weekly Report, Supplements* 60, no. 1 (January 14, 2011): 84–88, Center for Disease Control, www.cdc.gov/mmwr/ preview/mmwrhtml/su6001a18.htm?s_cid=su6001a18_w (accessed February 6, 2011). For non-Hispanic whites the rates of asthma among the poor were 10 percent; among the nearly poor, 9.5 percent; and among the nonpoor, 8.2 percent.

13. Illinois Department of Public Health, "Health Assessment and Screening: Preventing and Screening for Childhood Lead Poisoning," www.idph.state.il.us/HealthWellness/lead_ref_guide.htm (accessed

February 6, 2011); the rate of lead poisoning among children has been declining among those tested in the state of Illinois.

14. State of Illinois, Illinois Department of Public Health, "The Impact of Lead: Illinois Lead Program Annual Surveillance Report, 2008," December 2009, www.idph.state.il.us/envhealth/pdf/Lead_Surv_Rpt_08.pdf (accessed February 6, 2008).

15. See U.S. Department of Transportation, National Highway Traffic Safety Administration, "Traffic Safety Facts, Illinois 2004–2008," www-nrd.nhtsa.gov/departments/nrd-30/ncsa/stsi/17_IL/2008/17_IL_2008.pdf. In this report of a five-year trend for the top ten counties of Illinois, St. Clair County ranked fifth in the state for fatalities in 2008 (8).

CHAPTER SEVEN

1. On this migration, see, for example, Carole Marks, *Farewell—We're Good and Gone: The Great Black Migration* (Bloomington: Indiana University Press, 1989); Andrew Weise, *Places of Their Own: African American Suburbanization in the Twentieth Century* (Chicago: University of Chicago Press, 2004); Kimberley Phillips, *Alabama North: African-American Migrants, Community, and Working-Class Activism in Cleveland, 1915–1945* (Urbana: University of Illinois Press, 1999); Daniel R. Fusfeld and Timothy Bates, *The Political Economy of the Urban Ghetto* (Carbondale: Southern Illinois University Press, 1984); and E. Franklin Frazier, *Negro Families in the United States* (South Bend, IN: University of Notre Dame Press, 2001).

EPILOGUE

1. Adam Liptak, "Supreme Court Eases Limits on Evidence," *New York Times,* January 15, 2009.

2. Jesse McKinley, "Oakland Turns Violent over Shooting," *New York Times,* January 9, 2009; Malia Wollan, "Ex-Officer Charged in Killing in Oakland," *New York Times,* January 15, 2009.

3. Steven Greenhouse, *The Big Squeeze: Tough Times for the American Worker* (New York: Knopf, 2008), 4.

4. Bob Herbert, "Risking the Future," *New York Times,* February 3, 2009.

5. Interview with Mayor Alvin Parks, Tuesday, May 19, 2009, office of the mayor, City Hall, East St. Louis.

6. Ibid.

7. Ibid.

8. Ibid.

9. Nicholas J. C. Pistor, "Layoffs to Gut East St. Louis Police Force," *St. Louis Post-Dispatch,* July 30, 2010, www.stltoday.com/news/local/illinois/article_dfb230c2–9bf3–11df-9731–0017a4a78c22.html (accessed February 6, 2011).

10. Carolyn P. Smith, "Cash, Booze and Sex: Ex-Deputy Liquor Commissioner Accused of Shakedowns," *Belleville News-Democrat,* Thursday, August 20, 2009, www.bnd.com/news/crime/story/889645 .html.

11. Carolyn P. Smith, "Financial Expert: East St. Louis Is Broke; Budget Shows $2.7 Million Deficit," *Belleville News-Democrat,* Tuesday, September 8, 2009, www.bnd.com/homepage/story/913615.

12. "East St. Louis Begins Furloughs for Non-Union Employees," *Belleville News-Democrat,* Wednesday, September 2, 2009, www.bnd/news/local/story/905719.html; Carolyn P. Smith, "East St. Louis Will Lay Off 14 Employees including 11 Firefighters," *Belleville News-Democrat,* Tuesday, September 15, 2009. www.bnd/news/local/story/923694.html.

13. Heidi Shierholz, "There Were 5.5 Job Seekers per Job Opening in February," Economic Policy Institute: Research and Ideas for Shared Prosperity, April 6, 2010, www.epi.org/publications/entry/there_were_5.5_job_seekers_per_job_opening_in_february/; Ajamu Dillahunt, Brian Miller, executive director, Mike Prokosch, Jeannette Huezo, Dedrick Muhammad, "State of the Dream 2010: DRAINED, United by a Fair Economy," www.faireconomy.org/dream (accessed April 2, 2010).

14. Dillahunt et al., "State of the Dream 2010."

SELECTED BIBLIOGRAPHY

Amato, Paul R., and Joan G. Gilbreth. "Nonresident Fathers and Children's Well-Being: A Meta-Analysis." *Journal of Marriage and the Family* 61 (1999): 557–73.

Anderson, Elijah. *Code of the Street: Decency, Violence, and the Moral Life of the Inner City.* New York: Norton, 1999.

———. *Streetwise: Race, Class, and Change in an Urban Community.* Chicago: University of Chicago Press, 1990.

Bassett, Mary T., and Nancy Krieger. "Social Class and Black-White Differences in Breast Cancer Survival." *American Journal of Public Health* 76, no. 12 (1986): 1400–1403.

Berger, Bennett M. *Working-Class Suburb: A Study of Auto Workers in Suburbia.* Berkeley: University of California Press, 1969.

Berube, Alan, and Elizabeth Kneebone. *Two Steps Back: City and Suburban Poverty Trends 1999–2005.* Living Cities Census Series Report. Washington DC: Brookings Institution, 2006.

Blackman, Dionne J., and Christopher M. Masi. "Racial and Ethnic Disparities in Breast Cancer Mortality: Are We Doing Enough to Address the Root Causes?" *Journal of Clinical Oncology* 24, no. 14 (2006): 2170–78.

Blankenhorn, David. *Fatherless America: Confronting Our Most Urgent Social Problem.* New York: Basic Books, 1995.

Blau, Peter, and O. D. Duncan. *The American Occupational Structure.* New York: Free Press, 1967.

Bluestone, Barry, and Bennett Harrison. *The Deindustrialization of America: Plant Closings, Community Abandonment, and the Dismantling of Basic Industry.* New York: Basic Books, 1982.

Bobo, Lawrence, and James R. Kluegel. "Opposition to Race-Targeting: Self-Interest, Stratification Ideology, or Racial Attitudes?" *American Sociology Review* 58, no. 4 (1993): 443–64.

———. "Whites' Stereotypes, Social Distance, and Perceived Discrimination toward Blacks, Hispanics, and Asians: Toward a Multiethnic Framework." Paper presented at the eighty-sixth annual meeting of the American Sociological Association, Cincinnati, Ohio, August 23–27, 1991.

Bonilla-Silva, Eduardo. *White Supremacy and Racism in the Post–Civil Rights Era.* Boulder, CO: Rienner, 2001.

Bourgois, Phillip. *In Search of Respect: Selling Crack in El Barrio.* Cambridge: Cambridge University Press, 2002.

Braddock, Jomills Henry, II, and James M. McPartland. "How Minorities Continue to Be Excluded from Equal Employment Opportunities: Research on Labor Market and Institutional Barriers." *Journal of Social Issues* 43, no. 1 (1987): 5–39.

Brodsky, A. "Resilient Single Mothers in Risky Neighborhoods: Negative Psychological Sense of Community." *Journal of Community Psychology* 24 (1996): 347–63.

Budig, Michelle J., and Paula England. "The Wage Penalty for Motherhood." *American Sociological Review* 66, no. 2 (2001): 204–25.

Bullard, Robert D., and Beverly Wright. *Race, Place, and Environmental Justice after Hurricane Katrina: Struggles to Reclaim, Rebuild, an Revitalize New Orleans and the Gulf Coast.* Westview Press, 2009.

Burton, L. "Family Structure and Nonmarital Fertility: Perspectives from Ethnographic Research. Report to Congress on Out-of-Wedlock Childbearing." Pub. No. PHS 95–1257, 147–65. Washington DC: Department of Health and Human Services, 1995.

Butrica, Barbara. "Older Americans' Reliance on Assets." Urban Institute, pub. 411632, 2008. www.urban.org.

Butrica, Barbara, Joshua H. Goldwyn, and Richard W. Johnson. "Understanding Expenditure Patterns in Retirement." January 18, 2005. Urban Institute, Washington DC, www.urban.org/publications/411130.html.

Butrica, Barbara, Dan Murphy, and Sheila Zedlewski. "How Many Struggle to Get By in Retirement?" Working paper, Center for Retirement Research, Boston College, 2007.

Caiazza, Amy, April Shaw, and Misha Werschkul. "Women's Economic Status in the States: Wide Disparities by Race, Ethnicity, and Region." In *The Status of Women in the States,* ed. Amy Caiazza, April Shaw, and Misha Werschkul. Institute for Women's Research Policy, Washington DC, www.iwpr.org/pdf/R260.pdf (accessed February 6, 2011).

Callis, Robert. 2008. *Census Bureau Reports on Residential Vacancies and Homeownership, CB08–11.* U.S. Census Bureau News: U.S. Department of Commerce, Washington DC, January 28, 2008.

Carlson, Marcia J., and Sara S. McLanahan. "Fragile Families, Father Involvement, and Public Policy." In *Handbook of Father Involvement,* ed. Catherine Tamis-Lemonda and Natasha Cabrera, 461–88. Mahwah, NJ: Erlbaum, 2008.

Carlson, Virginia, and Nikolas C. Theodore. *Are There Enough Jobs? Welfare Reform and Labor Market Reality.* Illinois Job Gap Project. DeKalb: Office for Social Policy Research, Northern Illinois University, 1995.

Cha-Jua, Sundiata K. *America's First Black Town: Brooklyn, Illinois, 1830–1915.* Urbana: University of Illinois Press, 2000.

Coile, Courtney. "Health Shocks and Couples' Labor Supply Decisions." NBER Working Papers: 10810. National Bureau of Economic Research, Inc., Cambridge, MA. September 2004. www.nber.org/papers/w10810.

Coile, Courtney, and Jonathan Gruber. "Social Security Benefits for Retirement." In *Themes in the Economics of Aging,* ed. David A. Wise,

311–41. NBER Conference Report series. Chicago: University of Chicago Press, 2001.

Coles, Roberta L. "Black Single Father: Choosing to Parent Full-Time." *Journal of Contemporary Ethnography* 31, no. 4 (2002): 411–39.

Coley, Rebekah Levine, and P. Lindsay Chase-Lansdale. "Stability and Change in Paternal Involvement among Urban African American Fathers." *Journal of Family Psychology* 13 (1999): 416–35.

Conley, Dalton. *Being Black, Living in the Red.* Berkeley: University of California Press, 1999.

"Crossing Racial Lines, Coalition Reaches to Fathers." *USA Today,* June 17, 1999, 10D.

Dash, Leon. *Rosa Lee: A Mother and Her Family in Urban America.* New York: Plume, 1996.

Denton, Nancy A., and Douglass S. Massey. "Patterns of Neighborhood Transition in a Multiethnic World: U.S. Metropolitan Areas: 1970–1980." *Demography* 28, no. 1 (1991): 41–63.

DeSena, J. *Protecting One's Turf: Social Strategies for Maintaining Urban Neighborhoods.* New York: University of America Press, 1990.

Dey, A. N., J. S. Schiller, and D. A. Tai. *Summary Health Statistics for U.S. Children: National Health Interview Survey.* U.S. Department of Health and Human Services, Division of Health Interview Statistics, Centers for Disease Control and Prevention, National Center for Health Statistics, Hyattsville, MD. *Vital Health Stat 10* 221 (March 2004): 1–78.

Dobriner, William M. *Class in Suburbia.* Englewood Cliffs, NJ: Prentice-Hall, 1963.

Dodson, Lisa, Tiffany Manuel, and Ellen Bravo. "Keeping Jobs and Raising Families in Low-Income America: It Just Doesn't Work." Cambridge, MA: Harvard University, Radcliffe Institute for Advanced Study, 2002. www.radcliffe.edu/pubpol/boundaries.pdf.

Duneier, Mitchell. *Sidewalk.* New York: Farrar, Straus and Giroux, 2000.

Dwyer, J. "Outdoor Recreation Participation: An Update on Blacks, Whites, Hispanics and Asians in Illinois." In *Managing Urban and High Use Recreation Settings,* 119–21. USDA Forest Service, Gen. Tech. Rep. NC 163 (1993).

Dwyer, J., and P. Gobster. "Black/White Outdoor Recreation Preferences and Participation: Illinois State Parks." In *Proceedings of the 1991 Northeastern Recreation Research Symposium*, 20–24. USDA Forest Service, Gen. Tech. Rep. NE-160 (1992).

Edin, Kathryn, and Laura Lein. *Making Ends Meet: How Single Mothers Survive Welfare and Low-Wage Work*. New York: Russell Sage, 1997.

Edin, Kathryn, and T. Nelson. "Working Steady: Race, Low-Income Work, and Family Involvement among Noncustodial Fathers in Philadelphia." In *Problem of the Century: Racial Stratification in the United States*, ed. E. Anderson and D. Massey, 374–404. New York: Russell Sage Foundation, 2001

Fava, Sylvia Fleis. "Suburbanism as a Way of Life." *American Sociological Review* 21 (February 1956): 34–37.

Ferguson, Ann Arnett. *Bad Boys: Public Schools in the Making of Black Masculinity*. Ann Arbor: University of Michigan Press, 2001.

Ferguson, Ronald F. "The Working-Poverty Trap." *Public Interest* 58 (2005): 71–82.

Fordham, Signithia. *Blacked Out: Dilemmas of Race, Identity, and Success at Capital High*. Chicago: University of Chicago Press, 1996.

Frazier, E. Franklin. *Black Bourgeoisie: The Book That Brought the Shock of Self-Revelation to Middle-Class Blacks in America*. 1st paperback ed. New York: Free Press, 1997.

Furstenberg, F. "How Families Manage Risk and Opportunity in Dangerous Neighborhoods." In *Sociology and Public Agenda*, ed. William Julius Wilson, 231–58. Newbury Park, CA: Sage, 1993.

———. "Parenting in the Inner City: Paternal Participation and Public Policy." In *Fatherhood: Contemporary Theory, Research and Social Policy*, ed. William Marsiglio, 119–47. Thousand Oaks, CA: Sage, 1995.

Gans, Herbert, J. *The Levittowners: Ways of Life and Politics in a New Suburban Community*. New York: Columbia University Press, 1967.

———. *The War against the Poor*. New York: Basic Books, 1996.

Garfinkel, Irwin, Ronald B. Mincy, and Sara McLanahan. "Fragile Families, Welfare Reform, and Marriage." CCF Briefs 10. Brookings Institution, Washington DC, December 2001. www.brookings.edu/papers/2001/12childrenfamilies_mclanahan.aspx.

Glass, Jennifer, and Valeri Camarigg. "Gender, Parenthood, and Jo-Family Compatibility." *American Journal of Sociology* 98, no. 1 (1992): 131–51.

Greenhouse, Steven. *The Big Squeeze: Tough Times for the American Worker.* New York: Knopf, 2008.

Guinier, Lani, and Gerald Torres. *The Miner's Canary: Enlisting Race, Resisting Power, Transforming Democracy.* Cambridge, MA: Harvard University Press, 2002.

Hamer, Jennifer. *What It Means to Be Daddy: Fatherhood for Black Men Living Away from Their Children.* New York: Columbia University Press, 2001.

Hamer, Jennifer, and Kathleen Marchioro. "Becoming Custodial Dads: Exploring Parenting among Low-Income and Working-Class African American Fathers." *Journal of Marriage and the Family* 64, no. 1 (2002): 116–29.

Hamer, Jennifer, and Helen Neville. "Revolutionary Black Feminism: Toward a Theory of Unity and Liberation." *Black Scholar* 28, no. 3–4 (1998): 22–29.

———. "We Make Freedom: An Exploration of Revolutionary Black Feminism." *Journal of Black Studies* 31, no. 4 (March 2001): 437–61.

Harrington Meyer, Madonna. "Family Status and Poverty among Older Women: The Gendered Distribution of Retirement Income in the United States." *Social Problems* 37, no. 4 (1990): 551–63.

Hochschild, J. L. *Facing Up to the American Dream: Race, Class, and the Soul of the Nation.* Princeton, NJ: Princeton University Press, 1995.

Holzer, Harry. *What Employers Want: Job Prospects for Less Educated Workers.* New York: Russell Sage, 1996.

Horton, Hayward D., Beverlyn Lundy, Cedric Herring, and Melvin E. Thomas. "Lost in the Storm: the Sociology of the Black Working Class, 1850 to 1990." *American Sociological Review* 65, no. 1 (2000): 128–37.

Illinois Department of Children and Family Services. "DCFS Rules: Title 89: Social Services, Chapter III: Department of Children and Family Services, Subchapter E: Requirements for Licensure, Part

411, Licensing Standards for Secure Child Care Facilities." June 2000. www.state.il.us/dcfs/docs/411.pdf.

Illinois Department of Public Health. *Health Statistics.* Springfield: State of Illinois, 2002.

Insurance Information Institute. "Facts and Statistics, Auto Insurance." www.iii.org/media/facts/statsbyissue/auto/.

Jackson, Kenneth T. *Crabgrass Frontier: The Suburbanization of the United States.* New York: Oxford University Press, 1985.

Jargowsky, Paul A. *Poverty and Place: Ghettos, Barrios, and the American City.* New York: Russell Sage, 1997.

Jarrett, Robin. "African American Family and Parenting Strategies in Impoverished Neighborhoods." *Qualitative Sociology* 20 (1998): 275–88.

———. "African American Mothers and Grandmothers in Poverty: An Adaptational Perspective." *Journal of Contemporary Family Studies* 29, no. 3 (1994): 387–95.

Jarrett, Robin, Kevin Roy, and Linda Burton. "Fathers in the Hood: Qualitative Research on Low-Income African American Men." In *Handbook of Father Involvement: Multidisciplinary Perspectives,* ed. Catherine Tamis-Lemonda and Natasha Cabrera, 211–48. Mahwah, NJ: Erlbaum, 2008.

Jayakody, Rukhmalie, Linda Chatters, and Robert Joseph. "Family Support to Single and Married African American Mothers: The Provision of Financial, Emotional, and Child Care Assistance." *Journal of Marriage and Family* 55, no. 2 (1993): 261–76.

Jaynes, Gerald D., and Robin M. Williams. *A Common Destiny: Blacks and American Society.* Washington DC: National Academy Press, 1989.

Jimenez, Jillian. "The History of Grandmothers in the African American Community." *Social Service Review* 76, no. 4 (December 2002): 523–51.

Johnson, David S., and Timothy M. Smeeding. "Who Are the Poor Elderly? An Examination Using Alternative Poverty Measures." Working paper, 2000–14. Center for Retirement Research at Boston College, December 2000. http://crr.bc.edu/images/stories/Working _Papers/wp_2000–14.pdf?phpMyAdmin = 43ac483c4de9t5ıd9eb41.

Johnson, Jennifer. *Getting By on the Minimum: The Lives of Working Class Women.* New York: Routledge, 2002.

Johnson, Waldo E., Jr. "The Determinants of Paternal Involvement among Unwed Fathers." *Children and Youth Services Review* 23, no. 6–7 (2001): 513–36.

Jones, Jacqueline. *Labor of Love, Labor of Sorrow: Black Women, Work, and the Family from Slavery to the Present.* New York: Basic Books, 1985.

Jonsson, Greg. "Mother of Boy Killed by Dogs Will Go to Son's Funeral: Authorities Give Her Permission to Travel." *St. Louis Post-Dispatch,* March 15, 2001, B2.

Kefalas, Maria. *Working-Class Heroes: Protecting Home, Community, and Nation in a Chicago Neighborhood.* Berkeley: University of California Press, 2003.

Kington, Raynard S., and James Smith. "Socioeconomic Status and Racial and Ethnic Differences in Functional Status Associated with Chronic Diseases." *American Journal of Public Health* 87, no. 5 (1997): 805–10.

Kirschenman, Joleen, and Kathryn M. Neckerman. "'We'd love to hire them, but . . . ': The Meaning of Race for Employers." In *The Urban Underclass,* ed. Christopher Jencks and Paul E. Peterson, 203–32. Washington DC: Brookings Institution, 1991.

Kluegel, James R., and Lawrence D. Bobo. "Perceived Group Discrimination and Policy Attitudes: The Sources and Consequences of the Race and Gender Gaps." In *Urban Inequality: Evidence from Four Cities,* ed. Alice O'Connor, Chris Tilly, and Lawrence Bobo, 163–213. New York: Russell Sage, 2001.

Kornblum, William, and Terry Williams. *Growing Up Poor.* Lanham, MD: Lexington Books, 1985.

Kozol, Jonathan. *Savage Inequalities.* New York: HarperCollins, 1992.

Kreader, J. Lee, Jessica Piecyk, and Ann M. Collins. *Scant Increases after Welfare Reform: Regulated Child Care Supply in Illinois and Maryland, 1996–1998.* National Center for Children in Poverty, Mailman School of Public Health, Columbia University, June 2000. www.nccp.org/publications/pdf/text_388.pdf.

Kruse, Kevin M., and Thomas J. Sugrue, eds. *The New Suburban History.* Chicago: University of Chicago Press, 2006.

Kusmer, Kenneth. "African Americans in the City since World War II: From the Industrial to the Post-Industrial Era." *Journal of Urban History* 21 (1995): 458–504.

Lamont, Michele. *The Dignity of Working Men: Morality and the Boundaries of Race, Class, and Immigration.* New York: Russell Sage, 2000.

Lazear, Edward P., Katherine Baicker, and Mary Slaughter. *Council of Economic Advisors, Economic Report of the President.* Washington DC: GPO, 2007.

Lerman, R., and E. Sorensen. "Father Involvement with Their Non-marital Children: Patterns, Determinants, and Effects on Their Earnings." *Marriage and Family Review* 29 (2002): 75–95.

Letiecq, Bethany L., and Sally A. Koblinsky. "Parenting in Violent Neighborhoods: African American Fathers Share Strategies for Keeping Children Safe." *Journal of Family Issues* 25, no. 6 (2004): 715–34.

Lewis, Oscar. *Children of Sanchez.* New York: Vintage, 1979.

———. *Five Families: Mexican Case Studies in the Culture of Poverty.* 1959. Reprint, New York: HarperCollins, 1975.

Light, Audrey. "Job Mobility and Wage Growth: Evidence from the NLSY79." *Monthly Labor Review* 128, no. 2 (2005): 33–39.

Litt, J. "Managing the Street, Isolating the Household: African American Mothers Respond to Neighborhood Deterioration." *Race, Gender and Class* 6, no. 3 (1999): 90–101.

Marks, Carole. *Farewell—We're Good and Gone: The Great Black Migration.* Bloomington: Indiana University Press, 1989.

Massey, Douglas S., and Nancy A. Denton. *American Apartheid: Segregation and the Making of the Underclass.* Cambridge, MA: Harvard University Press, 1993.

———. "The Elusive Quest for the Perfect Index of Concentration: Reply to Egan, Anderton, and Weber." *Social Forces* 76, no. 3 (1998): 1123–33.

Mauer, Marc. *Race to Incarcerate.* New York: New Press, 1999.

Mishel, Lawrence, Jared Bernstein, and Sylvia Allegretto. *The State of Working America 2004/2005.* Ithaca, NY: Cornell University Press, 2005.

Mohr, Wanda K., John W. Fantuzzo, and Saburah Abdul-Kabir. "Safeguarding Themselves and Their Children: Mothers Share Their Strategies." *Journal of Family Violence* 16, no. 1 (2001): 75–92.

Moss, Philip, and Chris Tilly. *Stories Employers Tell: Race, Skill and Hiring in America.* New York: Russell Sage, 2001.

————. *Why Black Men Are Doing Worse in the Labor Market: A Review of Supply-Side and Demand-Side Explanations.* New York: Social Science Research Council, 1996.

Moynihan, Daniel P. *The Negro Family: The Case for National Action.* Washington DC: U.S. Department of Labor, 1965.

Murphy, Alexandra K. "The Suburban Ghetto: The Legacy of Herbert Gans in Understanding the Experience of Poverty in Recently Impoverished Suburbs." *City and Community* 6, no. 1 (2007): 21–37.

Neckerman, Kathryn, and Joleen Kirschenmann. "Hiring Strategies, Racial Bias, and Inner-City Workers." *Social Problems* 38 (1991): 433–47.

Neubeck, Kenneth J., and Noel A. Cazenave. *Welfare Racism: Playing the Race Card against America's Poor.* New York: Routledge, 2001.

Newman, Katherine S. *No Shame in My Game: The Working Poor in the Inner City.* New York: Knopf and Russell Sage, 1999.

News and Views. "Leaving Half a Generation Behind: Only a Slim Majority of Young Blacks Ever Finish High School." *Journal of Blacks in Higher Education* 43 (April 30, 2004): 52.

Oliver, Melvin, and Thomas Shapiro. *Black Wealth / White Wealth: A New Perspective on Racial Inequality.* 2nd ed. New York: Routledge, 2006.

Orfield, Gary, Daniel Losen, Johanna Wald, and Christopher B. Swanson. "Losing Our Future: How Minority Youth Are Being Left Behind by the Graduation Rate Crisis." Urban Institute, February 2004. www.urban.org/url.cfm?ID = 410936.

Partridge, Mark D., and Dan S. Rickman. *The Geography of American Poverty: Is There a Need for Place-Based Policies?* Kalamazoo, MI: Upjohn Institute for Employment Research, 2006.

Patillo-McCoy, Mary. *Black Picket Fences: Privilege and Peril among the Black Middle Class*. Chicago: University of Chicago Press, 1999.

Pearlin, Leonard. "The Social Context of Stress." In *Handbook of Stress: Theoretical and Clinical Aspects*, ed. Leo Goldberger and Shlomo Breznitz, 303–15. 2nd ed. New York: Free Press, 1993.

"Placing Blacks in College: States and Cities Vary in Their Success and Failures." *Journal of Blacks in Higher Education* 34 (Winter 2001/2002): 116–21.

Porter, Kathryn H., Kathy Larin, and Wendell Primus. *Social Security and Poverty among the Elderly: A National and State Perspective*. Washington DC: Center for Budget and Policy Priorities, 1999.

Puntenney, D. "The Impact of Gang Violence on the Decision of Everyday Life: Disjunctions between Policy Assumptions and Community Conditions." *Journal of Urban Affairs* 19 (1997): 143–61.

Quillian, Lincoln. "The Decline of Male Employment in Low-Income Black Neighborhoods, 1950–1990." *Social Science Research* 32, no. 2 (June 2003): 220–50.

Roberts, Dorothy. *Shattered Bonds: The Color of Child Welfare*. New York: Basic Books, 2002.

Rose, Stephen J., and Heidi I. Hartmann. *Still a Man's Labor Market: The Long-Term Earnings Gap*. Washington DC: Institute for Women's Policy Research, 2004.

Ross, Norman E., Dionne Ferguson, and Veda D. Berry. *Economic Recovery Model Project: For the Revitalization of the East St. Louis Area*. Vol. 1. East St. Louis, IL: Greater East St. Louis Chamber of Commerce, 2002.

Roy, Kevin. "Three-Block Fathers: Spatial Perceptions and Kin-Work in Low-Income African American Neighborhoods." *Social Problems* 51, no. 4 (November 2004): 528–48.

Rudwick, Elliot. *Race Riot at East St. Louis, July 2, 1917*. Illini ed. Chicago: University of Illinois Press, 1982.

Schwartzman, David. *Black Unemployment: Part of Unskilled Unemployment*. London: Greenwood, 1997.

Selvin, Elizabeth, and Kate M. Brett. "Breast and Cervical Cancer Screening: Sociodemographic Predictors among White, Black, and

Hispanic Women." *American Journal of Public Health* 93, no. 4 (2003): 618–23.

Skiba, Russell J., Robert S. Michael, Abra Carroll Nardo, and Reece L. Peterson. "The Color of Discipline: Sources of Racial and Gender Disproportionality in School Punishment." *Urban Review* 34, no. 4 (2002): 317–42.

Smeeding, Timothy M. "Income Maintenance in Old Age: Current Status and Future Prospects for Rich Countries." Paper delivered at the United Nations Conference on Status of the Older Population: Prelude to Twenty-first Century, Switzerland, 1999.

Smelser, Neil, William Julius Wilson, and Faith Mitchell, eds. *America Becoming: Racial Trends and Their Consequences National Research Council Commission on Behavioral and Social Sciences and Education.* Washington DC: National Academy of Sciences Press, 2000.

Stack, Carol B. *All Our Kin: Strategies for Survival in a Black Community.* New York: Basic Books, 1974.

Stack, Carol B., and Linda M. Burton. "Kinscripts." *Journal of Comparative Family Studies* 24 (1993): 157–70.

Stanback, Thomas M, Jr. *The New Suburbanization: Challenge to the Central City.* Boulder, CO: Westview Press, 1991.

Stanfield, Rebecca, Robert Manning, Megha Budruk, and Myron Floyd. "Racial Discrimination in Parks and Outdoor Recreation: An Empirical Study." In *Proceedings of the 2005 Northeastern Recreation Research Symposium,* ed. and comp. John G. Peden and Rudy M. Schuster, 247–53. April 10–12, 2005, Bolton Landing, NY. Gen. Tech. Rep. NE-341. Newtown Square, PA: U.S. Forest Service, Northeastern Research Station, 2006.

Stern, Mark J. "Poverty and Family Composition since 1940." In *The Underclass Debate: Views from History,* ed. Michael B. Katz, 220–53. Princeton, NJ: Princeton University Press, 1993.

Stier, Haya, and Marta Tienda. *Pathways to Family, Welfare, and Work.* Chicago: University of Chicago Press, 2001.

Stohr, Kathy, Susie Lee, and Sessy Nyman. "The Illinois Child Care Experience since 1996: Implications for Federal and State Policy."

Day Care Action Council of Illinois, 2002. www.clasp.org/admin/ site/publications_states/files/0006.pdf.

Tamis-Lemonda, Catherine, and Natasha Cabrera, eds. *Handbook of Father Involvement: Multidisciplinary Perspectives.* Mahwah, NJ: Erlbaum, 2008.

Theising, Andrew J. "East St. Louis: Made in the U.S.A." PhD diss., University of Missouri–St. Louis, 1997.

———. *Made in USA: East St. Louis: The Rise and Fall of an Industrial River Town.* St. Louis, MO: Virginia Publishing, 2003.

Tilly, Chris. "Raw Deal for Workers." *Dollars and Sense,* August 2003, 41–44.

U.S. Bureau of the Census. "Fact Sheet: 2005–2007 American Community Survey 3-Year Estimates: East St. Louis City, Illinois." http:// factfinder.census.gov/servlet/ACSSAFFFacts?_event = &Active GeoDiv = geoSelect&pctxt = fph&_lang = en&_sse = on&geo_id = 16000US1722255&_state = 04000US17 (accessed August 2009).

———. *Profile of Selected Housing Characteristics: 2000. Geographic Area: East St. Louis City, Illinois.* Washington DC: GPO, 2001.

———. *2001 Supplementary Survey Profile, St. Clair County.* Washington DC: GPO, 2002.

U.S. Department of Agriculture, Forest Service, Northeastern Forest Experiment Station. "Black/White Outdoor Recreation Preferences and Participation: Illinois State Parks." In *Proceedings of the 1991 Northeastern Recreation Research Symposium,* by John F. Dwyer and Paul H. Gobster, 20–24. Saratoga Springs, NY, April 7–9, 1991. Gen. Tech. Rep. NE-160. USDA Forest Service, 1992.

———. "Outdoor Recreation Participation: An Update on Blacks, Whites, Hispanics and Asians in Illinois." In *Managing Urban and High Use Recreation Settings,* by John F. Dwyer, 119–21. Gen. Tech. Rep. NC 163. 1993.

U.S. Department of Health and Human Services. "Minority Women's Health: African Americans." , 2008. www.4women.gov/minority/ africanamerican (accessed November 10, 2008).

———. *Vital and Health Statistics.* Summary Health Statistics for U.S. Adults: National Health Interview Survey, series 10, no. 225, 2003.

DHHS publication no. (PHS) 2005–155. Washington DC: National Center for Health Statistics, Centers for Disease Control and Prevention, July 2005. www.cdc.gov/nchs/data/series/sr_10/sr10_225.pdf.

———. Office of the Secretary. "Annual Update of the HHS Poverty Guidelines." *Federal Register* 69, no. 30 (February 13, 2004): 7336–38. http://frwebgate.access.gpo.gov/cgi-bin/getpage.cgi.

U.S. Department of Housing and Urban Development. *Now Is the Time: Places Left Behind in the New Economy.* Washington DC, 1999. www.hud.gov/library/bookshelf18/pressrel/leftbehind/menu.html.

———. Office of Policy Development and Research. *The State of the Cities 2000: Megaforces Shaping the Future of the Nation's Cities.* 4th annual report. Washington DC: June 2000. www.huduser.org.

U.S. Department of Labor, Bureau of Labor Statistics. "Barbers, Cosmetologists, and Other Personal Appearance Workers." Office of Occupational Statistics and Employment Projections, 2005. http://stats.bls.gov/.

———. Economic News Release, Mass Layoff Summary, November 17, 2005. www.bls.gov/mls/.

———. *Geographic Profile of Employment and Unemployment, 2002.* Bulletin 2564, 2005. http://stats.bls.gov.

———. *State and Selected Claimant Characteristics: Extended Mass Layoff Events and Initial Claimants for Unemployment Insurance, Private Nonfarm Sector, Second and Third Quarters.* Washington DC: U.S. Department of Labor, Bureau of Labor Statistics, 2005.

———. "Worker displacement." USDL 04–1381, July 30, 2004. www.bls.gov/news.release/archives/disp_07302004.pdf.

Valentine, Bettylou. *Hustling and Other Hard Work: Life Styles in the Ghetto.* New York: Free Press, 1978.

Venkatesh, Sudhir. *Off the Books: The Underground Economy of the Urban Poor.* Cambridge, MA: Harvard University Press, 2006.

Vigil, James Diego. *Barrio Gangs: Street Life and Identity in Southern California.* Austin: University of Texas Press, 1988.

Wacquant, L. "Scrutinizing the Street: Poverty, Morality, and the Pitfalls of Urban Ethnography." *American Journal of Sociology* 107, no. 6 (2002): 1468–574.

Weise, Andrew. *Places of Their Own: African American Suburbanization in the Twentieth Century.* Chicago: University of Chicago Press, 2004.

Werschkul, Misha, and Erica Williams. *The Status of Women in the States.* Washington DC: Institute for Women's Policy Research, 2004.

Williams, David R. "Racial Variations in Adult Health Status: Patterns, Paradoxes and Prospects." In *America Becoming: Racial Trends and Their Consequences,* ed. Neil Smelser, William Julius Wilson, and Faith Mitchell, 370–410. National Research Council Commission on Behavioral and Social Sciences and Education. Washington DC: National Academy of Sciences Press, 2000.

Wilson, William Julius. *More Than Just Race: Being Poor and Black in the Inner City.* New York: Norton, 2009.

———. *The Truly Disadvantaged: The Inner-City, the Underclass, and Public Policy.* Paperback ed. Chicago: Chicago University Press, 1990.

———. *When Work Disappears: The World of the New Urban Poor.* New York: Vintage, 1997.

Young, Alford. *The Minds of Marginalized Black Men.* Princeton, NJ: Princeton University Press, 2004.

Zweig, Michael. *The Working Class Majority: America's Best Kept Secret.* Ithaca, NY: ILR Press, 2001.

Text:	10.75/15 Janson MT Pro
Display:	Janson MT Pro
Compositor:	BookMatters, Berkeley
Indexer:	J. Naomi Linzer
Printer and Binder:	Sheridan Books, Inc.

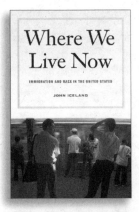

Where We Live Now

Immigration and Race in the United States
JOHN ICELAND

"A unique work that takes on immigration, race, and ethnicity in a novel way. It presents cutting-edge research and scholarship in a manner that policy makers and other nonspecialist social scientists can easily see how the trends he examines are reshaping American life."

—**Andrew A. Beveridge, Queens College and the Graduate Center of City University of New York**
$21.95 paper 978-0-520-25763-4

Neon Wasteland

On Love, Motherhood, and Sex Work in a Rust Belt Town
SUSAN DEWEY

"A riveting and compelling book. Dewey's reflections and analyses are richly descriptive and insightful. She poignantly relates the stories of these women but also never lets the reader forget the stark social inequalities that are part of these women's daily lives." —**Jennifer K. Wesely, PhD, co-author of *Hard Lives, Mean Streets***
$26.95 paper 978-0-520-26691-9

Promises I Can Keep

Why Poor Women Put Motherhood Before Marriage
KATHRYN EDIN and MARIA KEFALAS

"The most important study ever written on motherhood and marriage among low-income urban women." —**William Julius Wilson, author of *The Bridge over the Racial Divide***

William J. Goode Best Book-Length Contribution to Family Sociology Award, American Sociological Association
$24.95 paper 978-0-520-27146-3

www.ucpress.edu